Islam and Muslim Resistance to Modernity
in Turkey

Gokhan Bacik

Islam and Muslim Resistance to Modernity in Turkey

Gokhan Bacik
Palacký University Olomouc
Olomouc, Czech Republic

ISBN 978-3-030-25900-6   ISBN 978-3-030-25901-3   (eBook)
https://doi.org/10.1007/978-3-030-25901-3

This Palgrave Macmillan imprint is published by the registered company Springer Nature Switzerland AG
The registered company address is: Gewerbestrasse 11, 6330 Cham, Switzerland

To Jaroslav Miller and Jiri Lach, whose support made this book possible

PREFACE

The Islamic cause had seen big promises in Turkey: economic prosperity, high standards of law, and a decent status in global politics. Simply, its pledge was to bring Turkey back to the "Golden Age of Muslims," which is believed to have happened somewhere in history. Millions of Turks have made sacrifices in different ways to contribute to the Islamization of Turkey, but all efforts were affiliated with making Turkey a better country with Islam. People sincerely believe that Islamization will solve Turkey's problems. For the millions who supported it, Islamization was a stand-alone magic cure. A Turkish slogan "İslam gelecek, dertler bitecek" (Islam is the solution for all problems) summarizes that mindset.

However, Islamization in Turkey has brought the country to the brink of a multifaceted catastrophe. In less than two decades, Islamism transformed Turkey into an authoritarian regime with a host of structural problems ranging across the economy and foreign policy. Naturally, the Islamist failure provoked a debate on Islam, Islamic movements, and anything related to Islam. Yet it would not be fair to explain the failure of Islamism in Turkey in terms of Islam alone. In other words, the failure of Islamists in not *ipso facto* the failure of their religion: A fair number of other factors have also had a role. Then again, the failure is bound to have some links with how certain cuts of Islamist interpret and practice Islam. Turkey's brand of "What went wrong?" literature has grown quickly. This book can be read as one of many in the "What went wrong?" bracket of scholarly literature about contemporary Turkey.

Usually, books in the "What went wrong?" bracket analyze how different interpretations of Islam are relevant in understanding the interplay between Islam and Muslims. In this book, I present a rarely analyzed dimension in the interplay between people and religion: the Islamic Idea of Nature. The Islamic Idea of Nature is the collection of beliefs about how nature works that a Muslim acquires during religious socialization. My aim is to shed light on an almost-ignored aspect of the interplay between Islam and Muslims in Turkey. So I try to explain how Islam is interpreted in Turkey in regard to the key issues in the Idea of Nature, such as causality, free will, and knowledge. Such an analysis will provide a completely different perspective on Islamization in Turkey.

The idea for writing this book emanated from my personal experiences with, and observations of, Islamic scholar, academics, politicians, and Islamic movement leaders. While following closely all sorts of Islamic actors in Turkey in the last two decades, I came upon a specific brand of Islamic outlook on nature, causality, and the relevant issues. I noticed that the Islamic actors under my scrutiny share a similar outlook on those concepts, which, I believe, has its origins in Islamic socialization. One readily detects this Islamic outlook when the committed comment on a natural events like an earthquake, or they speculate on the limits of freedom. This perception led me to what became the subject matter of this book: It might be interesting to study how Islam is taught in Turkey in regard to some fundamental issues such as human free will, causality, and knowledge. Islamic socialization and education are not only about law, but also about acquiring a creed-specific "complex knowledge." Reading the major texts that shape Islamic socialization, and even education, in Turkey, I noticed that they tend to be long articulations of the Islamic Idea of Nature, and they devote relatively little attention to Islamic law.

While writing this book, I have benefited from the help of many people and institutions. Soon after I began to work on it, I was forced to leave Turkey, and I found myself in survival mode in Europe. I am therefore greatly indebted to Scholar Rescue Fund (SRF) for its officers' prompt response to my application. I thank also Sean Lamberg for his cooperation with me during my correspondence with the SRF. I am deeply indebted also to Prof. Jaroslav Miller, the President of Palacky University, for all his generous support. I would like to declare my sincerest appreciation of him. I am grateful also to Prof. Jiri Lach for his help during my transition to the Czech Republic, as well as for his continuing support. I also acknowledge the help of Ahmet T. Kuru, Tomas Lebeda, Sophie Johnson, Fevzi Bilgin, Ozgur Koca, İsa Afacan, Tercan Basturk, and Yasir Yılmaz. Last but not least, I owe a special debt of gratitude to my family, Semra, Bensu, and Leyla.

Olomouc, Czech Republic   Gokhan Bacik
June 2019

CONTENTS

LIST OF TABLES

CHAPTER 1

Introduction

On November 12, 2017, a powerful earthquake rocked northern Iraq. That earthquake also shook the whole population of Turkey, which falls within an active seismic zone. As usual, geologists were quick to appear on television to explain the earthquake. Among them was Professor Ahmet Ercan, who spoke on state television. The channel cut his speech immediately after he made the following comment:

> Eighty percent of people who lose their lives in earthquakes are from Muslim countries, because there is neither democracy nor scientific and technological capability in Muslim countries. (*Birgün*, November 13, 2017)

There is a considerable body of literature on how Islam is interpreted, and it entails the rationalizations of the several problems of Muslim societies. Accordingly, the interpretation and the concomitant practice of Islam are identified as the causes of the various problems that beset Muslim societies. The geologist's comments are also a reflection of a widely shared understanding that posits a causal link between how Islam is interpreted and the problems that plague various Muslim societies. By referring to the democracy gap in Muslim countries, Ercan called to mind the popular thesis that a democratic and transparent political regime is critical for economic and social development. But he also added that Muslims are performing in various fields without the necessary scientific capability. His comments raise two questions: Why do many Muslim societies lack fully functional democracy? And why do they generally lack scientific capability?

© The Author(s) 2020
G. Bacik, *Islam and Muslim Resistance to Modernity in Turkey*,
https://doi.org/10.1007/978-3-030-25901-3_1

The first question pertains to the well-known literature on democracy and law in explaining various problems in Muslim societies. These studies focus on the effects of Islamic law on the economy and the other spheres of Muslim countries.[1] For example, according to Timur Kuran, Islamic law could not produce worldviews that could keep up with the transition from the medieval to the modern economy (characterized by corporations and banking). This failure also inhibited the accumulation of capital in Muslim societies.[2] In another vein, François Facchini proposes that the Islamic legal tradition did not provide a basis for strong property rights, which in turn explains economic underdevelopment in Muslim societies.[3] Muslims' economic success in earlier periods of history is attributed to trade-friendly interpretations of Islamic law.[4] Later on, the emergence of inflexible regulating institutions and the evolution of Muslim inheritance law discouraged growth values and practices. Accordingly, the state and religious authorities were concerned only with preserving the status quo that emerged in the ninth century and was consolidated by the eleventh century. That period's law and institutions gradually directed Muslims to be "strongly against competition" and made them anti-market.[5]

Economic and political institutions in Muslim societies doubtlessly reflect contemporary interpretation and practice of Islam. However, mainstream scholarship assumes too readily that factors such as how Islamic law is interpreted or the current democracy gap are likely to be the major causes of the problems of the Muslim world today. Social and historical developments are also understood as the outcomes of the evolution of Islamic law or Islamic politics. The upshot of this is the projection that a more democratic, gender-friendly, and market-oriented interpretation of Islamic law would ameliorate Islam's impact on Muslim societies.

The interplay between Islam and Muslims is however complex, and there are also other fields that are highly pertinent in the quest to understand Muslim societies. Analyzing certain problems that have their origin in a lack of scientific and technological capabilities, the second point that geologist Ahmet Ercan raised requires a different analytical perspective in regard to the interplay between Islam and Muslims. In this regard, various problems such as slow technological advancement and low agricultural productivity in Muslim societies can be seen as the result of their failure to understand the relevant causal relations. This brings us to the main purpose of this book: *to introduce a new analytical tool, the "idea of nature," in explaining the interpretation and practice of Islam affecting various situations in the Muslim world by studying selected cases from Turkey. The Islamic idea of nature is the collection of beliefs concerning how nature works that a Muslim acquires during religious socialization.* Transmitted from one generation to the next in the continuity of the Islamic faith, the Islamic idea of nature is an observable phenomenon. It occupies a large space in contemporary Islamic socialization. In many Muslim societies, religious socialization therefore entails engagement with the interpretation and transmission of the Islamic idea of nature. Like law, the Islamic idea of nature has serious implications for how Muslims interpret Islam, particularly with respect to key issues like causality, knowledge, and free will.

However, the role of the Islamic idea of nature has received scant attention, and we therefore remain uninformed about this vital historical and intellectual enterprise, which produced some of the foundational postulates according to which all Islamic thought, including legal theory, operates. Instead, scholars of Islamic studies who examine social, economic, and political problems in Muslim societies have favored legal and scriptural-hermeneutic approaches while generally overlooking the role of theology.[6]

1.1 Framing the Research Questions

Let us attend to some data on how Muslim societies perform in various fields. No Muslim-majority state ranks among the top ten exporters of manufactured goods, according to the World Trade Organization's statistics. Nor is any one of them on the list of the top ten exporters of chemicals and pharmaceuticals. There is also no Muslim-majority state among the top ten exporters of agricultural products.[7] Belgium, which has relatively little natural resources and a small population, performs far better in terms of agricultural production than many larger, more resource-rich Muslim-majority countries. Muslim societies' poor performances in such fields are direct or indirect reflections of the lack of relevant scientific data and methods. With 57 Muslim-majority states as members, the Organization of Islamic Conference (OIC) represents nearly a quarter of the world's population but only 2.4% of its research expenditure, 1.6% of its patents, and 6% of its publications. Over half of the world's gross expenditure on research and development (R&D) comes from the United States and the more advanced economies within the European Union (EU), at 30.6% and 22.6%, respectively, while the OIC's collective share stands at around 2.4%. Japan alone generates 10.3% of the world's gross expenditure on R&D, almost five times more than that of the OIC's 57 Muslims countries combined. Furthermore, between 2000 and 2011, OIC countries were granted only 1.5% of all patents worldwide.[8] The knowledge gap is also observable

in education. Average year of schooling in Muslim-majority countries is
5.6 years, well below the 7.7-year global average. The average year of
schooling among Jews is 13.4 years; among Christians, it is 9.3 years. Yet,
based on adults ages 25 years or older, Muslims along with Hindus have
the largest shares of adherents with no formal education: 36% and 41%,
respectively.[9] Nearly four in ten Muslims have no formal schooling.

Two interrelated problems that this knowledge gap creates are a failure
to apply scientific methods and knowledge to various fields of life, and the
lack of dissemination of scientific thinking among the general population.

How is religion relevant here? Islam as studied and taught in Muslim
societies still claims sweeping authority in shaping Muslims' understanding of nature. As a result, religious ideas on nature, which are acquired
during socialization and education, still determine Muslims' understandings of nature. They bear directly on what the interpretation of religion
promotes in significant issues such as human autonomy and the theory of
knowledge. They also influence people's understanding of how nature
works in relation to laws of causation. Thus, the Islamic idea of nature,
very much like Islamic law, is another level of analysis to observe the
impact of Islam on Muslims. Methodologically, working on the impact of
Islam on Muslims at this level requires answering two questions:

- What does the Islamic idea of nature promote?
- Does the Islamic idea of nature differ from modern, scientific one,
  and if so, does that difference explain Muslim societies' poor perfor-
  mance in various material fields?

This book will answer these questions by studying how Muslims in
Turkey are taught about nature in their religious socialization. We will
see how the scientific and material deficiencies of Muslim societies are
related to their mainstream understanding of nature. Before explaining
Turkey's relevance as a case study, below I will elaborate on why we still
need to take a religious idea of nature into consideration while examining the interaction between Islam and Muslims. In addition, I will explain
the need of the sociohistorical framework of "Sunni orthodoxy" for
studying the Islamic idea of nature in the Turkish case. Though Islam has
survived in the Turkish context with the peculiarities of culture and other
sociological dynamics, the general patterns of Islamic law and theology
as determined by Sunni orthodoxy have been the historical framework in
dictating the interpretation of religion.

1.2   ISLAM'S RESILIENCE

Unlike in Christianity, religious authorities in Islam have been successful in retaining their traditional powers in modernity, and this is the historical reason for studying how the Islamic idea of nature affects the interplay between Islam and Muslims.

To demonstrate the differences between Islam's and Christianity's experiences with modernity, a brief discussion of the development of modernity in Western societies is required. In the Middle Ages, religion was a major organizer of human affairs and human relations with nature.[10] Religion was everywhere, interwoven with everything else, and in no sense constituted a separate sphere of its own.[11] To a large extent, the law that ruled people was inspired by religion. People turned to religion to explain their own existence and character, nature, and the universe.[12]

For this study, one of the most significant effects of modernity was to deprive religion of its authority in legislation and explanation. The modern state acquired legislative power, excluding religion as the source of law. Modernity also developed as a new way of thinking and permitted learned non-clerical men to investigate and explain the natural world and its relationship to human beings. Gradually, modern science displaced religion as the means of understanding the nature. Similarly, modern medicine diminished religion's traditional role in healing.[13] Today, only a doctor's medical report, and not a shaman's or another religious person's, can exempt an employee from work or a student from an exam. In short, Christianity gradually lost many of its traditional powers to modern institutions. It accepted modernity's demand that it transform into a spiritual authority that inspires people without coercion.

Modernity's demand from religion was that it narrows its all-encompassing reach and withdraws from all spheres beyond its own episteme. Modern society is an entity that accommodates clearly demarcated sets of beliefs, practices, and institutions, unlike premodern societies, where religion permeated everywhere.[14]

Unlike Christian religious authorities, religious authorities in Islam did not and still have not completely ceded their powers to modern norms and institutions. Undeniably, Islamic societies have not been unaffected by modernizing dynamics.[15] However, modernizing trends in their cases never paralleled those in Western countries. In other words, Islam survived, though sometimes only partially, the fight with modern institutions over the authority to legislate and to explain nature. For example, apart from strict Islamic states like Saudi Arabia and Iran, there are many states, like Egypt, where Islamic law is recognized as the source of legislation and is the reference for matters like marriage and divorce. Similarly, Islamic law is in effect in many states like Malaysia and Jordan, though in differing degrees and forms. A volume edited by Jan Michiel Otto, *Sharia Incorporated; A Comparative Overview of the Legal Systems of Twelve Muslim Countries in Past and Present*, studies 12 different Muslim countries and concludes that in all these states except Turkey, Islamic law has been incorporated into the legal system.[16] Islam's resilience is also observable at the social level: As a PEW Survey finds, many Muslims say that they want Islamic law to be the official law of the land.[17] Such cases demonstrate Islam's resilience in staying as the source of law.

Law is not the sole field to observe Muslims' different response to modernity. The contemporary Islamic narrative, as we observe in the Turkish case as well as in many other Muslim countries, argues that Islam should remain the ultimate point of reference in other fields like politics as well as in explaining nature. But this is not only a claim: In Turkey, Islamic creed about nature is part of the official school curriculum. There are also thousands of officially sponsored religious clergy who continuously transmit it, and there are many Islamic movements that intensively incorporate it into their indoctrination and activism. Thus, cases like Turkey prove that the encounter of Muslims with modernity should also be studied at different levels in addition to that of the law. Nevertheless, the study of modernity in the context of Muslim societies is usually reduced to a legal and institutional level.

Reflecting that reading, Muslims' various experiences, mainly as part of their urban lives, are often cited as proof of their modernization. For example, an Islamic movement having a radio station is typically interpreted as a sign of modernization. This practice-oriented approach might well account for the wrong expectations among experts. In 1998, Dale F. Eickelman claimed that a Muslim reformation was taking place across the Muslim world at a rate and caliber similar to those of the Protestant Reformation in the sixteenth century.[18] Such analyses and expectations were the result of a particular reading of Muslim politics from institutional and legal perspectives with regard to Muslims' encounter with modernization.

However, as illustrated in Table 1.1, modernization is a complex phenomenon with a paradigmatic aspect that exists beyond the practice level of analysis. Islamic actors who adopt modern practices may still be in

Table 1.1 Different experiences of modernization

Modernity as paradigm	Modernity as practice
Rationality, science, secularism, gender relations	Urbanization, citizenship, modern state, modern international system
Dissociation of fields, rational boundaries	

conflict with modernity at the paradigmatic level. As we shall observe in the case studies of this book, Turkish Islamic actors use modern institutions like media organizations and schools to propagate ideas that are incompatible with modernity. For example, we find many Islamic actors rejecting causality in explanations of natural events while happily employing modern instruments and institutions. The discrepancy in their engagement with modernity at the practical and paradigmatic levels requires closer inspection.

As a result, we do not observe complex secularization, as Jose Casanova defines it, either as the annihilation of the impact of religion in various areas, or as the abolition of its impact by separating religion from fields such as politics.[19] In its full-fledged progress toward modernity, Christianity conceded, after initial resistance, that modern norms and institutions hold the mandate for defining and determining norms and institutions. In exchange for this recognition, the modern system gives freedom to religious faiths and practices, as long as they do not breach the boundaries set by modernity. In this model, there is still a negotiation between religion and modernity; however, it is the pattern of this negotiation for religion to lose any battle against modernity. All too clearly, negotiation between Islam and modernity at the paradigmatic level in Muslim societies does not involve the weakening of religion as it does in Western societies. Islam has not yielded to modernity by recognizing it as the superior framework, obviating the possibility of a Western type of disassociation of fields.

1.3   The Historical Complexity: Sunni Orthodoxy

To study religion's impact on a society is to follow the footsteps of Max Weber, who studied the relationship between various forms of Christianity and capitalism. Weber's method is usually criticized for being essentialist. However, Weber himself confirmed the essentialist aspect in his studies by noting that the principal explanation of the difference between various confessions "must be sought in the permanent, intrinsic character of their religious beliefs, and not only in their temporary external historico-political situations."[20] In striking contrast, contemporary approaches are no longer interested in essentialist analysis; rather, they develop their arguments in relation to temporal, social, and other contexts.

Without an external reference, arguments about an idea of nature would simply be essentialist. Islam is no exception, for like other religions and even political ideologies, its interpretation is constantly contested. Comparison of the various interpretations of Islam is methodologically tautological in the absence of a logically articulated comparator. Therefore, unless one picks up an external reference point to determine one's position, debates that are constructed on certain concepts of a normative or authentic Islam are only essentialist, and often tautological. Thus, the only available method is to approach Islam in a given temporal, social, and other context, the very method that Weber rejected.

I suggest in this book that *Sunni orthodoxy is the incumbent sociohistorical complexity that determines mainstream interpretation of Islam in Turkey like many other Sunni-Muslim societies, including the Islamic idea of nature.* By Sunni orthodoxy, I mean two interrelated phenomena. The first is the interpretation of Islam in terms of law and faith, the proponents of which hold that it is the only valid and correct belief.[21] At this level, orthodoxy is the set of arguments about faith and law that is usually referred to as Sunni Islam. However, orthodoxy is a claim, and it is a claim that can be enforced only through a distinct relationship of power.[22] Therefore, the construction of any orthodoxy requires not only religious scholars, but also state agents in some capacity through a complex network of power relations. Finally, people's participation is also critical, for their engagement is required in propagating and forging religious orthodoxy.[23] Thus, as its second meaning, Sunni orthodoxy refers to a distinct mode of social and political relations in a given society according to which religion is interpreted, institutionalized, and propagated.

Sunni orthodoxy is methodologically important, since it provides us with the sociohistorical complexity, that is, the external reference, according to which we can study how Sunni Muslims have interpreted Islam. It will be the reference frame, or independent variable, in our study, since the very same complexity commands the interpretation of the Islamic idea of nature in contemporary Turkey.

Starting with the second level, that is, the enabling relations of power, Sunni orthodoxy emerged in various complex political, social, and intellectual formations that have shaped the Muslim world since the eleventh century. In the turbulent post-Abbasid period, a convergence of political, economic, and political factors generated complexity in the Muslim world that produced a new ideas and structures. The vacuum left by the fall of the Abbasid order engendered new social and political structures in Islamic societies.[24] Gradually, Sunni orthodoxy consolidated as the dominant perspective way of interpreting and transmitting Islam in Sunni societies. The period included many large-scale changes such as:

- The destruction of Muslim centers of science like Baghdad by the Moghul armies;
- The end of the Abbasid order;
- The rise of a new state traditions of importing foreign cultural and administrative patterns into the Islamic heartland[25]; and
- Important intellectual developments that led to the emergence of a new understanding of Islam epitomized by Abu Hamid al-Ghazali (1055–1111) and his attack on the rationalist philosophers.[26]

The most critical feature of the post-Abbasid Muslim world was the shift to a hierarchical society. Though the first organized intermediaries had emerged to formulate Islamic opinions in the latter periods of the Abbasid state, that earlier era was comparatively anarchical: a variety of opinions and interpretations coexisted, and the legal and theological schools were still in the process of formation. Contending opinions overlapped and intersected. Similarly, there was no fixed model of the kind of hierarchical relationship that was to emerge later and lead to the alignment of political and religious authorities. Such conditions created an anarchical atmosphere in which disparate actors exercised a considerable degree of freedom.[27]

However, developments in the post-Abbasid period introduced a more centralized society that narrowed the space for autonomy-seeking actors likes merchants. There was a creeping militarization of the state, and to some extent, even of the social and economic arrangements of Islamic society, according to traditional Turkic and Persian practices. The new model gradually introduced state ("bureaucratic") rationality as the main factor to dominate all social arrangements, including the erstwhile economic rationality.

Militarization was not limited to the coercive apparatus of the state. It introduced a new type of economic administration into the economy, particularly regarding the use of land, which led to the consolidation of a new state-society model. In general, this was the transition process that brought about the hierarchical social order inspired mainly by the Sassanid political tradition. It differed from the previous, comparatively anarchical and autonomy-granting order, which had been inspired by a Greco-Arabic model.[28]

The Islamic world thus found itself with a model that reorganized society hierarchically and displaced the previous, comparatively autonomous model. The new model, designed mainly along the model of the Sassanid state tradition, reorganized the relationship between state and religion to empower actors to forge a religious orthodoxy.[29] Rational philosophers not only lost their previous influence over rulers but also found themselves under the strict control of both religion and state, their autonomy gradually disappearing. In this new hierarchical model, the military, bureaucrats and civil servants, and the clergy captured the most powerful positions, which reduced the autonomy of civilian groups like merchants and men of science. This was a new government, structurally less receptive to the societal dynamics and prone to imposing its bureaucratic rationality as the key principle of governance.[30] We now see the main political features of the historical move of Islamic societies toward the hierarchical model of the post-Abbasid era.

Going back to the first level of Sunni orthodoxy, that is, the interpretation of Islam in terms of faith and law, the period also determined what is usually referred to as Sunni Islam. To begin with, in this historical context, the intellectual rivalry between philosophy and religion, epitomized by al-Ghazali's attack on philosophy, was less a debate among equals than an attempt by al-Ghazali to reinterpret the relevant issues in the emerging hierarchical model. His challenge to philosophy was not only an effort to correct Aristotelian scholars. It was also a demand that philosophy adapt to the Sunni orthodoxy, as articulated by the allied religious and political authorities. The fight against philosophy was therefore a reflection of the emergence of a new, hierarchical Islamic society. Al-Ghazali's writings themselves symbolized the new power relations between state and religion in the post-Abbasid order and were pivotal in the reorganization of Islamic thought.[31]

Second, and equally importantly, the consolidation of the Sunni orthodoxy also resulted in the formalization of organized theological schools. By the eleventh century, the Mu'tazila had been almost completely destroyed by the Ash'ari school of theology, which was flourishing with official support thanks to the new alliance between Sunni orthodoxy and the Seljuqi state. The rise of the Ash'ari school was a critical change, since it became the dominant theological framework among the Sunni Muslims, securing its place as the dominant paradigm for interpreting the Islamic idea of nature.

Having its origins in the post-Abbasid period, Sunni orthodoxy has survived to this day and remains the dominant framework for interpreting the Islamic idea of nature in contemporary Turkey. Studying the impact of the Islamic idea of nature upon Muslims in Turkey is in fact to study how the Sunni paradigm of nature is reproduced and transmitted in this country. Furthermore, a key legacy of the Sunni orthodoxy, that is, the power relations between clergy and the agents of state, also survives in Turkey, in nearly the same historical form.

1.4 The Islamic Idea of Nature in Turkey

This book studies selected cases from contemporary Turkey to analyze how Muslims are taught about nature in their religious socialization. The purpose of such a study is to explain how the idea of nature relates to the interplay between Islam and Muslims, a relationship that is usually approached in terms of Islamic law or politics.

The Islamic narrative about nature we encounter in Turkey, to be elaborated in later chapters, can be summarized as follows. Natural law has limited power, since nature is governed by divine causation. Natural law is often presented as if it were illusory, enticing human beings away from an understanding of the real power relations in the universe. The narrative teaches either refusal to believe in causality, or the maintenance of a rigorous skepticism about it.[32] God is not only the creator but also the agent of all changes in the nature. The overarching message is God's direct rule. As a personal deity, God governs nature with frequent interventions that result in the suspension of the natural order.[33] Being primarily a theology of God's ultimate power and sovereignty, the Islamic idea of nature in Turkish Islam is very reluctant to recognize an autonomous space for man's will.[34] Its priority is to secure God's sovereignty, so man's freedom is either a secondary issue or merely a matter of moral responsibility. Muslims are advised to appeal directly to God, that is, to divine causation, for it is the real causal agent. Such thinking contributes to a very skeptical stance vis-à-vis modern scientific knowledge. Thus, challenging, and even sometimes deriding, modern science is a common controversy in the contemporary Islamic discourse on nature.[35]

Results from several surveys indicate the same outlook summarized above. A PEW survey conducted in 2012 found that 92% of Turkish people believe in predetermination in life.[36] 63% of Turks believe in the supernatural.[37] This "supernatural" includes miracles, the suspension of the natural order, and God's direct intervention in the world; the common logic behind all such cases is the belief in a divine causation. Almost half of Turks believe that dead ancestors' spirits have the ability to intervene in their life.[38] According to a more recent survey, only 6% of Turkish Muslims believe in a natural order without God's intervention.[39] 84% report that they believe in a God of intervention who governs the universe. Moreover, this intervention is incessant: 91% of Turks believe that God continuously attends to each and every one of them.[40] The flipside of this emphasis on God's intervention is a weak conception of human will: Only 15% of Turks believe that free will determines human actions.[41] Almost 50% of Turks do not accept that a person has the capacity to change the course of his or her life.[42] Reflecting their understanding of causality and divine intervention, most Turks (92.5%) pray very frequently.[43] The survey tells us that almost 60% of them pray daily.[44] Looking in more details, we see that they mainly pray for God's direct intervention in their personal lives in various issues like solving financial problems, having a good marriage, getting good scores on exams, and even having the soccer team they support defeat their rivals.[45] 63% of Turks have no doubt that God responds positively to their prayers.[46]

The above table could be summarized by what Ali Çarkoğlu, a Turkish scholar who conducted various surveys on religiosity in Turkey, once said about the religious understanding of nature in Turkey: Accordingly, it recognizes a higher (or metaphysical) causality that determines events (*Milliyet*, November 17, 2009). Reflecting this, a more critical fact is the strong influence of that understanding as it is conveyed via religious socialization and Islamic activism. Unsurprisingly, its role in many different realms, such as the communications of daily politics and the discourses about science and the West by Islamic agents, is easily observed.

When discussing environmental issues or workplace accidents, megaconstruction projects, or healthcare policies and education, the idea of nature is therefore one of the major discursive frameworks in which competing ideologies clash. A short analysis of several topics in Turkish politics reveals how the Islamic narrative of nature is relevant in the political communication between Islamists and their followers, as well as in the political rivalry between Islamists and secularists. Consider the example of responses to a 2014 mine accident in Soma, a city in western Turkey, in which 301 people were killed. Commenting on the event, Turkish Prime Minister R. Tayyip Erdoğan explained the accident by referring to *fıtrat*, that is, the inherent nature of things as designed by God, leaving no place for human agency in the explanation (*Cumhuriyet*, May 14, 2014). Joining the public debate on the accident to support the government, a professor of Islamic studies noted that the accident is itself an intervention by God. Accordingly, such events are beyond human comprehension since they are directly linked to God's discretion. Reflecting the view that God's acts are above human reasoning, including moral inquiry, the professor advised the victims' families to praise God since they could have faced worse ways of dying (*Hürriyet*, May 14, 2015). In response to a previous mine accident in 2010, Erdoğan emphasized destiny and argued that those with no faith could not understand the disaster (*Milliyet*, May 19, 2014).

The secular response to such events is different. For example, the Turkish Chamber of Mechanical Engineers, a union dominated by secular leftists, publishes regular reports on work accidents and the Islamist government's various projects. These reports often criticize the Islamic interpretation of the nature.[47] Recently, İsmail Saymaz, a journalist popular among secularists, published a book in which he criticizes the Islamist account of causality in the case of work accidents.[48]

As many other cases also reveal, the debate between Islamists and secularists is reminiscent of the debate that European societies had some time ago about the secularization of explanations of issues like poverty, economic status, and nature.[49] It is a debate where we observe how Islamic and secular narratives differ from each other in explaining natural events.

These examples also illustrate how Turkey's recent Islamization, despite its having been subjected to various levels of modernization in the last two centuries, deserves special attention in this inquiry into the function and impact of the Islamic idea of nature. Turkey has passed through a number of critical turning points during this period, such as the Ottoman modernization programs, the early radical Kemalist modernization, and the later modernization to satisfy requirements for European Union membership candidacy.

However, despite that long and intensive modernization, Islamic actors have also exerted considerable influence in line with their Islamist agenda and its highly authoritarian elements as recently as the 2000s. Therefore, Turkey's case is particularly important to understand how and why the Islamic idea of nature remains relevant in such a country. Analysis of this phenomenon provides insights, at a paradigmatic level, into the Turkish society's complex encounter with Islam and modernity. Unlike many other cases, Islamic socialization and Islamization in Turkey have not followed a law-first approach. Analyzing the narratives of Islamic socialization or Islamization, one rarely observes a clear and sophisticated call to make Islamic law the official law of the land. Turkey so far has not incorporated Islamic law into the state system. Instead, Islamization efforts have their most intense clash with modernity in debates about the idea of nature. As this book will demonstrate in detail, the realms of Islamic texts and speeches—which shape the narratives of Islamization in Turkey—are full of long articulations of the Islamic idea of nature while with relatively little attention to Islamic law.

1.5   Studying the Islamic Idea of Nature in Turkey

The study of the Islamic idea of nature is substantively about the sociological interactions of Muslims in socialization, education, and religious activism, and about the interpretation and transmission of the Islamic idea of nature in the context of these interactions.

Logically, this endeavor brings us to the details of how Turks communicate Islam in their particular historical and sociological contexts.[50] Turkish Muslims are a part of the greater Islamic *umma*. However, their relationship with Islam reflects various particularities, especially in the reception and interpretation of Islam in Turkish. Though sharing the general patterns of Islamic theology, Turkish Islam has evolved in its particular sociohistorical context, with its own scholars and texts. The situation is similar in contemporary Turkey when it comes to the interpretation and transmission of the Islamic idea of nature. Contemporary Islamic actors promote engagement with the Islamic idea of nature through the favored discourse structures of the times. In keeping with historical experience, linguistic and cultural factors continue to interact in the interpretation of theology. Corroborating this insight are the several Turkish texts and actors as well as various social movements and institutions that have shaped the evolution of theological thought among Turkish Muslims.

In this account, I examine the interpretation and transmission of the Islamic idea of nature in five cases: the Directorate of Religious Affairs (Diyanet), compulsory religion classes in public education, and the religious movements of İskenderpaşa, Işıkçılar, and Erenköy.

Methodologically, Islam in the Turkish context requires that two inter-related sociological levels be taken into consideration. First, Turkey being a predominantly Muslim society, the average individual is subjected to Islamic socialization. Like other aspects of Islam, the idea of nature is acquired as part of religious socialization. Second, Turkey is home to many Islamic movements that, in their various forms, strive for the Islamization of society. Their efforts result in renewed and more intensive religious indoctrination, which is also key to understanding how these movements interpret and transmit the Islamic idea of nature. The individual person's experience with Islam should be studied at both levels.

Socialization is naturally the most common way for people to learn about religion in Turkey. Two cases are selected for the study of how the Islamic idea of nature is interpreted and transmitted at this level: (i) the Diyanet and (ii) the eight consecutive years of compulsory religious courses for public school students.

The Diyanet is a constitutional organ responsible for managing all religious affairs. The law designates the Diyanet as the monopolist institution in all religious domains, including the articulation of faith. Simply put, it has the constitutional power to define Islamic orthodoxy for the Turkish state.[51] With so many means and opportunities to transmit its interpretation as official Islam, the Diyanet is a major actor in religious socialization.[52] Organized across the country, the Diyanet had 112,725 employees as of 2016.[53] It enjoys official as well as social support. In a survey, 60% of Turks responded that they see Diyanet imams as the prime authorities in religious matters.[54] As is observable in several surveys, there is a consensus in society that the Diyanet is the second source of religious socialization and learning, after the family.[55] Thus, the ways in which the Diyanet interprets the Islamic idea of nature are critical to this study.

Compulsory religious courses are the second important case to observe how Turkish people are taught about the Islamic idea of nature in schools. It is a constitutional requirement that students attend courses of religious instruction during eight consecutive years. As a consequence, students have religious courses from fourth through twelfth grade. Primary education in Turkey consists of four years of elementary (1–4) school and four years of middle school (5–8). It is followed by secondary education (high school), another 4 years (9–12). The courses are instruments by which the state promotes official Islam in line with its societal vision.[56] These courses are critical to this project, since they provide students with their first rigorous instruction about the Islamic idea of nature. Religious textbooks have detailed sections on the various aspects of nature, falling under the sub-themes of causality, free will, and the theory of knowledge. Naturally, examining how the Islamic idea of nature is interpreted and transmitted through these courses is an important part of this study.

Both in the case of the Diyanet and the compulsory religious courses, religious socialization and learning take place in early, formative years. A survey shows that 86.9% of Turks get most of their religious knowledge before age 17.[57] Having social and legal support, the Diyanet and compulsory religious courses dominate early Islamic socialization and learning. In the classical Durkheimian sense, they are typical examples of a formal and systematic socialization.[58]

To study the Islamic idea of nature in the context of Islamic movements, this book takes three cases: İskenderpaşa, Işıkçılar, and Erenköy. Turkey historically has been a hub of many Islamic movements. The three selected social movements offer typical examples of Islamic socialization, each dating back to the nineteenth century. They provide rich evidence concerning the phenomenon we study in this book. In addition, their impact on their followers, as well as on the public, has been decisive in the recent Islamization of Turkey. Furthermore, the rise of Islamic politics and society in Turkey has been advanced by various actors, including the three Islamic movements studied in this book. The analysis of these three cases from the perspective of the Islamic idea of nature provides us with important insights into the motivations and strategies of the Islamizing actors, from a perspective that differs from that of the more common law- or politics-oriented studies.

1.6   THE STRUCTURE OF THE BOOK

The subject of this study requires that this book follows two tracks: the historical and the contemporary. Though the prime purpose is to understand how the Islamic idea of nature is interpreted and transmitted in contemporary Turkey, the book addresses historical questions as well, for that is methodologically required for tracing the origins and consolidation of the Islamic idea of nature, and how Islam in the Turkish case is linked to those origins.

Chapter 2, "Origins: Sunni Orthodoxy," introduces the grand social and historical complexity that determines the mainstream interpretation of Islam in Turkey. To paraphrase Weber here, this is the external historico-political situation in which Islam is interpreted. I previously quoted Shahab

Ahmad's definition of orthodoxy as both a set of ideas as well as a reflection of certain power relations. Accordingly, this chapter is about the power relations between religion and political authorities. Our findings in this chapter are methodologically important: it is almost the same mode of connections between Sunni orthodoxy and political power that empower Islamic agents' to promote their interpretations as the correct ones in Turkey today.

Chapter 3 explains the contending narratives of nature within the Sunni Islamic theological tradition. Briefly, a religious idea of nature is defined as the collection of theological propositions about how nature works that Muslims acquire in their religious socialization. Those propositions are expounded in an immense body of literature. I attempt to systematize them in a plain and consistent framework. Accordingly, the Islamic idea of nature is examined in terms of four major constitutive elements: causality, free will, knowledge, and the concept of God. I submit that this is a reliable method for investigating the understanding the "Islamic idea of nature" across the five cases. I explain these four topics according to the Ash'ari, the Maturidi, and the Mu'tazili schools of theology. We need to outline the main Islamic perspectives on these four issues to make sense of how the Islamic idea of nature is interpreted in present-day Turkey. This will enable us to understand and categorize what Islamic socialization teaches about the Islamic idea of nature.

Debates about nature involve arguments drawn from the various schools of Islamic theology, including the Ash'ari, the Maturidi, and the Mu'tazila. The Islamic idea of nature is fundamentally a theological issue, since Islamic authorities often advance their propositions about nature in theological terms. Historically, discussions of the idea of nature in Islamic societies have been transmitted mainly through the Islamic schools of theology. Thus, Chap. 4 examines the historical evolution of Turkish Islam (i.e. the negotiations of Turks and the Islamic theological schools) by studying how Islam in Turkey has positioned itself in the general debates about Islamic theology between two schools: the Ash'ari and the Maturidi. This chapter is methodologically important for investigating the historical patterns of continuity and differentiation that have affected Turks' theological views.

Chapter 5, "Mapping the Cases: Official Islam and Islamic Movements," surveys the five selected cases in terms of their genealogy, historical evolution, structure, and methods of activism. The main purpose of the chapter is to introduce the reader to the selected cases of the book. The chapter also explains the rationale behind the selection of these five cases and clarifies their relevance to the understanding of the Islamic idea of nature in the Turkish context. In this vein, given that three of the cases are Islamic movements (Işıkçılar, İskenderpaşa, and Erenköy), the chapter includes a discussion on how to interpret them within the larger frame of Islamic activism by proposing three models: reformism, renewalism, and revivalism.

Chapter 6 studies the five selected cases' interpretation and transmission of the Islamic idea of nature in terms of causality, free will, knowledge, and the concept of God. The purpose of this chapter is to explore how Islamic actors interpret and transmit the Islamic idea of nature to their followers as well as to the larger public in Turkey. While studying how Islamic authorities and actors articulate their respective ideas of nature, the chapter also explains where their narratives are situated within the Islamic tradition. Drawing from the works of scholars and leading thinkers of Islamic movements, the chapter offers a critical analysis of the Islamic idea of nature as interpreted and transmitted in Turkey.

This book's account of Muslims' encounter with modernity at the paradigmatic level and examination of the dimensions of the debate on the Islamic idea of nature together offer new insights into the limits of change in Muslims' interpretation of Islam. Therefore, the book concludes with a general discussion of how its findings are relevant to understanding Muslim societies with respect to debates over change, reform, and modernization.

NOTES

1. Kuran, "The Absence of the Corporation in Islamic Law," 785–834. Kuran, "The Islamic Commercial Crisis," 415.
2. Kuran, *The Long Divergence*, 7. Kuran, "Why the Middle East is Economically Underdeveloped," 71.
3. Facchini, "Religion, Law and Development," 103–129.
4. Çizakça, *Islamic Capitalism and Finance Origins*, xiv–xv.
5. Guiso, Sapienza and Zingales, "People's Opium Religion and Economic Activities," 228–229.
6. Halverson, *Theology and Creed in Sunni Islam*, 5.
7. World Trade Organization, "Statistical Tables," Accessed June 1, 2017. https://www.wto.org/english/res_e/statis_e/wts2016_e/wts16_chap9_e.htm
8. Clarke, Eryetli and Selçuk, *The Atlas of Islamic World*, 8, 19, 36.

9. PEW Research Center, "Religion and Education Around the World, 13 December 2016," Accessed July 5, 2018. http://www.pewforum. org/2016/12/13/religion-and-education-around-the-world/

10. Southern, *Western Society and the Church*, 16.

11. Taylor, *A Secular Age*, 2.

12. Luxton, "The Reformation and Popular Culture," 62–63.

13. Marcum, *Humanizing Modern Medicine*, 18.

14. Taylor, *A Secular Age*, 15.

15. My assumptions here are to a great extent also valid for Shi'a Islam in the case of Iran. The fusion of Shi'ism and state after 1979 proves Islam's resilience in retaining its traditional authorities in many fields. Moazami, *State, Religion and Revolution in Iran*. Unsurprisingly, a typical case is to observe this resilience is education in Iran. Mahran and Adli, "Female Education in the Islamic Republic," 15–35.

16. Otto, "Introduction: investigating the role of sharia," 27.

17. PEW Research Center, "The World's Muslims: Religion, Politics and Society, 30 April 2013," Accessed August 8, 2018. http://www.pewforum.org/2013/04/30/the-worlds-muslims-religion-politics-society-overview/

18. Eickelman, "Inside the Islamic Reformation," 82.

19. Casanova, "Rethinking Secularization," 7. Casanova, *Public Religions in the Modern World*, 12–20.

20. Weber, *The Protestant Ethic*, 7.

21. Ahmad, *Before Orthodoxy*, 3.

22. Ibid.

23. Al Shamsy, "The Social Construction of Orthodoxy," 97.

24. Hodgson, *The Venture of Islam Vol. II*, 12.

25. Lapidus, *A History of Islamic Societies*, 111.

26. Hirschler, *Medieval Arabic Historiography*, 44.

27. Saliba, *Islamic Science*, 87.

28. Walbridge, *God and Logic in Islam*, 19.

29. Spuler, *Iran in the Early Islamic Period*, 2–3. Lambton, *State and Government*, 68.

30. Safi, *The Politics of Knowledge*, 112.

31. Griffel, *Al-Ghazali's Philosophical Theology*, 102–103.

32. Işık, *Tam İlmihal*, 82. Coşan, *Tabakatü's-Sufiyye Sohbetleri II*, 582. Topbaş, *Gönül Bahçesinden*, 176.

33. Karaman, Bardakoğlu and Apaydın, *Ilmihal I*, 66. Karaman et al., *Kur'an Yolu Türkçe Meal ve Tefsir III*, 405.

34. Işık, *Faideli Bilgiler*, 233. Topbaş, *Gönül Bahçesinden*, 177.

35. Coşan, *Tabakatü's-Sufiyye Sohbetleri II*, 231. Işık, *Namaz*, 155. Topbaş, *The Islamic Approach to Reasoning*, 82.

36. PEW Research Center, "The World's Muslims: Unity and Diversity, 9 August 2012," Accessed August 4, 2018. www.pewforum.org
37. Ibid.
38. Çarkoğlu and Kalaycıoğlu, *Türkiye'de Dindarlık*, 18.
39. Kulat, *Türkiye'de Toplumun Dine ve Dini Değerlere Bakışı*, 4.
40. Ibid., 8.
41. Ibid., 9.
42. Çarkoğlu and Kalaycıoğlu, *Türkiye'de Dindarlık*, 7.
43. Subaşı, *Türkiye'de Dini Hayat*, 101.
44. PEW Research Center, "The Age Gap in Religion Around the World, 13 June 2018," Accessed August 5, 2018. https://www.pewforum.org/2018/06/13/the-age-gap-in-religion-around-the-world/
45. Çarkoğlu and Kalaycıoğlu, *Türkiye'de Dindarlık*, 30.
46. Ibid., 31.
47. http://sendika10.org/2016/08/mmo-olumler-bu-isin-fitratinda-degil/ Accessed October 24, 2016.
48. Saymaz, *Fıtrat: İş Kazası Değil, Cinayet*, 1–25.
49. Wandel, "The Poverty of Christ," 22.
50. Ocak, *Türk Sufiliğine Bakışlar*, 79.
51. Kara, "Diyanet İşleri Başkanlığı," 183.
52. Gözaydın, *Diyanet Türkiye Cumhuriyeti'nde Dinin Tanzimi*, 1–24. Kara, "Din ve Devlet Arasına Sıkışmış Bir Kurum," 29.
53. Diyanet İşleri Başkanlığı, "İstatistikler," Accessed January 11, 2018. https://www.Diyanet.gov.tr/tr-TR/Kurumsal/Detay//6/Diyanet-isleri-baskanligi-istatistikleri
54. Subaşı, *Türkiye'de Dini Hayat*, 139.
55. Ibid., 122.
56. Cesari, *The Awakening of Muslim Democracy*, 89.
57. Subaşı, *Türkiye'de Dini Hayat*, 112.
58. Durkheim, *Education and Sociology*, 124.

References

Ahmad, Shahab. 2017. *Before Orthodoxy: The Satanic Verses in Early Islam*. Cambridge, MA: Harvard University Press.

Çarkoğlu, Ali, and Ersin Kalaycıoğlu. 2009. *Türkiye'de Dindarlık: Uluslararası Bir Karşılaştırma*. Istanbul: IPM.

Casanova, Jose. 1980. *Public Religions in the Modern World*. Chicago and London: The University of Chicago Press.

———. 2006. Rethinking Secularization: A Global Comparative Perspective. *The Hedgehog Review* 8 (1/2): 7–22.

Cesari, Jocelyne. 2014. *The Awakening of Muslim Democracy: Religion, Modernity and the State*. New York: Cambridge University Press.

Çizakça, Murat. 2011. *Islamic Capitalism and Finance: Origins, Evolution and the Future*. Cheltenham: E. Elgar.

Clarke, Luke, H.H. Eryetli, and Z.Z. Selçuk. 2014. *The Atlas of Islamic World Science and Innovation Final Report*. San Francisco: Creative Commons.

Coşan, M. Esad. 2016. *Tabakatü's-Sufiyye Sohbetleri II*. Ankara: M. Erkaya.

Durkheim, Emile. 1956. *Education and Sociology*. New York: The Free Press.

Eickelman, Dale F. 1998. Inside the Islamic Reformation. *The Wilson Quarterly* 22 (1): 80–89.

El Shamsy, Ahmed. 2008. The Social Construction of Orthodoxy. In *The Cambridge Companion to Classical Islamic Theology*, ed. Tim Winter, 97–118. Cambridge: Cambridge University Press.

Facchini, François. 2010. Religion, Law and Development: Islam and Christianity—Why is it in Occident and Not in the Orient that Man Invented the Institutions of Freedom? *European Journal of Law and Economics* 29 (1): 103–129.

Gözaydın, İştar. 2009. *Diyanet: Türkiye Cumhuriyeti'nde Dinin Tanzimi*. Istanbul: İletişim.

Griffel, Frank. 2017. *Al-Ghazali's Philosophical Theology*. Oxford: Oxford University Press.

Guiso, Luigi, Paola Sapienza, and Luigi Zingales. 2003. People's Opium Religion and Economic Activities. *Journal of Monetary Economics* 50 (1): 225–282.

Halverson, Jeffry R. 2010. *Theology and Creed in Sunni Islam: The Muslim Brotherhood, Ash'arism, and Political Sunnism*. New York: Palgrave Macmillan.

Hirschler, Konrad. 2006. *Medieval Arabic Historiography: Authors as Actors*. London: Routledge.

Hodgson, Marshall G.S. 1977. *The Venture of Islam Vol. II*. Chicago: The University of Chicago Press.

Işık, Hüseyin Hilmi. 2014a. *Faideli Bilgiler*. Istanbul: Hakikat.

———. 2014b. *Tam İlmihal Se'adet-i Ebediyye*. Istanbul: Hakikat.

———. 2017. *Namaz*. Istanbul: Hakikat.

Kara, İsmail. 2000. Din ve Devlet Arasına Sıkışmış Bir Kurum: Diyanet İşleri Başkanlığı. *Marmara İlahiyat Fakültesi Dergisi* 18 (1): 29–55.

———. 2005. Diyanet İşleri Başkanlığı. In *İslamcılık*, ed. Yasin Aktay, Tanıl Bora, and Murat Gültekingil, 45–66. Istanbul: İletişim.

Karaman, Hayreddin, Ali Bardakoğlu, and H. Yunus Apaydın. 1998. *Ilmihal I*. Ankara: Diyanet İşleri Başkanlığı.

Karaman, Hayreddin, I. Mustafa Çağrıcı, Kafi Dönmez, and Sadrettin Gümüş. 2012. *Kur'an Yolu Türkçe Meal ve Tefsir III*. Ankara: DİB.

Kulat, Mehmet Ali. 2017. *Türkiye'de Toplumun Dine ve Dini Değerlere Bakışı*. Ankara: MAK.

Kuran, Timur. 2003. The Islamic Commercial Crisis: Institutional Roots of Economic Underdevelopment in the Middle East. *The Journal of Economic History* 63 (2): 414–446.

———. 2004. Why the Middle East is Economically Underdeveloped: Historical Mechanisms of Institutional Stagnation. *Journal of Economic Perspectives* 18 (3): 71–90.

———. 2005. The Absence of the Corporation in Islamic Law: Origins and Persistence. *American Journal of Comparative Law* 53 (4): 785–834.

———. 2011. *The Long Divergence: How Islamic Law Held Back the Middle East.* Princeton: Princeton University Press.

Lambton, Ann K.S. 1991. *State and Government in Medieval Islam.* London: Routledge.

Lapidus, Ira. 2002. *A History of Islamic Societies.* Cambridge: Cambridge University Press.

Luxton, Imogen. 1977. The Reformation and Popular Culture. In *Church and Society in England: Henry VIII to James I*, ed. Felicity Heal and Rosemary O'day, 57–77. New York: Macmillan.

Marcum, James A. 2008. *Humanizing Modern Medicine: An Introductory Philosophy of Medicine.* New York: Springer.

Mehran, Golnar, and Fariba Adli. 2019. Female Education in the Islamic Republic of Iran: Understanding the Paradox of Tradition and Modernity. In *Women, Islam, and Education in Iran*, ed. Goli M. Rezai-Rashti, Golnar Mehran, and Shirin Abdmolaei, 15–34. New York: Routledge.

Muazami, Behrooz. 2013. *State, Religion, and Revolution in Iran, 1796 to the Present.* New York: Palgrave Macmillan.

Ocak, Ahmet Y. 1996. *Türk Sufiliğine Bakışlar.* Istanbul: İletişim.

Otto, Jan Michiel. 2010. Introduction: Investigating the Role of Sharia in National Law. In *Sharia Incorporated; A Comparative Overview of the Legal Systems of Twelve Muslim Countries in Past and Present*, ed. Jan Michiel Otto, 17–50. Leiden: Leiden University Press.

Safi, Omid. 2006. *The Politics of Knowledge in Premodern: Islam Negotiating Ideology and Religious Inquiry.* Chapel Hill: The University of North Caroline Press.

Saliba, George. 2007. *Islamic Science and the Making of the European Renaissance.* Cambridge and London: The MIT Press.

Saymaz, İsmail. 2017. *Fıtrat: İş Kazası Değil, Cinayet.* Istanbul: İletişim.

Southern, R.W. 1990. *Western Society and the Church in the Middle Ages.* London: Penguin.

Spuler, Bertold. 2015. *Iran in the Early Islamic Period: Politics, Culture, Administration and Public Life between the Arab and the Seljuk Conquests, 633–1055.* Brill: Leiden and Boston.

Subaşı, Nejdet. 2014. *Türkiye'de Dini Hayat Araştırması*. Ankara: Diyanet İşleri Başkanlığı.

Taylor, Charles. 2007. *A Secular Age*. Cambridge: Belknap.

Topbaş, Osman Nuri. 2016a. *Gönül Bahçesinden Son Nefes*. Istanbul: Erkam.

———. 2016b. *The Islamic Approach to Reasoning and Philosophy*. Istanbul: Erkam.

Walbridge, John. 2011. *God and Logic in Islam: The Caliphate of Reason*. Cambridge: Cambridge University Press.

Wandel, Lee P. 2003. The Poverty of Christ. In *The Reformation of Charity: The Secular and the Religious in Early Modern Poor Relief*, ed. T. Max Safely, 15–29. Boston: Brill.

Weber, Max. 2005. *The Protestant Ethic and the Spirit of Capitalism*. London and New York: Routledge.

Origins: Sunni Orthodoxy

Sunni orthodoxy has framed the trajectory of the Islamic concept of nature in Turkey. Therefore, before analyzing the Turkish case, I first examine the origins of Sunni orthodoxy, the significance of the idea of nature within that tradition, and how that tradition historically has reflected power relations between religion and political power.

Sunni orthodoxy emerged slowly over centuries through political as well as religious debate both among Muslims and between Muslims and non-Muslims.[1] We are interested in the political and intellectual developments that played a role in the formation of what became the Islamic idea of nature, which brings us to a peculiar set of complex political, social, and intellectual formations that developed between the eleventh and thirteenth centuries. While weakening and even abolishing some previous political, intellectual, and economic structures, various dynamics and patterns gradually differentiated themselves to form the new understanding of Islam that emerged roughly in the period between the demise of the Abbasid order and the rise of the Seljuqi state as a new norm-creating polity.[2]

Both mainstream and revisionist historical narratives recognize this period as one of critical change in Islamic political culture, though they differ in their assessments of its consequences. Mainstream accounts generally interpret the period as the beginning of the decline of Islamic civilization, while revisionist accounts reject that judgment and argue that the decline of Islamic civilization was a "myth."[3] The period is a laboratory specimen of Islamic history, displaying critical developments such as the

© The Author(s) 2020   25
G. Bacik, *Islam and Muslim Resistance to Modernity in Turkey*,
https://doi.org/10.1007/978-3-030-25901-3_2

end of the Abbasid order; the introduction of cultural and administrative forms from the Steppes to the Islamic heartland; and the emergence of a new understanding of Islam that is epitomized by al-Ghazali and his attacks on philosophy.[4]

I suggest a three-part periodization of the development of Sunni orthodoxy over the course of history of Islam:

The Formative Period: This is roughly the first century of Islam, when the Prophet Muhammad and his companions and first successors lived. During this period, normative practice was based on the example of the Prophet Muhammad and his companions rather than on scholarly texts or an established school of law/thought. All Muslims who lived in this period had an ability to affect the evolution of new religion, though at differing degrees. Even an unknown companion who put a question to Prophet had a formative effect on the emerging conception of Islam. The formative period opened with Muhammad's declaration of his prophecy in 610 and lasted until the death of the last companion, Abu et-Tufayl Amir ibn Wathilah, in c. 724.[5] The critical legacy of this period is the revelation and the practices of Muhammad and his companions.

The Age of Autonomy: This is more or less the same period of time that Marshall Hodgson calls "the Earlier Middle Period."[6] It spans from the early eighth century into the twelfth century. In that period, the first organized intermediaries emerged to formulate Islamic teachings in systematic forms. However, the key dynamics that forged the essential characteristic of the age were comparatively anarchic and let divergent interpretations coexist.

Muslim philosophers' engagement with Greek thought occurred in this period. The legal and theological schools were still in the process of formation; no solid borders had yet demarcated the schools, and the cordial intercourse of contending opinions was possible. As Daniel Gimaret explains, the general *zeitgeist* of the period supported "an extreme diversity of people and doctrines."[7] There was no established hierarchical divide between political and religious authorities. The absence of such a divide fostered an atmosphere in which actors could claim high level of autonomy.

A variety of power structures naturally governed society during the Age of Autonomy. However, there was no single institution that could define political and religious orthodoxy. This atmosphere tolerated rationalist scholars' influence on Muslim intellectual life and institutions. The rationalist scholars not only exerted influence over society but also exercised substantial agency in matters of religion. George Saliba notes scientists' close affiliation "with the religious functioning of the society," sometimes even serving at the "helm of religious offices."[8] There was no orthodoxy to deny their legitimacy as interpreters of Islam.

The Age of Orthodoxy: Sunni orthodoxy has its origins in the political turmoil that led to the collapse of the Arab-Muslim cosmopolitan order, that is, the latter period of the Age of Autonomy. The decline of Abbasid power rendered the caliphate a merely figurehead post by the mid-eleventh century. The period paved the way for new dynamics and institutions that would transform the Muslim community. New social-political structures emerged and determined the interplay between Muslims and their religion.[9] The most critical development of this period was the hierarchical structuring of society, according to which social, political, and religious/intellectual life was organized according to an institutionalized orthodoxy. This development marked the shift in Muslim societies from a Greco-Arab understanding of society and nature to an Islamic-Sassanid one.

As I discussed in the Introduction, doctrinal unity is only one aspect of religious orthodoxy; religious orthodoxy is also defined by its formulation, reproduction, and transmission in a contingent and complex relationship to political authority.[10] Thus religious orthodoxy requires three elements: doctrinal unity among religious authorities; consensus between religious and political authorities; and the transmission of religious doctrine into a society by available means. The historical significance of this period is the hierarchical organization of society and the development of the three elements required for the institutionalization of religious orthodoxy.

In this chapter, I will first examine the transition to the post-Abbasid order, the historical conjuncture when Sunni orthodoxy emerged. I will then discuss the general characteristics of that orthodoxy's doctrine as pertains to the Islamic concept of nature.

2.1   THE DECLINE OF AUTONOMOUS STRUCTURES

The collapse of the Abbasid order cleared a space for a new Islamic regional order in which contending actors, including the Seljuqs, aspired to power and promoted their own cultural and political traditions.[11] At times, these contending powers went to war with the Abbasid caliphate; at other times, they traded and cooperated across overlapping borders.[12]

The transition was a prolonged one. Local political powers and military groups nominally under Abbasid rule asserted greater and greater autonomy, which in turn led to economic problems, particularly in agricultural production and taxation. This fragmentation of authority was an opportunity for political actors who had already parceled out their lands on the periphery, and for the autonomous military groups aspiring to dominance.[13] Gradually, these changes engendered a more militaristic and hierarchical state-society relations the Islamic heartland.[14]

Rising states such as the Samanids in Transoxiana, the Ghaznavids in Afghanistan, and the Seljuqs, who had moved from Transoxiana to Anatolia, introduced new ideas and practices from other cultural zones.[15] These ideas and practices generally came from non-Arab regions and included interpretations of Islam that were different from that of the Abbasid order. Unlike in the western regions like Iraq and Syria, where Arabic was the predominant language, in the eastern lands where many rising states originated, Persian dominated. Thus, not only the Samanids and Buyids but also the Ghaznavids and Seljuqs spread Persian administrative culture.[16] At the same time, these state's institutional foundation was the tribe organized around the military. This organization resulted in the militarization of state and society. For example, Seljuqs were organized on the basis of military and tribal federations and were in most parts bereft of urban culture. However, the issue was a matter not only of administrative incompetence but also of cultural difference. For example, the Buyids quickly patronized the arts and literature once they established themselves as regional power; however, the way they linked these activities to political authority differed from the Abbasid precedent.[17]

These rising states promoted a new type of militaristic state and transformed state-society relations into a strictly hierarchical configuration, which harmed the interests of merchants. Thus, militarization redefined the composition of political power and established vertical power relations where political authority was almost free from societal influences.

This militarization had its origins in the rise of various warring tribes, including the Turks, as early as the ninth century.[18] It is possible to trace the Turks' fame as highly skilled warriors; al-Jahiz (775–868) reports that Turks were mostly known for their military service.[19] Such groups quickly became useful to Arab rulers who needed warriors but also faced a loyalty problem within their own communities. Al-Ghazali also hints at the historic transformation associated with the arrival of the Turks. He called them "the holders of power" in his explanation of why the Caliph needed them. Al-Ghazali believed that beyond their military ability, the Turks had no political means of attaining power, such as a system of urban culture or a sophisticated administrative tradition.[20] Apparently, the Abbasids saw eastern lands like Khorasan "as a prime source of manpower."[21] Thus, warring groups like Turks were valued as mercenaries who obviated the need to forge additional political allegiances for they were seen as military groups isolated from the larger community.

But this initially military arrangement gradually affected Abbasid politics. Even as early as the Caliph Mutawakkil (reign 847–861), there was criticism that the Turkic military groups were isolating the ruler.[22] Later, in 870, Caliph Muhtadi (reign 869–870) was forced to negotiate with his mercenary soldiers, even over their share of state revenues—strong evidence that the military groups were evolving as an autonomous group.[23] The early image of the professional warrior expired as these soldiers gradually transformed into *de facto* political groups with their distinct interests and internal loyalty.

Organized though they had become as a political-military group, they were still nomadic and economically collectivist.[24] For example, the tribe had a central role in the allocation of land for habitation and grazing. Moreover, the tribe as a collective unit generally did not want to share its sovereignty over the land with the ruler. This, as Lambton observes in the case of the Seljuqs, rendered the ruler the leader of the people but not a territorial sovereign.[25] The tribal unit itself also had military aspects. For the Seljuqs, the *uymaq* (household state) was also a military formation, and all groups' loyalty was expressed as military allegiance to the leader.[26] Seljuq political order and economic infrastructure were linked through tribal and military networks.

Unlike in the previous Abbasid-Islamic state, in the Seljuq state, politics and the economy were militarized, and the warriors were set apart from the rest of society.[27] This differentiation secured for the warriors special privileges and a status at the top of the hierarchy. Soldiers' autonomy far exceeds that of other social groups. Marshall Hodghson glosses the new model thus:

> Properly speaking, such a state had no capital city: the capital was the army, wherever it happened to be camped at the moment. The monarch was monarch because he was commander-in-chief, and he was expected not to act by deputy; unlike the first caliphs … in principle, all forces were concentrated in one army and so in one expedition. Indeed, the whole state apparatus was organized as a single massive army.[28]

An examination of the *iqta* system also reveals the way this new military-dominated hierarchy affected the economy. In the Abbasid system, regular military troops were paid salaries from the central budget, which was fed by taxes and other revenues.[29] In several rising states, the *iqta* system, that is, the distribution of land to soldiers, replaced this salary model.[30] For example, the *iqta* system became the main pillar of the Seljuqi order.[31] *Iqta* played a key role in Nizam al-Mulk's strategy of developing an absolutist theory of land ownership, relying on the Sassanid tradition, where the sultan was the sole owner of the soil.[32]

The essential problem with the *iqta* system was that it turned professionally irrelevant people like soldiers into stakeholders in the economy.[33] When the Buyids implemented the system, Ibn Miskawayh (d. 1030) predicted that its negative impact would be seen first in agricultural productivity and taxation.[34] He warned that the *iqta* might be destructive if it failed to keep pace with economic realities. Confirming his prediction, the practice of *iqta* was resented by a considerable number of merchants, and some of them even left urban centers. Regression in the agricultural economy was also inevitable. As Ibn Miskawayh remarked, the officials in the *iqta* did nothing to increase agricultural productivity, and even cultivation was given up entirely.[35] "Soldiers make bad landlords," as Heribert Busse wrote, and the whole system caused a severe and long-lasting impoverishment of the country, with the additional cost of the displacement of the peasantry.[36] Lacking the needed expertise, new landlords conducted endless debates about the proper exchange of *iqta* assignments. This preoccupation resulted in serious problems, like the neglect of irrigation.[37] A further result was the abandonment of large tracts of land and their transfer from private to state ownership. Like that of the Buyids, the Seljuqs' *iqta* system also set in motion the transfer of land tenure out of the control of hereditary families.[38] Over and over again, land was distributed to soldiers. Under this system, the military, as the leading group of officials, were linked to the economic and fiscal segments of the state through the new land tenure system, which harmed classes like the merchants and cultivators. *Iqta* also weakened the market: Since a large portion of the dues was presumably paid in kind, it resulted in agricultural products to be consumed without being routed through markets.[39] It also pushed merchants to invest primarily in state-linked businesses and generally to fall in line with the state agenda.[40] Thus, the general consequence of *iqta* was an economy built into the hierarchical state bureaucracy and in which autonomy-seeking actors like merchants were allowed little space.[41]

2.2   THE NEW IDEA OF RULERSHIP

If the new militaristic and nomadic patterns formed the basis of state-society relations in the post-Abbasid period, then the Sassanid administrative tradition provided the super-structural framework.[42]

Even after the spread of Islam throughout Persia, Persian intellectual elites retained preserved much of their pre-Islamic culture.[43] Paradoxically, the Islamization of the Persian people provided an unprecedented opportunity for the Persian culture to go beyond its historical geographical domain by reframing itself as Islamic (and not merely Persian).[44] At the same time, with the Islamization of the Iranian people, Islam had spread beyond the Arabs.[45] Thus, Islam's encounter with Persia entailed a reconciliation between and synthesis of two great cultural traditions. This was especially the case when it came to administration and governance, as ancient Sassanid ideas of rulership were incorporated into Islamic political thought.[46]

The term "Turco-Persian" normally refers to two different linguistic zones. However, the Persian linguistic zone, with its administrative and cultural heritage, was the ascendant model even among the Turkic groups. In the course of the interaction of the two cultures, several successor states, including the Seljuqs, helped the Persian elements bring their impact on the Islamic tradition. In fact, the Eastern lands had already become the new center of gravity in the Islamic world as early as the eighth century. Al-Tabari's *History* indicates many events that occupied the agenda of Caliph Hisham (724–743) were linked to developments in the Eastern lands.[47] The early Persian influence through translation and newly adopted administrative practice dates back to his rule. Another example of Persian influence is the financial practices of Caliph Abd al-Malik in the late seventh century.[48] Thus, starting with the Umayyads and accelerating with the Abbasids, the Arab caliphate had incorporated Persian elements that ranged from the literary to the administrative.[49]

In this vein, the rise of transcendental concepts of statehood and kingship among Muslims was one of the most significant developments. Before, there was no concept of leadership as an organized form of a transcendental mythos. It was only after the incorporation of the Sassanid model of rulership that Islamic political thought would assert a transcendental authority.

In the Sasanian system, the monarch was the central figure and enjoyed a privileged position in the esteem of the Stars and the Sun. People saluted him as "king of the four corners of the world,"[50] reminiscent of the Roman tradition of sacred kingship. Both the Roman and the Persian conceptions of sacred kingship were transcendental and independent of religious endorsement. In both cultures, kingship was as sacred as a religious narrative could be. In a letter to the Roman Emperor Maurice, the Sasanian King Kosrow II described the Roman and the Sassanid empires as the two eyes through which God affects the world. The portrayal by Kosrow II of the Roman and the Sassanid empires encapsulates the Sassanid model of sacred kingship, in which the king mediates between heaven and earth.[51]

Unlike the Sassanid king, the Arab-Muslim caliph was never a transcendental leader. Not having a mythological quality, the caliphate was a practical solution that the Muslim community devised after the death of the Prophet.[52] As al-Mawardi theorized, the caliph succeeded to prophethood as a means of protecting the faith managing the affairs of this world. In this narrative which would be mostly embraced by the Sunnis, the necessity of Islamic leadership is mostly defended by rational argument rather than by claims of the transcendent authority of the leader.[53] The caliph never engaged in any sacred mediation between God and man. The caliphate was a religious office and held the utmost authority in matters of religion—"all political and religious authority being concentrated in it" as Patricia Crone and Martin Hinds note.[54] However, the caliph had no independent transcendental attributes that were either above or equal to religion.

Thus, since the first day of Abu Bakr's reign, the caliph did not enjoy any divine authority. Neither Islam nor the traditional Arabic tribal code allowed him to claim such a status. The caliphate had no spiritual dimension.[55] If we put communal support or homage (*bay'a*) aside, the only symbolic authority a caliph could claim was that of being a successor to the Prophet. Yet even that is realized differently in practice. For example, the original title of the first caliph, Abu Bakr, was *khalifat rasul Allah* (successor of the Prophet). Following the same logic, for a while the Muslims called the second caliph, Umar, *khalifatu khalifati rasul Allah* (successor of the Prophet's successor). In other words, Umar was the successor of Abu Bakr who was the successor of the Prophet.

Indeed, the caliphate evolved into an Arab-style kingship in the Umayyad period, whose rulers thereby distinguished themselves from the early caliphs.[56] The Umayyads used a myriad of instruments to claim legitimacy, ethnic and as well as religious. For example, in the eighth century, the Arab theory of rulership was quite different from that of the early Islamic caliphate and shared some elements with Sassanid theories of rulership. However, the eighth-century Arab theory of rulership never acquired any transcendental aspect, so even during the reigns of Hisham (724–743) and Walid II (743–744), the basis of legitimacy for the Umayyad caliphs rested largely on the consensus of the Umayyad elites and not on any religious doctrine.[57]

Under the influence of Sassanid administrative techniques implemented by the Seljuqs and other successor states, Islamic rulership acquired a transcendental quality.[58] Moreover, transcendentalization of royal authority transformed the state's relationship to religious authority as well. The state now also had a transcendental power comparable to that of religion, so a redefinition of the relations between the two became necessary. Beyond its standard instruments, the state could now define religion according to its own agendas and intervene in matters of faith.

In *Denkard*—the collection of Zoroastrian beliefs and practices written down in the tenth century—religion and state are described as inseparably connected. An oft-quoted statement summarizes this link: "Know that kingship is religion and religion is kingship."[59] Similarly, the *Testament of Ardasir*, a book attributed to King Ardasir (180–242), states: "religion and government are twin brothers, no one of which can survive without the other."[60] Inspired by the Sassanid administrative culture, successor states like the Seljuqs developed an Islamic iteration of the Sassanid model. Now the state had become as sacred as religion, and political power was fully equipped to determine and enforce religious orthodoxy.

As a result, the boundary between state and religion was erased. A major outcome of this transformation was the rise of new Islamic scholars loyal equally to both the state and religion. Naturally, the state's elevation to a transcendental level also affected the status of religious authorities vis-à-vis the state. The Islamic tradition would soon have a clergy situated in a hybrid space controlled by both religious and political authorities.[61] As Lambton has written, the incorporation of the transcendent sultan into the Islamic government constituted an entirely new model in which political authority was a matter of religious orthodoxy.[62]

More critical than the subjugation of the clergy was the consolidation of power in the state, a development that led to the hierarchical organization of society in which social groups acquired their status through submission to political authority.[63] Social groups' positions were no longer determined by the competitive bargaining among them, but exclusively on the basis of where they attached to the vine of the hierarchy of state power and interests. In Sassanid society, warriors were below the priests, and merchants sat at the lowest stratum.[64] Many classical Persian texts describe society as comprising four classes. The priesthood was the most powerful group and sat at the highest echelon of Sassanid society. The second class was the warriors, who were described as "the hands." The cultivators, described as "the belly," were the third, and the artisans including the merchants, "the feet of society," were the lowest group.[65]

Stanislaw Andreski observes that the reorganization of Sasanian society to empower the military groups over all others weakened the status of peasants and merchants.[66] Similarly, the new Islamic polities that succeeded the Abbasid order would adhere to this model, in which state authority governs both relations within society (i.e. between different groups) and between each group and the state. As a result of the amalgamation of the Turco-Persian elements and the Islamic ones, a "power state" emerged. C.E. Bosworth derives the term "power state" from the Ghaznavids, another example of the Turco-Persian model, "in which the sultan and his servants, both military and civilian, stood over and against the mass of subjects."[67] The power state was a hierarchy dominated by the state that relegated autonomy-seeking actors to a low stratum. The system maintained a sharp division between the ruling class and the ruled.[68] The rise of a new concept of statehood, as well as a new type of relationship between state and religion, were the two path-breaking developments that allowed Islamic society to acquire the capacity to develop a religious orthodoxy.

2.3   The Seljuqs: Religious Orthodoxy and the State

Seljuq state brought Turco-Persian elements of political organization—chiefly nomadism, militarism, and the Sassanid theory of rule—together with the preexisting Arab-Islamic caliphate. In so doing, they adopted the Sassanid administrative culture and integrated it into mainstream Sunni Islamic thought. The writings of major thinkers of the Seljuq period, including al-Ghazali and Nizam al-Mulk, reflect the early interaction of the nascent Sunni orthodoxy and the political authority that defined the Seljuq state.

Nizam al-Mulk, the influential and long-serving *wazir* of the Seljuqi state, wrote in *Siyasatnamah*:

The most important thing which a king needs is sound faith, because kingship and religion are almost brothers, whenever disturbances breaks out in
the country religion suffers too; heretics and evil-doers appear; and whenever religious affairs are in disorder, there is a confusion in the country;
evil-doers gain power and render the king impotent and despondent; heresy
grows rife and rebels make themselves felt.[69]

For Nizam al-Mulk, when state weakens, heretics appear, and they are
naturally the enemies of the state. Furthermore, rebels benefit if religious
affairs are in disorder. The message is very clear: To avoid the problem of
heretics, religion should protect the state; and to avoid the problem of
rebels, the state should protect religion. This is one of example of Nizam
al-Mulk's political philosophy, which marks a shift from early Islamic politics to the Sasanian absolutist statehood.[70]

Siyasatnamah presents a Persian tradition of kingly rule as the basis of
its theory of political power.[71] In his list of advice to the Seljuqi Sultan,
Nizam al-Mulk underlines the virtues of running an empire according to
the traditional Irano-Islamic model.[72] His administrative philosophy
rooted Seljuqi power in the Sassanid idea of absolute monarchy.[73] As in the
Sassanid model, in his model, state and religion—though they may appear
to be two organizations with different functions—are in fact symbiotes,
that is, each is essential to the survival of the other.[74] Similarly, the idea of
kingship in Nizam al-Mulk's writings was also based on the Persian concept of kingship: God directly chooses the king and confers upon him the
mission and power to rule over countries and people.[75] Divinely empow-
ered, the king is above everyone and everything.

Al-Ghazali was no different: he did not refrain from citing traditions
(*hadith*), including some of dubious authenticity, where the Prophet was
said to have accepted that the state and religion are twins.[76] Under the
pretext of the need for a strong state for Islam, al-Ghazali accepted the
Sasanian maxim that religion and temporal power are twins.[77] What mat-
tered for al-Ghazali was "political stability and the existence of a strong
government in order to produce the right conditions for the conduct of
good religion."[78] In explicating his theories, it is clear that al-Ghazali had
the sultan in his mind.[79]

In his time, the political and ideological challenge by the Fatimid Shi'a
state pressured the Seljuqi state to promulgate its orthodox interpretation
of Islam. This threat was compounded by Fatimid missionaries, the *dai*,
who preached Ismaili doctrine in Seljuqi lands.[80] The Ismaili threat indeed
informed al-Ghazali's thinking.[81]

Observing the cooperation between state and religion under the Seljuqs, al-Ghazali developed his political theory based on a combination of two different frameworks: the *purely theological* and the *politically theological*. At times, al-Ghazali was therefore a man of his political-theological paradigm and prioritized the political causes. For example, though al-Ghazali incorporated Sufi theories of knowledge into his work, he also wrote the *Kitab al-Mustazhiri*, in which he attacked the idea of divine knowledge of the Fatimid *imamate*. The book was written to establish the legitimacy of the Abbasid Caliph Al-Mustazhir against Fatimid ideology.[82] As Ebrahim Moosa has written, al-Ghazali used sometimes theology in the service of Seljuqi politics.[83] Thus, his position straddled different frameworks, at times producing contradictory opinions, which was criticized by Ibn Rushd:

> He adhered to no single doctrine in his books. Rather, with the Ash'arite he was an Ash'arite, with the Sufis a Sufi, and with the philosophers a philosopher.[84]

Al-Ghazali's thinking not only reflects his anxiety over the Fatimid threat, but also the new hierarchical society maintained in part by the cooperation of state and religion. His *Nasihat al-Muluk* is worth studying to observe how he links politics and theology. After underlining the superiority of the sultan, he reminds the reader that a sultan's consultation with the ulema is a virtue.[85] He lists kings as the second group of superior people, after the prophets. For al-Ghazali, the sultan is the shadow of God on earth. Power is granted to the sultans by God, so they must be obeyed, loved, and followed.[86] In developing such arguments, al-Ghazali theorized the new *de facto* situation in which, as Safi said, the semantics of state and religion now overlapped.[87] Reading al-Ghazali's political arguments, we observe Islamic thought on the march toward a Sunni orthodoxy.[88]

Al-Ghazali was therefore never alarmed by the rise of an absolute statehood that weakened the autonomy of merchants and tradesmen. As a scholar of a Seljuqi madrasa, al-Ghazali's indifference to the complexity of the interdependence of politics and the economy is telling. Al-Ghazali imagined the state as a completely autonomous phenomenon that stands above society, an administrative body directly above the people. In both *Ihya* and *The Alchemy of Happiness*, he approaches economy as a mechanical system governed by administrative and moral principles.[89] Thus, we have no reason to think that al-Ghazali was concerned about the negative repercussions of the nascent absolutist statehood on religion or economy.

Both Nizam al-Mulk and al-Ghazali theorized the relationship of state and religion as it was understood in the Sassanid administrative tradition. They were both agents of the legitimation and transmission of the Sassanid concept of statehood in the Seljuq state.[90]

Thus in the case of Seljuqis, we observe a nascent Sunni orthodoxy dependent on collaboration between state and religion. Such collaboration also entailed official patronage of scholars who adhered to and promoted orthodoxy. This support was particularly necessary in the face of an ideological threat, for example of the Ismailis. The Seljuqi state governed and enforced a particular interpretation of religion, which came to be taken as orthodoxy. Nizam al-Mulk's invitation of influential Ash'ari scholars, such as al-Juwayni (d. 1085), to protect and enforce the official religion was a harbinger of a new type of cooperation between clergy and officials.[91] A critical piece of this new system was the state-sponsored *madrasa*, which was expected to define and defend Sunni orthodoxy.[92] Ibn al-Athir (1160–1233) gave details of several cases in which Nizam al-Mulk personally appointed lecturers at the madrasa.[93] In return for political and financial support, the Seljuqs imposed a certain measure of doctrinal uniformity upon the interpretation of religion.[94] With this institutional network, the Seljuqs laid down a state-controlled religious orthodoxy by methods such as promoting *madrasa* scholars and popular Islamic saints and defining Sunni orthodoxy itself.

Thus, there was no longer competition between political and religious actors (as had been the case during the Age of Autonomy). In the Seljuqi period, political and religious authorities were mutually dependent. In their time, the Abbasids persecuted groups they deemed to be heretical. However, as Zaman notes, the Abbasid policies were "rather the effort, on the part of the Abbasid caliphs, to lay claim to the sort of competence the ulama were known to possess" and did not even come close to the Seljuqi model, which officials were the patrons of orthodox Islam.[95] Clearly, then, the Seljuq state was the first Islamic polity with the capacity to formulate and enforce religious orthodoxy.

2.4   AL-GHAZALI: SUNNI ORTHODOXY AS DOCTRINE

An equally important topic is the reflection of the Islamic societies' move toward a hierarchical model in the post-Abbasid era, which I have analyzed above in the case of Seljuqis, unto the intellectual life. On this account, what we observe, in Foucauldian terms, is the birth of a "regime of truth" reflecting the new "circular relation within systems of power."[96] In this vein, al-Ghazali's attack on philosophy epitomized the rivalry between philosophy and religion and marked a turning point in Islamic intellectual history. It was both a correction of perceived errors in Aristotelian thought and also a demand that philosophy (and even the rationalist tradition in Islam) recognize the new hierarchy of society that placed religious and political authority together at the top.[97]

Al-Ghazali's writings reflect the new power relations in the post-Abbasid order and played a key role in the reorganization of Islamic thought. Al-Ghazali's leadership in the theorizing and legitimizing of the developing paradigm of religion–state collaboration made him the top scholar of mainstream Islam, a distinction that ensured his enduring influence. An oft-heard expression runs thus: "If there had been a prophet after Muhammad, it would have been al-Ghazali."

The Age of Autonomy witnessed a flourishing of Islamic philosophy. During that period, translated Greek philosophers shaped the essentials of the Islamic thought. Muslims made extensive use of Greek philosophy when they formulated their ideas of God, nature, causality, free will, and other key concepts.[98] Thus, as already noted, the theological basis of the Age of Autonomy can be described as Greco-Arab or Greco-Islamic. This influence was apparent since the writings of al-Kindi—dubbed the first Muslim philosopher—who began his *On First Philosophy* with the Aristotelian discourse on the four causes of being.[99] No later age would witness such an intensive and fruitful fusion of Islamic thought and rationalist philosophy.

The institutionalization of Sunni orthodoxy during the Seljuq period however drove philosophy to a remote outpost. The prestige of philosophy declined dramatically. It was deemed a threat to religion. Moreover, through the attack on philosophy, Sunni orthodoxy imposed a hierarchy in which rationalists were forced to accept the vague concept of a higher authority, which was in practice a group of religious and political scholars/authorities. Islamic thought was brought into line with the hierarchical organization of Islamic society in the post-Abbasid period.

It is possible to identify how philosophy came to be seen as a somehow distressing phenomenon through several examples. For example, Imam al-Nawawi (1233–1277) noted in his *Etiquette with the Quran*, a book that represents the main tenets of Sunni orthodoxy, that when he read *the Qanun* of Ibn Sina, darkness filled his heart, and he was unable to work for several days. It was only after he sold Ibn Sina's book that al-Nawawi was able to come to his senses and feel "light fill his heart."[100] Ibn al-Salah, who taught hadith in thirteenth-century Damascus, explained his position on philosophy in a way that reflected the social conditions of the new age:

> Philosophy is the basis of foolishness and weakness [in belief], the base of confusion and error, the teaching of deviation and heresy. Whoever philosophizes, his sight becomes blind to the beauties of the sharia, which are supported by proofs. Whoever adopts it will be afflicted by disappointment and deprivation, the devil will take possession of him and his heart will be darkened for the prophethood of Muhammad…Thus, it is the duty of the ruler to protect the Muslims from the evil of these sinister individuals, to expel them from the madrasas and to exile them.[101]

Not satisfied with declaring philosophers heretics, Ibn al-Salah also wanted the state to punish them. Ibn al-Salah adopts the same position as Nizam al-Mulk, who ruled that religion and kingship are brothers, that is, a symbiotic unit with common enemies.

There are many other examples that attest to the new negative attitude toward philosophy as well as rationalist interpretations of religion. Studying the same period, Konrad Hirschler observes that the trend against the rationalist thinking even forced several scholars to retreat to small towns for security and financial reasons. The hostility toward philosophy could lead to accusations of promulgating incomplete or non- existent belief, and potentially to suspect scholars being barred from teaching.[102]

These examples do not suggest that philosophical and rationalist thought was extinguished. However, they do indicate a general trend in favor of religious sciences at the expense of rational philosophy across the Muslim world.

Al-Ghazali's intellectual activism promoted such skepticism toward philosophy. Downgrading the status of philosophy and philosophers was his one of key purposes.[103] He was disturbed by their influence, and as he wrote in *Ihya*, his aim was to let the theologian know the limits of the philosophers' position.[104] He successfully downgraded philosophy with respect to function and status.[105] Moreover, his severe criticism of philosophers, sometimes going as far as claiming that they were infidels with no right to be part of the Muslim community, left an enduring legacy among Muslims in the form of a skeptical view to philosophy.[106]

However, as stated earlier, the more critical issue, far greater than the impact of al-Ghazali's attack on philosophy, is the legacy of his role in the reorganization of Islamic thought. Al-Ghazali challenged some opinions of Aristotelian philosophers like Farabi and Ibn Sina. However, he was not satisfied with arguing that they were wrong; he also asserted that their proclamation of certain views made them heretics.[107] In al-Ghazali's own words, those heretical views included:

> One of them is the question of the world's pre-eternity and their statement that all substances are pre-eternal. The second is their statement that God's knowledge does not encompass the temporal particulars among individual [existents]. The third is their denial of the resurrection of bodies and their assembly at the Day of Judgment.[108]

Claiming that an argument is heretical is not the same as claiming that it is wrong. The cost of a heretical argument is far greater than the cost of a wrong one. Consider how al-Ghazali puts a question to himself, in his famous *The Incoherence of the Philosophers*, about those who defend the three opinions listed above:

> If someone says: You have explained the doctrines of these [philosophers]; do you then say conclusively that they are infidels and that the killing of those who uphold their beliefs is obligatory?[109]

The charge of being an infidel was central to al-Ghazali's opposition to the philosophers.[110] He was not reluctant to broach the issue of whether it is religiously permissible to kill those who endorse philosophers' beliefs, not only the philosophers themselves. This sweeping opposition was known to his contemporaries like Ibn Tufayl (1105–1185), who criticized al-Ghazali for charging philosophers with unbelief because they deny the resurrection of the body and affirm that only souls are rewarded and punished.[111]

Al-Ghazali questioned the faith of philosophers and even indicted them as heretics.[112] He also rejected some philosophical opinions because they conflicted with "the political authority of the religious law."[113] This judgment was based on a hierarchy in which religion is the final arbiter in matters of philosophy. There is no doubt, as Leor Halevi shows, that in the event of any non-concurrence of religion and philosophy, al-Ghazali would know that "right resides on the authority of religion," and would not entertain the possibility that the philosophers could be right.[114] What we observe here is a more than a repudiation of philosophy; it is the insertion of a regime of religious correctness into Islamic thought.

One result of such a hierarchical method is the subjugation of the sciences to religious verification. In *Munkidh*, having listed some sciences like mathematics, logic, and geometry, al-Ghazali declared that none of their results "are connected with religious matters, either to deny or to affirm them."[115] However, those words may be misleading, since al-Ghazali in fact imagined some sciences as merely technical disciplines unable to draw insights for important questions of theology such as existence, the nature of God, or the eternality of the universe. For example, he considered astronomy to be a neutral discipline without precepts that trespass onto the religious domain. This exculpation of astronomy by al-Ghazali was, however, conditional upon its staying within that neutral territory. Thus, as long as sciences were neutral on philosophical or religious issues, al-Ghazali recognized them as ways of gaining knowledge. On the other hand, he insisted—for example in *Ihya*—that even sciences like geometry and arithmetic are permissible only "for those who are firm in faith" and maintained that some parts of physics contradicted religion and therefore are incorrect.[116]

However, notwithstanding al-Ghazali's qualified acceptance, sciences like astronomy can in fact have philosophical and theological implications and thus were not always seen as "neutral" in those domains. In contrast to al-Ghazali, Nasir al-Din Tusi (1201–1274), a scholar known for his synthesis of Aristotelian thought with Islamic thought, argued that astronomy is based on metaphysics, geometry, and natural philosophy.[117] Thus, it was problematic that al-Ghazali pinned his conditional tolerance of astronomy on its not intruding into the domain of religion. Al-Ghazali insisted on the propriety of religious verification of all sciences that make philosophical arguments that might be at odds with religious ones. In so doing, al-Ghazali generated a hierarchy in Islamic thought by asserting the propriety of religious verification. A clear example of this subjugation of science to religion can be found in his *Al-Qistas Al-Mustaqim*. In this book, al-Ghazali proposed that an analogy should be made as it is explained in Qur'an. Al-Ghazali rejected the appeal to reasoning (*qiyas*) and opinion (*ra'y*) according to the "rules of the devil" and insisted that these faculties be exercised according to "the rule of God. (*qistas al-mustaqim*)"[118] In this line of thinking, al-Ghazali recognized logic as a legitimate science, but only after subordinating it to religion. Thus, his understanding of religion and science permitted the former to interfere with the autonomy of the latter.

Sunni orthodoxy thus gradually elevated religious knowledge as the authoritative test by which all other knowledge was verified or disproved. Orthodoxy never recognized any non-religious discipline as having an independent epistemology not subject to religious verification. An enduring impact of orthodoxy was the prevention of the full differentiation of various disciplines and religion.

Al-Ghazali's innovation was indeed different than the rationalist scholars' approach. To get a sense of the latter approach, consider how Al-Hasan ibn al-Haytham (965–1040), one of the earliest empiricist scholars, whose studies created a new optic theory that survived until Kepler's time. Al-Haytham's method was distinguished by a rigor remarkably similar to that of the modern science.[119] His method combined the natural and the mathematical; he relied on both the sense-based observation of natural things and mathematical calculations (reasoning).[120] He thus recognized key elements of the scientific method as the independent and ultimate means of verification. By contrast, Sunni orthodoxy would develop a dim view of independent (non-religious) verification that led to the inhibition of the differentiation of distinct disciplines and realms of knowledge.

Another aspect of al-Ghazali's legacy is his articulation of an alternative type of knowledge. In developing his idea of inner knowledge, al-Ghazali first argued that human knowledge is limited because human senses are restricted.[121] As he wrote in his autobiography, he had searched for an infallible body of knowledge but ultimately found that he "could no longer trust sense-perception."[122] Al-Ghazali's critical ideas on the boundaries of human knowledge are valid. However, having confessed his reservations about human knowledge, he introduced the possibility of an inner type of knowledge. This formulation drew on Sufi thought and practice and incorporated them into the Islamic framework. Thus, another important legacy of al-Ghazali was the reconciliation of Sunni orthodoxy with the teachings of Sufism.[123] This accommodation was tantamount to adding a new discipline to the curriculum of Islamic knowledge—as Ahmet T. Karamustafa called it, "Inner Science."[124]

In rational knowledge, human beings acquire knowledge through the senses, and what is collected through senses is processed by brain. In this model, the senses are limited, and therefore what people know about objects changes over time, as new methods enhance human observation. By contrast, al-Ghazali suggests a different method for acquiring knowledge. In *Al-Risalat al-Laduniyya*, al-Ghazali recognizes two different methods for acquiring knowledge: *from without* and *from within*.[125] Knowledge *from without* is rational knowledge that is drawn through sensory perception and reasoning. Knowledge *from within* is acquired without sensory perception or reasoning, through self-realization that transcends all spatio-temporal dimensions. As al-Ghazali defined knowledge *from within*:

> This did not come about by systematic demonstration or marshalled argument, but by a light which God most high cast into my breast. That light is the key to the greater part of knowledge. Whoever thinks that the understanding of things Divine rests upon strict proofs has in his thought narrowed down the wideness of God's mercy.[126]

Al-Ghazali's inner knowledge refers to the possession of direct access to truth. His discussion is not abstract speculation. He makes it clear who are the actors, as well as the masters, of inner knowledge: the mystics. Al-Ghazali describes the mystics as men of real experiences and not merely men of words. He tells the reader that the mystics can easily and quickly achieve the intellectual progress that al-Ghazali himself only accomplished over a long time and with great effort.[127] For al-Ghazali, the mystics' ability to acquire knowledge is beyond doubt, since it depends on and is bestowed by God's grace.[128]

At the same time, inner knowledge is not confined within the spiritual realm. It can be applied to a range of questions, including to the investigation of nature. Writing on intellectual changes in the post-Abbasid period, Ira Lapidus has highlighted the rise of inner knowledge and its impact on the broader Islamic tradition:

> It also carried with it a theosophical view of the universe which explained the structure of the cosmos and the possibility of religious ascent toward union with God. Finally, it encompassed belief in the miraculous powers of saints as channels for God's action in the world. Sufism thus encompassed piety and ethical behavior, ascetic and ecstatic practices, theosophical metaphysics, and magical beliefs. It embraced at once a scripturalist, an agnostic, and a miraculous concept of Islam."[129]

Al-Ghazali's conception of inner knowledge reflected the elevation of religion over sciences, even physics in explaining the workings of the universe.[130] He was not against reason, but he redefined it. He invented a *subservient reason*, which had no independent ability to determine truth. Rather, it could endorse one idea among alternatives only if it was supported by religion. Reason was given a subordinate role.[131] Moreover, while reason was limited, inner knowledge reigned supreme over both material and spiritual matters. Magid Fakhry thus described al-Ghazali's legacy as "sowing the seeds of misology."[132] Similarly, Mohammed Abed al-Jabri likened his legacy to a deep wound inside reason, which is still bleeding.[133]

2.5   Conclusion

Sunni orthodoxy emerged during the waning of Muslims' brilliant ages. Those were the times when "the mood of confidence," in the words of Tarif Khalidi, which had blossomed during the enormous economic growth in 900–1100, was fading. During the period that followed, 1100–1500, the mood of confidence disappeared.[134]

Under the new paradigm, the Islamic society was reorganized into a hierarchy, which replaced the previous model of distinct autonomous spheres. At the core of the new model was the concept of transcendental statehood that expanded at the expense of autonomy-seeking groups. The new paradigm reorganized the relationship between state and religion, empowering authorities to interpret and enforce religious orthodoxy. The developments radically altered the relationship among religion, state, and science as well. Rationalist philosophers not only lost their authority to help interpret Islam but were also subjected to the strict scrutiny of both religion and state. Piety-minded scholars grew more popular and influential. Sufi thought emerged as a strong component of the Sunni orthodoxy.[135] Reflecting the new hierarchical model, military officers, bureaucrats, civil servants, and the clergy captured the most powerful roles and thereby reduced the autonomy of civilian groups like the merchants and the men of science.

At its outset, Islamic civilization institutionalized relatively egalitarian and cosmopolitan values, giving considerable weight to mercantile interests.[136] New social and economic structures that gave birth to the new orthodoxy reversed this dynamic and dominated urban and mercantile elites as well as independent scholars. The emergence of Sunni orthodoxy marked the Islamic world's break from its earlier engagement with the Greek *logos*. Instead, the Sassanid administrative tradition became the new source of inspiration. The Sassanid tradition prioritized submission to power, order, and hierarchy, not *logos*.[137]

Thus, it may be argued that Islamic society in the Age of Autonomy were organized rather like what Aristotle defined as a political community dependent on the middle ground. In his *Politics*, Aristotle said of such a society that its balance is held steady by the tradesmen who are able to bargain.[138] However, gradually destroying the autonomous space for such middle classes, new power relations in the post-Abbasid period instituted a new hierarchy. Islamic society was reorganized into a polity where non-state actors' capacity to generate and claim political, social, economic, and intellectual autonomy weakened dramatically, if not completely. Sunni orthodoxy, including its idea of nature, evolved within this broader social structure. The content of the Sunni orthodox idea of nature will be the subject of the following chapter.

Notes

1. Berkey, *The Formation of Islam*, ix.
2. Makdisi, "The Sunni Revival," 155–168.
3. El-Rouayheb, *Islamic Intellectual History*, 7. El-Rouayheb, "The Myth of 'The Triumph of Fanaticism'," 196–221.
4. Sezgin, *Science and Technology in Islam*, 155–165. Gutas, "The Study of Arabic Philosophy," 5–25.
5. For example, *Sunan*, one of the most authoritative *hadith* books, includes a tradition narrated by Amir ibn Wathilah. al-Nasa'i, *Sunan*, 346.
6. Hodgson, *The Venture of Islam Vol. 2*, 3.
7. Gimaret, "Mu'tazila," 784.
8. Saliba, *Islamic Science*, 87.
9. Akhtar, *Philosophers, Sufis, and Caliphs*, 238–240.
10. Ahmad, *Before Orthodoxy*, 3. Shamsy, "The Social Construction of Orthodoxy," 97.
11. Hodghson, *The Venture of Islam Vol. 2*, 12.
12. Kurt, "Devlet Kurma Sürecinde Samanoğulları," 109–129.
13. Larkin, *Al-Mutanabbi*, 12.
14. Lapidus, *A History of Islamic Societies*, 111.
15. Negmatov, "The Samanid State," 80.
16. Frye, "The Samanids," 145.
17. Ansari, *The Ethical Philosophy of Ibn Miskawaih*, 15.
18. Gordon, *The Breaking of A Thousand Swords*, 37.
19. Walker, "Jahiz of Basra to Al-Fath Ibn Khaqan," 666. Peacock, *Early Seljuq History*, 74–81.
20. Safi, *The Politics of Knowledge*, 112.
21. Daniel, *The Political and Social History of Khurasan*, 157.
22. Bonner, "The Waning of Empire," 309.
23. al-Tabari, *The History Vol. 36*, 104.

24. Durand-Guédy, "The Türkmen-Saljuq Relationship," 46.
25. Lambton, *Landlord and Peasant in Persia*, 60.
26. Lapidus, *A History of Islamic Societies*, 232. For the similar political consequences of the *uymaq* system in Iran, see: Reid, "The Qajar Uymaq in the Safavid Period," 117–143.
27. Andreski, *Military Organization and Society*, 31.
28. Hodghson, *The Venture of Islam Vol. 2*, 408.
29. Kennedy, "The Military," 114.
30. Lambton, "The Evolution of the Iqta'," 41. For example, Ghaznavids employed *iqta* for military stability, see: Tusigitaka, *State and Rural Society in the Medieval Islam*, 18–38.
31. Cahen, "Tribes, Cities and Social Organizations," 313. Barthold, *Turkestan Down to the Mongol Invasion*, 307.
32. Lambton, *Landlord and Peasant in Persia*, 61.
33. Nadvi, "Al Iqta or Theory of Land Ownership in Islam," 261.
34. Ibn Miskawayh, *The Concluding Portion of the Experiences of Nations*, 98–99, 131–132. Amitai, "Turko-Mongolian Nomads," 152–171.
35. Tsugitaka, "The Iqta System of Iraq," 90–91.
36. Busse, "Iran Under the Buyids," 260.
37. Bosworth, "Military Organization Under the Buyids," 161.
38. Zaporozhets, *The Seljuks*, 182.
39. Heidemann, "Un-Islamic Taxes and Un-Islamic Monetary System in Seljuq Baghdad," 496.
40. Tramontana, "Khubz as Iqta," 109–110.
41. Ibid., 103. On the other hand, *iqta* was different from the European *fief*, since the former never generated a similar way of possessions as the *fief*, see: Crone, *Slaves on Horses*, 87.
42. Boswort, "Dailamis in Central Iran," 73.
43. Shaked, *From Zoroastrian Iran to Islam*. Also see: Davaran, *Continuity in Iranian Identity*, 136.
44. Spuler, *Iran in the Early Islamic Period*, 2–3.
45. Ibid., 125.
46. Tor, "The Islamisation of Iranian Kingly Ideals," 116.
47. al-Tabari, *The History Vol. 25*, 20, 33–44, 45–63.
48. Bosworth, "The Heritage of Rulership in Early Islamic Iran," 52.
49. el-Hibri, *Reinterpreting Islamic Historiography*, 73.
50. Daryaee, *Sasanian Persia*, 41.
51. Canepa, *The Two Eyes of the Earth*, 1.
52. Madelung, *The Succession to Muhammad*, 4. Azmeh, "Misconceptions About the Caliphate in Islam," 249. Ali, *The Early Caliphate*, 10.
53. al-Mawardi, *The Laws of Islamic Governance*, 10.
54. Crone and Hinds, *God's Caliph*, 1.

55. Arnold, *The Caliphate*, 14.
56. Hawting, *The First Dynasty of Islam*, 43, 77.
57. Alajmi, "Ascribed vs. Popular Legitimacy," 25–33.
58. Barthold, *Turkestan Down to the Mongol Invasion*, 306–307.
59. Daryaee, *Sasanian Persia*, 81.
60. Shaked, *From Zoroastrian Iran to Islam*, 37.
61. Pourshariati, *Decline and Fall of the Sasanian Empire*, 47, 44.
62. Lambton, *State and Government in Medieval Islam*, 106–107.
63. Hillenbrand, "Aspects of the Court of the Great Seljuqs," 25.
64. Pourshariati, *Decline and Fall of the Sasanian Empire*, 45–49.
65. Tafazzoli, *Sasanian Society*, 2.
66. Andreski, *Military Organization and Society*, 46–47.
67. Bosworth, "The Ghaznavids," 117. Since military was the kernel of the state, when the military success fails, for example in the case of Ghaznavids, states also gradually doomed. Atai and Saddodin, "Transoxiana under the Rule of Abbasid," 6.
68. Bosworth, "The Early Ghaznavids,"182.
69. al-Mulk, *The Book of Government*, 63.
70. Lambton, "The Dilemma of Government in Islamic Persia," 57.
71. Leder, "Sultanic Rule in the Mirror of Medieval Political Literature," 97.
72. Peacock, "The Great Age of the Seljuqs," 9. Seljuqi rulers like Alp Arslan had a great admiration of the Persian past. Rice, *The Seljuqs in Asia Minor*, 33.
73. Omid Safi described Nizam al-Mulk as "not a government official; he simply was the state". Safi, *The Politics of Knowledge*, 44.
74. The Seljuqi Sultan Malik Shah is thus both *Jalal al-dawla wa'l-din* (the glory of religion and state): Nishapuri, *The History of the Seljuq Turks*," 57.
75. This trend would be followed by the Ottomans, who formulated their theory of kingship in a similar way. Colin Imber, "Ideals and legitimation in early Ottoman history," 139.
76. Rosenthal, *Political Thought in Medieval Islam*, 39.
77. Lambton, *State and Government*, 108.
78. Hillenbrand, "Islamic Orthodoxy or Realpolitik?," 90.
79. Binder, "Al-Ghazali's Theory of Islamic Government," 232.
80. Al-Ghazali was born in 1055, when the Fatimids were already in decline under the reign of al-Mustansir (1036–1094). The year "marked the closing phase of the classical Fatimid period. While it witnessed numerous vicissitudes, the overall fortunes of the Fatimid caliphate now clearly began their irreversible decline," Daftary, *The Ismailis Their History and Doctrines*, 193. Fatimid control over Sicily also weakened, ending completely in 1072. However, the Ismaili Revolt of 1099 probably gave al-Ghazali cause to continue to fear the spread of Ismailism.

81. Nizam al-Mulk's dedication of a long section of his *Siyasatnamah* of the Ismaili threat is symbolic here. For a discussion on the impact of this threat on Islamic political thought, see: Virani, *The Ismailis in the Middle Ages*, 73.

82. Mitha, *Al-Ghazali and Ismailis*, 13. For an analysis of al-Ghazali's political ideas within a pure theoretical framework with no reference to the political setting, see Moussa, *Politics of the Islamic Tradition*, 99–120.

83. Moosa, *Ghazali and the Poetics of Imagination*, 163.

84. Averroes [Ibn Rushd], *The Book of the Decisive Treatise*, 22.

85. al-Ghazali, *Council for Kings*, 14–19.

86. Ibid., 45. There were Islamic critiques of the new model as well. Ayn al-Qudat al-Hamadani was critical of the nascent model of state–religion cooperation. Safi quoted the argument of al-Hamadani that "to serve the Seljuqi sultans is not to serve God in reality". Safi, *The Politics of Knowledge*, 183–184. Al-Hamadani was later executed by the Seljuqi state for his "offense against society" and "sharing Ismaili views". Papan-Matin, *Beyond Death*, 40–46

87. Safi, *The Politics of Knowledge*, 5. Lambton argues that several parts of this book bear Zoroastrian influence. Lambton, *State and Government*, 118.

88. al-Juwayni's political ideas were similar. His stance was also a kind of pragmatist one similar to that of al-Ghazali. Siddiqui, "Power vs. Authority," 193–220. Also see: Kavak, "Cüveyni'ye Göre Halifenin Vasıfları," 284–295. Ünverdi, "Eş'ari Kelamında İmamiyet Nazariyesi," 63.

89. al-Ghazali, *Ihya Ulum-ad-Din Vol. II*, 37. al-Ghazali, *The Alchemy of Happiness*, 465–485.

90. Freshteh Davaran argues that the Sassanid influence is visible in other of al-Ghazali's works. For example, *The Alchemy of Happiness* is reminiscent of the Pahlavi *Pandnamah*. Davaran also argues that Nizam al-Mulk's opinions reflect the influence of many classical Persian texts. Davaran, *Continuity in Iranian Identity*, 181–187.

91. Arjomand, "The Law, Agency, and Policy in Medieval Islamic Society," 269.

92. Starr, *Lost Enlightenment*, 405.

93. al-Athir, *The Annals of the Saljuq Turks*, 207, 213, 247.

94. Campanini, "In Defense of Sunnism," 228–239. R. Levy defined the school as "founded officially as theological school, being recognized both by the religious leaders of Islam and by the State that provided its revenues, though by indirect means". Levy, *A Baghdad Chronicle*, 193–194.

95. Zaman, *Religion and Politics Under the Early Abbasid*, 105. Even the failure of the Abbasids in the *mihna* could be interpreted that they were not able to establish a religious orthodoxy.

96. Foucault, *Power/Knowledge*, 131. See also: Foucault, *Discipline and Punish*, 194.
97. The standard idea that presents al-Ghazali as the enemy of philosophy dates back to Ernest Renan (1823–1892). See: Griffel, "Preface," x. Griffel, "The Western Reception of Al-Ghazali's Cosmology," 33–39.
98. Gutas, *Greek thought, Arabic culture*, 1–10.
99. Ivry, *Al-Kindi's Metaphysics*, 56.
100. al-Nawawi, *Etiquette with the Quran*, xxi.
101. Hirschler, *Medieval Arabic Historiography*, 44.
102. Ibid., 59.
103. Moosa, *Ghazali and the Poetics of Imagination*, 172.
104. al-Ghazali, *The Book of Knowledge*, 53–57.
105. Shihadeh, "From Al-Ghazali to Al-Razi," 144.
106. Watt, *Muslim Intellectual*, 59.
107. Mukti, "Al-Ghazzali and His Refutation of Philosophy," 9.
108. al-Ghazali, *The Incoherence of the Philosophers*, 226.
109. Ibid. Also see: al-Ghazali, *Moderation in Belief*, 244.
110. Watt, *Muslim Intellectual*, 26.
111. Mahdi, "Philosophical Literature," 101.
112. Ormsby, *Ghazali*, 66.
113. Griffel, *Al-Ghazali's Philosophical Theology*, 102–103.
114. Halevi, "The Theologian's Doubts," 31.
115. al-Ghazali, *Al Munkidh*, 33.
116. al-Ghazali, *Ihya Ulum-ad-Din Vol. 1*, 45–60. Also see: Altıntaş, "Gazali'nin Felsefe ile İlgili Düşüncelerinde Çelişkiler," 442.
117. Ragep, *Nasir al-Din Tusi's Memoir on Astronomy*, 41.
118. al-Ghazali, *The Just Balance*, 2–5.
119. Lindberg, *Theories of Vision from Al-Kindi to Kepler*, 58.
120. Sabra, *The Optics of Ibn-Haytham Books I-III*, 4. Rashed, *Ibn al-Haytham's Geometrical Methods*, 140–141.
121. al-Ghazali, *Al Munkidh*, 23.
122. Ibid., 21–23.
123. Smith, *Al-Ghazali: The Mystic*, 225. al-Ghazali's relations with Sufism should not be thought without a reference to the general rise of Sufism in the Seljuqi period. Renterghem, "Social and Urban Dynamics in Baghdad," 180.
124. Karamustafa, *Sufism The Formative Period*, 107.
125. Smith, "Al-Risalat Al-Laduniyya," 186.
126. Ghazali, *Al Munkidh*, 25.
127. Ibid., 55.
128. Al-Attas, *Islam and Secularism*, 146.

129. Lapidus, *A History of Islamic Societies*, 158.
130. Macdonald, "The Meanings of the Philosophers by Al-Ghazali," 9–15.
131. Shuʿayb, "Al-Ghazzali's Final Word on Kalam," 157.
132. Fakhry, *A History of Islamic Philosophy*, 323.
133. al-Jabri, *The Formation of Arab Reason*, 361.
134. Khalidi, "The Idea of Progress in Classical Islam," 282–283.
135. Chaney, "Religion and the Rise and Fall of Islamic Science," 1.
136. Burke III, "Islamic History as World History," 257.
137. Walbridge, *God and Logic in Islam*, 19.
138. Aristotle, *Politics*, 120.

References

Ahmad, Shahab. 2017. *Before Orthodoxy: The Satanic Verses in Early Islam.* Cambridge, MA: Harvard University Press.

Akhtar, Ali Humayun. 2017. *Philosophers, Sufis, and Caliphs: Politics and Authority from Cordoba to Cairo and Baghdad.* Cambridge: Cambridge University Press.

al-Athir, Ibn. 2002. *The Annals of the Saljuq Turks: Selections from al-Kamil fi'l-Taʾrikh of ʿIzz al-Din Ibn al-Athir.* Translated by D.S. Richards. New York: Routledge-Curzon.

Al-Attas, Syed Muhammad Naquib. 1993. *Islam and Secularism.* Kuala Lumpur: ISTAC.

al-Ghazali. 1963. *Deliverance From Error [Al Munkidh min Ad Dallal].* Translated by W.M. Watt. Lahore: Sh. M. Ashraf.

———. 1964. *Ghazali's Book of Council for Kings [Nasihat al-Muluk].* Translated by F.R.C. Bagley. London: Oxford University Press.

———. 1978. *The Just Balance [Al-Qistas Al-Mustaqim].* Translated by D.P. Brewster. Lahore: Sh. M. Ashraf.

———. 1979. *The Book of Knowledge; Being a Translation with Notes of the Kitab al-ʿilm of al-Ghazzali's Ihya' ʿulum al-din Vol. 2.* Translated by Nabih Amin Faris. Lahore: Sh. M. Ashraf.

———. 1991. *The Alchemy of Happiness [Kimiya-yi Saʿadat].* Translated by Claud Field. Lahore: Sh. M. Ashraf.

———. 1993a. *Revival of Religious Learnings, Vol. 1 [Ihya Ulum Ad-din].* Translated by Fazl-ul-Karim. Karachi: Darul Ishaat.

———. 1993b. *Revival of Religious Learnings, Vol. 2 [Ihya Ulum-ad-Din].* Translated by Fazl-ul-Karim. Karachi: Darul Ishaat.

———. 2000. *The Incoherence of the Philosophers [Tahafut al-Falasifa].* Translated by Michael E. Marmura. Provo: Brigham Young University Press.

———. 2013. *Al-Ghazali's Moderation in Belief [Al-Iqtisad Fi Al-Iʿtiqad].* Alaaddin M. Yaqub. Chicago: The University of Chicago Press.

al-Jabri, Mohammed Abed. 2011. *The Formation of Arab Reason: Text, Tradition and the Construction of Modernity in the Arab World*. London: I. B. Tauris.

al-Mawardi. 1996. *The Ordinances of Government [Al-Ahkam al-Sultaniyya w'al-Wilayat al-Diniyya]*. Translated by Wafaa H. Wahba. Reading, UK: Garnet Publishing.

al-Mulk, Nizam. 1960. *The Book of Government or Rules of for Kings: The Siyasatname or Siyar al-Muluk [Siyar al-Muluk]*. Translated by H. Darke. New Haven: Yale University Press.

al-Nasa'i. 2007. *Sunan*. Riyadh: Maktaba Dar-us-Salam.

al-Nawawi, Imam Abu Zakariya Yahya. 2012. *Etiquette with the Quran [Al-Tibyan fi Adab Hamalat al-Qur'an]*. Translated by Musa Furber. London: Islamomosaic.

al-Tabari. 1992. *The History of al-Tabari Vol. 36*. New York: The State University of New York.

al-Tusi, Nasir al-Din. 1993. *Nasir al-Din Tusi's Memoir on Astronomy [al-Tadhkira fi 'ilm al-hay'a] Vol. I*. Translated by F.J. Ragep. New York: Springer Verlag.

Alajmi, Abdulhadi. 2013. Ascribed vs. Popular Legitimacy: The Case of al-Walid II and Umayyad ʿahd. *Journal of Near Eastern Studies* 72 (1): 25–33.

Ali, Maulana Muhammad. 1987. *The Early Caliphate*. Lahore: The Ahmadiyya Anjuman.

Altıntaş, Hayrani. 2000. Gazali'nin Felsefe ile İlgili Düşüncelerinde Çelişkiler. *İslami Araştırmalar Dergisi* 13 (3): 441–444.

Amitai, Reuven. 2007. Turko-Mongolian Nomads and the Iqtaʿ System in the Islamic Middle East (ca. 1000–1400 AD). In *Nomads in the Sedentary World*, ed. Anatoly M. Khazanov and Andre Wink, 152–171. London: Routledge.

Andreski, Stanislaw. 1968. *Military Organization and Society*. Cambridge: Cambridge University Press.

Ansari, M. Abdul Haq. 1964. *The Ethical Philosophy of Ibn Miskawaih*. Aligarh: The Aligarh Muslim University Press.

Aristotle. 1998. *Politics*. Indianapolis: Hackett.

Arjomand, Said Amir. 1999. The Law, Agency, and Policy in Medieval Islamic Society: Development of the Institutions of Learning from the Tenth to the Fifteenth Century. *Comparative Studies in Society and History* 41 (2): 263–293.

Arnold, Thomas W. 1924. *The Caliphate*. Oxford: Clarendon.

Atai, Farhad, and Sika Saddodin. 2018. Transoxiana under the Rule of Abbasid, Ghaznavid and Seljuk Empires: A Comparison of the Systems of Governance. *Journal of Iran and Central Eurasia Studies* 1 (1): 1–14.

Averroes [Ibn Rushd]. 2001. *The Book of the Decisive Treatise [Fasl al-maqal]*. Translated by Charles E. Butterworth. Utah: The Birmingham Young University.

Azmeh, Wayel. 2016. Misconceptions About the Caliphate in Islam. *Digest of Middle East Studies* 25 (2): 186–209.

Barthold, W. 1928. *Turkestan Down to the Mongol Invasion*. Oxford: Oxford University Press.

Berkey, Jonathan P. 2003. *The Formation of Islam: Religion and Society in the Near East, 600–1800*. Cambridge: Cambridge University Press.

Binder, Leonard. 1955. Al-Ghazali's Theory of Islamic Government. *The Muslim World* 45 (3): 229–241.

Bonner, Michael. 2011. The Waning of Empire, 861 945. In *The New Cambridge History of Islam Vol. 1: The Formation of the Islamic World Sixth to Eleven Centuries*, ed. Chase F. Robinson, 305–359. Cambridge: Cambridge University Press.

Bosworth, C.E. 1965/1966. Military Organization Under the Buyids of Persia and Iraq. *Oriens* 18/19 (1): 143–167.

———. 1970. Dailams in Central Iran: The Kakuyids of Jibal and Yazd. *Iran* 8 (1): 73–95.

———. 1973. The Heritage of Rulership in Early Islamic Iran and the Search for Dynastic Connections with the Past. *Iran* 11 (1): 51–62.

———. 1975. The Early Ghaznavids. In *The Cambridge History of Iran Vol. 4: The Period from the Arab Invasion to the Saljuqs*, ed. R.N. Frye, 162–197. Cambridge: Cambridge University Press.

———. 1998. The Ghaznavids. In *History of Civilizations of Central Asia Vol. 4*, ed. M.S. Asimov and C.E. Bosworth, 95–117. Paris: UNESCO.

Burke, Edmund, III. 1977. Islamic History as World History: Marshall Hodgson, The Venture of Islam. *International Journal of Middle East Studies* 10 (2): 241–264.

Busse, Heribert. 1975. Iran Under the Buyids. In *The Cambridge History of Iran Vol. 4: The Period From the Arab Invasion to the Saljuqs*, ed. R.N. Frye, 250–304. Cambridge: Cambridge University Press.

Cahen, Claude. 1975. Tribes, Cities and Social Organizations. In *The Cambridge History of Iran Vol. 4: The Period from the Arab Invasion to the Saljuqs*, ed. R.N. Frye, 305–328. Cambridge: Cambridge University Press.

Campanini, Massima. 2011. In Defense of Sunnism: Al Ghazali and the Seljuqs. In *The Seljuqs Politics, Society and Culture*, ed. Christian Lange and Songül Mecit, 228–239. Edinburg: Edinburg University Press.

Canepa, Matthew P. 2009. *The Two Eyes of the Earth: Art and Ritual of Kingship Between Rome and Sasanian Iran*. Berkeley: University of California Press.

Chaney, Eric. 2016. Religion and the Rise and Fall of Islamic Science, May. https://scholar.harvard.edu/files/chaney/files/paper.pdf

Crone, Patricia. 2003. *Slaves on Horses: The Evolution of the Islamic Polity*. Cambridge: Cambridge University Press.

Crone, Patricia, and Martin Hinds. 2003. *God's Caliph: Religious Authority in the First Centuries of Islam*. Cambridge: Cambridge University Press.

Daftary, Farhad. 2007. *The Ismailis: Their History and Doctrines.* Cambridge: Cambridge University Press.

Daniel, Elton L. 1979. *The Political and Social History of Khurasan Under Abbasid Rule 747–820.* Chicago: Bibliotecha Islamic.

Daryaee, Touraj. 2009. *Sasanian Persia: The Rise and Fall of an Empire.* London and New York: I.B. Tauris.

Davaran, Freshteh. 2010. *Continuity in Iranian Identity: Resilience of a Cultural Heritage.* London: Routledge.

Durand-Guédy, David. 2011. The Türkmen-Saljuq Relationship in Twelfth-Century Iran: New Elements Based on a Contrastive Analysis of Three *Insa'* Documents. *Eurasian Studies* 9 (1–2): 11–66.

El Shamsy, Ahmed. 2008. The Social Construction of Orthodoxy. In *The Cambridge Companion to Classical Islamic Theology,* ed. Tim Winter, 97–118. Cambridge: Cambridge University Press.

el-Hibri, Tayeb. 2004. *Reinterpreting Islamic Historiography: Harun al-Rashid and the Narrative of the Abbasid Caliphate.* Cambridge: Cambridge University Press.

El-Rouayheb, Khaled. 2008. The Myth of 'The Triumph of Fanaticism' in the Seventeenth-Century Ottoman Empire. *Die Welt des Islams* 48 (1): 96–221.

———. 2015. *Islamic Intellectual History in the Seventeenth Century: Scholarly Currents in the Ottoman Empire and Maghreb.* Cambridge: Cambridge University Press.

Fakhry, Magid. 2004. *A History of Islamic Philosophy.* New York: Columbia University Press.

Foucault, Michel. 1980. *Power/Knowledge.* Brighton: Harvester.

———. 1991. *Discipline and Punish: The Birth of Prison.* London: Penguin.

Frye, R.N. 1975. The Samanids. In *The Cambridge History of Iran Vol. 4: The Period from the Arab Invasion to the Saljuqs,* ed. R.N. Frye, 131–161. Cambridge: Cambridge University Press.

Gimaret, Daniel. 1993. Muʿtazila. In *Encyclopedia of Islam Vol. 7,* ed. P. Bearman, Th. Bianquis, C.E. Bosworth, E. van Donzel, and W.P. Heinrichs, 783–793. Leiden: Brill.

Gordon, Matthew S. 2001. *The Breaking of A Thousand Swords: A History of the Turkish Military of Samara (A.H. 200-275/815-889 C.E.).* New York: State University of New York Press.

Griffel, Frank. 2011. The Western Reception of Al-Ghazali's Cosmology from the Middle Ages to 21st Century. *Divan* 16 (30): 33–62.

———. 2016. Preface. In *Islam and Rationality: The Impact of Al-Ghazali,* ed. Frank Griffel, xii–xiv. Leiden: Brill.

———. 2017. *Al-Ghazali's Philosophical Theology.* Oxford: Oxford University Press.

Gutas, Dimitri. 1998. *Greek Thought, Arabic Culture: The Greco-Arabic Translation Movement in Baghdad and Early Abbasid Society.* New York: Routledge.

54   G. BACIK

———. 2002. The Study of Arabic Philosophy in the Twentieth Century: An Essay on the Historiography of Arabic Philosophy. *British Journal of Middle Eastern Studies* 29 (1): 5–25.

Halevi, Leor. 2002. The Theologian's Doubts: Natural Philosophy and the Skeptical Games of Ghazali. *Journal of the History of Ideas* 63 (1): 19–39.

Hawting, G.R. 2005. *The First Dynasty of Islam: The Umayyad Caliphate AD 661–750*. New York: Routledge.

Heidemann, Stefan. 2011. Un-Islamic Taxes and Un-Islamic Monetary System in Seljuq Baghdad. In *İslam Medeniyetinde Bağdat*, ed. İsmail Safa Üstün, 493–505. Istanbul: Marmara Üniversitesi Yayınları.

Hillenbrand, Carole. 1988. Islamic Orthodoxy or Realpolitik? Al-Ghazali's Views on Government. *Iran* 26 (1): 81–95.

———. 1998. Aspects of the Court of the Great Seljuqs. In *History of Civilizations of Central Asia Vol. 4*, ed. M.S. Asimov and C.E. Bosworth, 22–38. Paris: UNESCO.

Hirschler, Konrad. 2006. *Medieval Arabic Historiography: Authors as Actors*. London: Routledge.

Hodgson, Marshall G.S. 1977. *The Venture of Islam Vol. 2*. Chicago: The University of Chicago Press.

Ibn Miskawayh. 1921. *The Concluding Portion of the Experiences of Nations [Tajarib al-umam]*. Translated by H.F. Amedroz. London: B. Blackwell.

Ivry, Alfred L. 1974. *Al-Kindi's Metaphysics: A Translation of Yaqub bin Ishaq al-Kindi's Tretise On First Philosophy*. Albany: State University of New York Press.

Karamustafa, Ahmet T. 2007. *Sufism the Formative Period*. Edinburgh: Edinburgh University Press.

Kavak, Özgür. 2013. Cüveyni'ye Göre Halifenin Vasıfları Yahut Nizamülmülk'ü Hilafete Teşvik Etmek. In *Selçuklularda Bilim ve Düşünce*, ed. Mustafa Demirci, 284–295. Konya: Selçuklu Belediyesi.

Kennedy, Hugh. 2013. The Military. In *Crisis and Continuity at the Abbasid Court Formal and Informal Politics in the Caliphate of al-Muqtadir (295–20/908–32)*, ed. Maaike van Berkel, Nadia Maria El Cheikh, Hugh Kennedy, and Letizia OstiLeiden, 111–144. Leiden: Brill.

Khalidi, Tarif. 1981. The Idea of Progress in Classical Islam. *Journal of Near Eastern Studies* 40 (4): 277–289.

Kunt, Metin, and Christine Woodhead, eds. 1995. *Süleyman the Magnificent and His Age: The Ottoman Empire in the Early Modern World*. London: Longman.

Kurt, Hasan. 2003. Devlet Kurma Sürecinde Samanoğulları. *Ankara Üniversitesi İlahiyat Fakültesi Dergisi* 44 (2): 109–129.

Lambton, Ann K.S. 1967. The Evolution of the Iqta' in Medieval Iran. *Iran* 5 (1): 41–50.

———. 1969. *Landlord and Peasant in Persia: A Study of Land Tenure and Land Revenue Administration*. London and New York: I. B. Tauris.

————. 1981. *State and Government in Medieval Islam: An Introduction to the Study of Islamic Political Theory, the Jurists.* Oxford: Oxford University Press.

————. 1984. The Dilemma of Government in Islamic Persia: The Siyasatnama of Niẓam al-Mulk. *Iran* 22 (1): 55–66.

Lapidus, Ira. 2002. *A History of Islamic Societies.* Cambridge: Cambridge University Press.

Larkin, Margaret. 2008. *Al-Mutanabbi: Voice of the ʿAbbasid Poetic Ideal.* Oxford: Oneworld.

Leder, Stefan. 2015. Sultanic Rule in the Mirror of Medieval Political Literature. In *Global Medieval: Mirrors for princes revisited*, ed. Neguin Yavari and Regula Forster, 93–111. Harvard: Harvard University Press.

Levy, Reuben. 1929. *A Baghdad Chronicle.* Cambridge: Cambridge University Press.

Lindberg, David C. 1976. *Theories of Vision from Al-Kindi to Kepler.* Chicago: University of Chicago Press.

Macdonald, Duncan Black. 1936. The Meanings of the Philosophers by Al-Ghazali. *Isis* 25 (1): 9–15.

Madelung, Wilferd. 2004. *The Succession to Muhammad: A Study of the Early Caliphate.* Cambridge: Cambridge University Press.

Mahdi, Muhsin. 1990. Philosophical Literature. In *Religion, Learning and Science in the ʿAbbasid Period*, ed. M.J.L. Young and R.B. Serjeant, 76–105. Cambridge: Cambridge University Press.

Makdisi, George. 1973. The Sunni Revival. In *Islamic Civilization, 950–1150*, ed. D.H. Richards, 155–168. Oxford: Bruno Cassirer.

Mitha, Farouk. 2001. *Al-Ghazali and Ismailis: A Debate on Reason and Authority in Islam.* London: I.B. Tauris.

Moosa, Ebrahim. 2005. *Ghazali and the Poetics of Imagination.* Chapel Hill: The University of North Caroline Press.

Moussa, Mohammed. 2016. *Politics of the Islamic Tradition: The Thought of Muhammad al-Ghazali.* London: Routledge.

Mukti, Mohd Fakhrudin Abdul. 2005. Al-Ghazali and His Refutation of Philosophy. *Jurnal Usuluddin* 21 (1): 1–22.

Nadvi, Syed Habibul Haq. 1971. Al Iqta or Theory of Land Ownership in Islam. *Islamic Studies* 10 (4): 257–266.

Negmatov, N.N. 1998. The Samanid State. In *History of Civilizations of Central Asia Vol. 4*, ed. M.S. Asimov and C.E. Bosworth, 80–93. Paris: UNESCO.

Nishapuri, Zahir al-Din. 2001. *The History of the Seljuq Turks: The Saljuq-nama of Zahir al-Din Nishpuri from the Jamiʿ al-Tawarikh An Ilkhand Adaptation of the Saljuq-nama of Zahir al-Din Nishapuri.* Translated by Kenneth Allin Luther and edited by Edmund Bosworth. Richmond: Curzon.

Ormsby, Eric. 2000. *Ghazali.* London: Oneworld.

Papan-Matin, Firoozeh. 2010. *Beyond Death: The Mystical Teachings of 'Ayn al-Qudat al-Hamadhani*. London and Boston: Brill.

Peacock, A.C.S. 2010. *Early Seljuq History: A New Interpretation*. London and New York: Routledge.

———. 2016. The Great Age of the Seljuqs. In *Court and Cosmos: The Great Age of the Seljuq*, ed. Sheila R. Canby, Deniz Beyazit, Martian Rugiadi, and A.C.S. Peacock, 2–33. New York: The MMA.

Pourshariati, Parvaneh. 2008. *Decline and Fall of the Sasanian Empire: The Sasanian–Parthian Confederacy and the Arab Conquest of Iran*. London: I.B. Tauris.

Rashed, Roshdi. 2017. *Ibn al-Haytham's Geometrical Methods and the Philosophy of Mathematics: A History of Arabic Sciences and Mathematics Volume 5*. London: Routledge.

Reid, James J. 1978. The Qajar Uymaq in the Safavid Period, 1500–1722. *Iranian Studies* 11 (1): 117–143.

Renterghem, Vanessa Van. 2011. Social and Urban Dynamics in Baghdad During the Seljuq Period. In *İslam Medeniyetinde Bağdat*, ed. İsmail Safa Üstün, 171–194. Istanbul: Marmara Üniversitesi Yayınları.

Rice, Tamara Talbot. 1961. *The Seljuqs in Asia Minor*. London: Thames and Hudson.

Rosenthal, Erwin. 1958. *Political Thought in Medieval Islam: An Introductory Outline*. New York: Cambridge University Press.

Sabra, A.I. 1989. *The Optics of Ibn-Haytham Books I-III: On Direct Vision*. London: University of London.

Safi, Omid. 2006. *The Politics of Knowledge in Premodern Islam: Negotiating Ideology and Religious Inquiry*. Chapel Hill: The University of North Caroline Press.

Saliba, George. 2007. *Islamic Science and the Making of the European Renaissance*. Cambridge and London: The MIT Press.

Sezgin, Fuat. 2010. *Science and Technology in Islam*. Frankfurt: Institut für Geschichte der Arabisch–Islamischen Wissenschaften an der Johann Wolfgang Goethe-Universität.

Shaked, Shaul. 1995. *From Zoroastrian Iran to Islam: Studies in Religious History and Intercultural Contacts*. Vermond: Variorum.

Shihadeh, Ayman. 2005. From Al-Ghazali to Al-Razi: 6th/12th Century Developments in Muslim Philosophical Theology. *Arabic Sciences and Philosophy* 15 (1): 141–179.

Shu'ayb, Fiazuddin. 2011. Al-Ghazzali's Final Word on Kalam. *Islam & Science* 9 (2): 151–172.

Siddiqui, Sohaira. 2017. Power vs. Authority: Al-Juwayni's Intervention in Pragmatic Political Thought. *Journal of Islamic Studies* 28 (2): 193–220.

Smith, Margaret. 1938. Al-Risalat Al-Laduniyya. By Abu Ḥamid MuḤammad Al-Ghazali (450/1059–505/1111). *The Journal of the Royal Asiatic Society of Great Britain and Ireland* 70 (2): 177–200.

———. 1983. *Al-Ghazali: The Mystic*. Lahore: HIP.

Spuler, Bertold. 2015. *Iran in the Early Islamic Period: Politics, Culture, Administration and Public Life Between the Arab and the Seljuk Conquests, 633–1055*. Brill: Leiden and Boston.

Starr, Frederick. 2013. *Lost Enlightenment: Central Asia's Golden Age from the Arab Conquest to Tamerlane*. New Jersey: Princeton University Press.

Tafazzoli, Ahmad. 2000. *Sasanian Society*. New York: Bibliotheca Persica.

Tor, D.G. 2011. The Islamisation of Iranian Kingly Ideals in the Persianate Fürstenspiegel. *Iran* 49 (1): 115–122.

Tramontana, Felicita. 2012. "Khubz as Iqta," in "Four Authors from the Ayyubid and Early Mamluk Periods". *Mamluk Studies Review* 16 (1): 103–122.

Tsugitaka, Sato. 1992. The Iqta System of Iraq Under the Buwayhids. *Orient* 18 (1): 83–105.

———. 1997. *State and Rural Society in the Medieval Islam: Sultans, Muqta's and Fallahun*. Leiden: E. J. Brill.

Ünverdi, Veysi. 2018. Eş'ari Kelamında İmamiyet Nazariyesi. *Usul Islam Araştırmaları* 29 (1): 39–66.

Virani, Shafique N. 2007. *The Ismailis in the Middle Ages: A History of Survival, A Search for Salvation*. Oxford: Oxford University Press.

Walbridge, John. 2011. *God and Logic in Islam: The Caliphate of Reason*. Cambridge: Cambridge University Press.

Walker, C.T. Harley. 1915. Jahiz of Basra to Al-Fath Ibn Khaqan on the Exploits of the Turks and the Army of the Khalifate in General. *The Journal of the Royal Asiatic Society of Great Britain and Ireland* 23 (1): 631–197.

Watt, W. Montgomery. 1963. *Muslim Intellectual: A Study of Al-Ghazali*. Edinburg: Edinburgh University Press.

Zaman, Muhammad Qasim. 1997. *Religion and Politics Under the Early Abbasid: The Emergence of a Proto Sunni Elite*. Leiden: Brill.

Zaporozhets, V.M. 2012. *The Seljuks*. Hannover: European Academy of Natural Sciences e.V.

CHAPTER 3

The Islamic Idea of Nature

After a tour from Baghdad to Khorasan in 1082, Abu Ishak al-Shirazi, the head of the Nizamiya madrasa in Baghdad, noted that in almost every city, town, and village, he met a student of his who was serving as a scholar, imam or mufti.[1] Al-Shirazi made this remark 15 years after his inaugural lecture at the Baghdad Madrasa, attesting to the growing impact of the Seljuqi madrasas. Al-Ghazali was still not around. He would join the faculty in 1091. A graduate of the Nishapur madrasa, al-Ghazali himself was a proof of these madrasas' impact.[2]

This chapter aims to explain the Islamic idea of nature according to the Sunni view. It has its origins in the ninth-century synthesis of Islamic and the Greek philosophy, when the Mu'tazila nearly acquired the status of dominant intellectual school. By the eleventh century, the Mu'tazila had been almost completely destroyed by the Ash'ari school of theology, which was flourishing, as al-Shirazi's anecdote demonstrates, with official support thanks to the new alliance between Sunni orthodoxy and the Seljuqi state.

The consolidation of the Ash'ari school of theology was a result of the alliance between the state and religion, which Nizam al-Mulk had compared to twins. Ash'ari scholars now benefited from state funds and could even call on state authorities to punish their intellectual opponents. They were able to transmit their interpretations through the madrasa curriculum not only in Baghdad but also in cities like Isfahan, Damascus, and Mosul. During the second half of the eleventh century alone, the Seljuqis

© The Author(s) 2020
G. Bacik, *Islam and Muslim Resistance to Modernity in Turkey*,
https://doi.org/10.1007/978-3-030-25901-3_3

established 11 madrasas in Iraq and Syria, demonstrating how the madrasa became a central institution of the Muslim society.[3]

Al-Turtushi (1059–1126) was reported to have said that in his time, there was hardly a scholar from Jerusalem to Samarqand who did not enjoy Seljuqi state support.[4] The madrasas in Damascus increased from 23 to 89 during the twelfth and thirteenth centuries.[5] Undoubtedly, the growing network of madrasas benefited from the new state-religion alliance. Visiting Baghdad in 1185, Ibn Jubayr wrote about the most splendid Nizamiya madrasa and its impressive financial resources that paid the professor stipends.[6]

Political patronage naturally changed the balance of power among the various intellectual as well as theological groups. Official interventions like Nizam al-Mulk's decision that all students should read *Sahih al-Bukhari*, which resulted in the canonization of *al-Bukhari*, contributed to a new educational standardization and a homogeneous intellectual climate.[7] The piety-minded scholars who benefited from the state-sponsored education system quickly developed their outreach to the broader Muslim community.[8] However, public funds alone cannot explain all the expanding influence of the Ash'ari school.[9] The new paradigm was not only a matter of school curriculum. More decisive was the new alliance between state and Islam that enabled the clergy to religious clergy penetrate society to an unprecedented degree.

The Ash'ari School, which took its name from Abu'l-Hasan al-Ash'ari (873–935), a former Mu'tazila, had consolidated into a major school of theology by the eleventh century, dominating the classical heartland of the Islamic societies, that is, the modern-day Middle East. As underlined above, its consolidation virtually ended the largely Mu'tazila-dominated Islamic theological scene of the previous two centuries. It also had far-reaching consequences in law and other spheres of Islamic civilization.[10] E. Edgar Elder compared its rise with the history of Christian doctrine since the first Council of Nicaea (325).[11]

There were numerous challengers to the Ash'ari doctrine, the most consistent and well-known of whom was the Maturidi school (Table 3.1).[12]

Table 3.1 The spectrum of Islamic: theology between rationalism and traditionalism

The spectrum of Islamic theology			
Mu'tazila	Maturidi	Ash'ari	Hanbali

The significance of the Maturidi school was its success in remaining a legitimate school in the Sunni world despite the fact that it shared many views with the then delegitimated Mu'tazila.[13] The school took its name from Abu Mansur al-Maturidi (*c.* 852–944), who was born in Samarkand and whose teachings became dominant in Transoxiana. The Maturidi school tended to attribute more power to human agency and secondary causes than did the Ashari school. However, unlike the Mu'tazila, the Maturidi view resulted from a variation in interpretation rather than a theological rupture with the Ash'ari.[14]

3.1   DEFINING THE ISLAMIC IDEA OF NATURE

The Islamic idea of nature refers to the set of theological arguments about how nature works. There is no standard method to present the opinions and arguments on nature, which usually remain scattered in a number of books. Thus, a major purpose of this chapter is to systematically describe the Islamic idea of nature according to the Sunni theology. I analyze the Islamic idea of nature by focusing on four major themes: causality, free will, the theory of knowledge, and the idea of God.

3.1.1   *Causality*

Axiomatic in the Islamic approach is the need to develop a theological perspective on causality that recognizes God's central agency. But, how is it possible to develop a theory of causality that accommodates an intervening God who governs the universe?

Ash'ari theologians base their account of causality on the basic principle of God's omnipotence.[15] There is nothing God does not will.[16] Thus, for the Ash'ari school, no being or event in the world causes another, since God creates each event.[17] What people call causality is merely a sequence of events created by God. As al-Ash'ari wrote in *Kitab al-Luma'*, all the things that proceed from others are acts of God.[18]

We read in al-Ghazali how Ash'ari explains natural events: God creates them independent of any necessary connection of natural causes.[19] Logically, therefore, proposing that natural law has the capacity to cause natural events is to deny God's omnipotence, since it implies that something is acting on its accord.[20]

In the Third Discussion of *The Incoherence of Philosophers*, al-Ghazali developed a theory of movement that is ontologically dependent on agency. According to this theory, movement is possible only when there is an agent capable of volition. Nature, however, is not a living entity endowed with volition, and so it lacks the capacity to cause any movement.[21] God is the only agent, and there is no casual relationship between any two natural events.[22] He concluded that the term natural law is a misnomer: What we observe are God's actions; it is only the human mind that tends to frame them as laws.

The repudiation of natural law and the recognition of God's agency in nature produced a different concept of causality that makes reference to the relationship between this world and the divine one.[23] But, how is this relationship possible? Al-Ghazali has an analogy in which a mere physicist, who relies on natural law, is likened to an ant who, crawling on a sheet of paper and observing black letters spreading over it, sees the pen alone as the cause. However, for the astronomer with a wider vision, it is fingers that move the pen.[24] Causality is now a fuzzy shadow of God's customs. God is not part of time and space; therefore, it is not possible to understand exactly how he governs the universe. Likewise, natural laws are the human interpretations of God's actions. This is the space-time problem in Islamic philosophy. Ibn Rushd summarizes it in *The Incoherence of the Incoherence* as follows:

> One i.e. human in the nature of which there is motion and which cannot be separated from time; the other i.e. God in the nature of which there is no motion and which is eternal and cannot be described in terms of time.[25]

Al-Ghazali's concept of causality is based on God's agency and therefore refutes natural law.[26] As we will see later, Ibn Rushd, in contrast, based his concept of causality on the difference in their natures and suggested a distinction between human and the divine agency.

In this vein, the impact of Atomist philosophy on Muslim scholars, especially in regard of the formation of Islamic natural theology, requires attention, particularly if one is to understand Ash'ari skepticism toward natural causality. A selective reading of Atomism enabled Muslim scholars to reject the notion that the capacity or tendency to cause motion is inherent in the nature of atoms (or things).[27] According to Atomism, everything is composed of atoms and accidents.[28] Atoms can acquire properties only by accident. Accidents happen, but what they create immediately ceases to exist. There is no continuity or connection between one moment in time and another, nor one accident and another. In proving that there is no agent other than God, Ash'ari theologians filled these gaps with God's power, which creates the accident in each case, and at every instance of time.[29] This Ash'ari account also accorded with the atomist idea that human attempts to know reality through the senses are futile.[30] What was appealing about Atomism to Ash'ari theologians was the idea that no situation in nature is real, since each is in fact the appearance of atomic combinations.

Muslim scholars' selective reading of the Atomist view demonstrates that the main motivation was not to reject causality but to explain it in a way that does not violate God's agency in nature. This motivation is also evident in their engagement with Stoic thought. The Stoics had elaborated a theory of continuity to explain determinism in nature. According to this theory, things are connected to one another like a chain. The whole system of causation depends on "a chain of fate; and this chain of fate [is] held together by *pneumatic* force."[31] Stoic causation posits an ultimate, transcendental cause (the *pneuma*), the active divine spirit.[32] It includes the *logos*, which the Stoics identify as God pervading everybody in the universe and holding them together.[33] It ascribes all action to the supreme Deity, leaving no space for man's choice. Stoic determinism was also preferable for Ash'ari theologians, including al-Ghazali, since it explained God's continuous intervention with *pneuma*, which admits a God-driven causation into nature.[34] Ibn Rushd was thus correct when he criticized occasionalist Muslim scholars for adopting "the theory of those ancient philosophers of the Stoics" to repudiate natural law.[35]

The Ash'ari theologians concluded that an external agency is required to explain any action in nature. Thus, ours is a world of accidents, where God creates each of us independently of autonomous causal laws.[36] This amounts to placing all causal efficacy in the hands of God, on the authority of the doctrine of continuous creation.[37] However, Muslim scholars were also motivated to reconcile causality with God's absolute agency. Their efforts to do so produced the theory of Occasionalism.

As defined by Majid Fakhry, Occasionalism is the belief in the exclusive efficacy of God, according to which every natural event is the manifestation or occasion of God's direct intervention.[38] Occasionalism among Muslim scholars was a challenge to the Aristotelian concept of causation, which had come to be considered a threat to faith.[39] The Aristotelian view of nature, which holds that events take place according to certain causal procedures, is indeed not compatible with a God who is always active in nature. In contrast, Occasionalism offers a view of nature in which everything is composed of atoms, and every movement on this atomic foundation occurs as God wishes.[40]

Contending Ideas on Causality

Reading al-Ghazali we get detailed information on how Ash'ari occasionalism explains causality. The theory's basic framework is that whatever we see as a cause is not a real cause, and the sole reason for movement in nature is God's agency.[41] I will call this the God-first approach. The God-first approach first secures the idea that God's continuous creation causes all temporal events.[42] Having defined the constant, the God-first approach then explains how to understand nature, which basically amounts to an attempt to prove how natural laws do not exist. The priority is to define the substantial constants of the debate, and then attempt to explain the secondary issues. The constant is God's continuous creation, intervention, and rule over nature. Any explanation may not put the constant at risk.

Following a God-first approach, al-Ghazali first denies the impact of intermediate causes on events and things. He does not only deny (caused) effects; he denies the very existence of a cause-and-effect (natural law) order: "The connection between what is habitually believed to be a cause and what is habitually believed to be an effect is not necessary." How then do things occur? An effect occurs on the "prior decree of God, who creates side by side, not to its being necessary in itself, incapable of separation."[43] In fact, this interpretation is a typical Neoplatonist one. In the Neoplatonist account of causation, terminology like "before," "after," or "sequence" is metaphorical. Or, better put, these terms refer in reality to a "metaphysical order of priority and posteriority," and not to events as we understand them in a temporal sequence.[44] Causality in the Neoplatonic system is mainly about the ultimate soul that rules the universe, rather than some other explanation stemming from nature.[45] Similarly, in al-Ghazali's account of nature, rules or non-living things have no ability to initiate action; only willing agents can have such roles. Thus, by observing events in nature, we learn to accept that "existence [of one something] with a[nother] thing does not prove that it exists by [that thing]."[46] In other words, things may exist together, but that does not imply a causal link between them. Rather, their coexistence is a mere coincidence. For example, observing the ebb of the sea when there is a full moon does not prove that the moon causes the sea to ebb. Al-Ghazali is adamant on this:

crediting a non-living rule or law with action contradicts God's sovereignty, since all actions in nature are created exclusively by divine power.[47] To stress his thesis, he gave the following example:

> The movement of the stone downward is also compulsory, originating by God's creating motion in it. The same is to be said of the motion of all inanimate bodies.[48]

Another, probably the famous, example is the burning of cotton:

> The first position is for the opponent to claim that the agent of the burning is the fire alone, it being an agent by nature [and] not by choice—hence, incapable of refraining from [acting according to] what is in its nature after contacting a substratum receptive of it. And this is one of the things we deny. On the contrary, we say: The one who enacts the burning by creating blackness in the cotton, [causing] separation in its parts, and making it cinder or ashes is God, either through the mediation of His angels or without mediation.[49]

Al-Ghazali was not the first thinker to question the role of secondary causes; however, as Fakhry notes, his approach was outstanding in its systematic refutation of the concept of the necessary causal nexus of events.[50] In fact, al-Ghazali also left a legacy concerning other issues of Ash'ari theology such as knowledge and free will. However, his most important legacy was the positing of another, higher cause of natural events.[51] Magid Fakhry called this legacy the bipolarity in Muslim thought.[52] Thus, popular engagement with Islamic theology has tended to focus on divine causation, leaving a deep mistrust of the natural laws.[53]

Revisiting Ibn Rushd's approach to causality, which is different on many accounts, will help us reach a better understanding of the Ash'ari perspective. Ibn Rushd explained nature in terms of causal relations. He defined a natural agent as "one which performs one essential thing exclusively: For instance, warmth causes heat, and coldness causes cold."[54] As a qadi in the court of the Almohad rulers and author of significant books on Islamic law, he did not think that recognizing natural causes necessarily contradicts God's sovereignty.[55] Instead, he argued that there was a continuum of causality underlying structure of physical reality. For Ibn Rushd, there are rules and standards in nature, and they can be discovered through science.[56]

In elaborating his arguments, Ibn Rushd first criticizes al-Ghazali's interpretation of God's agency. Ibn Rushd believes that God's agency is not an easy topic to study, since there is "no counterpart to His will in the empirical world."[57] He finds al-Ghazali's presentation of God as the sole agent of natural events to be reductionist and flawed. God's being out of time and space makes impossible to find a counterpart of God's will in the empirical world. Given that God is outside of time and space, it is not clear how deliberation and choice are tied to time and space. Thus, he concluded that there is no equivalent to God's will within the empirical world. Ibn Rushd consequently differentiates between empirical or natural and divine agency. For Ibn Rushd, philosophers do not reject the view that God is the omnipotent creator. But al-Ghazali's proposal that God is the sole agent in the events of nature is problematic, since it is wrong to assume the possibility of observing an equivalent to God's will in the empirical world. Ibn Rushd opines that the way al-Ghazali and the Ash'ari theologians repudiate secondary causes on the basis of God's sovereignty ironically creates the problem of contradicting God's divine nature. A superior view according to Ibn Rushd is that while God is the creator of everything, things may depend on different agencies.[58] In other words, in Ibn Rushd's account, the admission of secondary causes does not contradict God's sovereignty; instead, that admission is made necessary by the impossibility of observing an equivalent to God's will in nature.

Ibn Rushd thus offered a formula to reconcile God's omnipotence with causation. He proposed a straightforward explanation of secondary causes: "… for what actualizes another thing, i.e. acts on it, is not called agent simply by a metaphor, but in reality, for the definition of agent is appropriate to it." Thus, all other attempts at theological explanation are either various linguistic metaphors of no importance.[59] The agency of secondary causes is so clear that denying them is sophistry. Arguing that God is an agent for everything in the world without an intermediary contradicts the evidence provided by human senses that things act upon (and in this sense cause) other things.[60]

What we observe in Ibn Rushd is a shift from the God-first approach to a different view that recognizes the agency of other things.[61] Ibn Rushd accepted that the agency that causes things to happen (either in the way of passing from potency to actuality, or from non-existence to existence) occurs sometimes by choice and sometimes by nature.[62] There is no doubt for Ibn Rushd that God's agency is "more perfect and glorious than any performed by the empirical agents," for he is the sole capable agent of drawing forth the universe from non-existence to existence.[63] However, by differentiating "passing from potency to actuality" and "passing from non-existence to existence," Ibn Rushd accepts a division of labor between agency-by-choice and agency-by-nature. In other words, he recognizes the capacity of natural laws to cause movement. In practice, Ibn Rushd rejects the mixing of the visible and the divine worlds, as al-Ghazali did. For al-Ghazali, such opinions that credit laws or things as the origin of movements are inadmissible:

> But [according to the philosophers] the stone has an action—namely, falling due to heaviness and an inclination toward [the earth's] center—just as fire has an action, which is heating, and the wall has an action—namely, the inclination toward the center and the occurrence of the shadow—for all [these latter things] proceed from [the wall]. But this is impossible.[64]

In contrast, Ibn Rushd is firm in his view that there are some principles in nature that govern motion—that is, that things move by their nature.[65] For him, those principles are the general ones that affect all things in similar ways.[66] Ibn Rushd's nature, therefore, is a nature of constant rules. Human beings can trust the natural laws. Further, he challenges the Ash'ari position that acts cannot proceed from natural things, on the grounds that such a position denies that living beings act. For Ibn Rushd, such a denial is wrong, even if its objective is to prove God's exclusive agency.[67] Ibn Rushd's masterstroke was to point out simply that the denial of constant laws would require a tyrannical idea of God.[68] On this logic, he made one of his strongest points against the Ash'ari idea of causality, which in his view renders God a tyrant:

> [...] agent to rule existents like a tyrannical prince who has the highest power, for whom nobody in his dominion can deputize, of whom no standard or custom is known to which reference might be made. Indeed, the acts of such a prince will undoubtedly be unknown by nature, and if an act of his comes into existence the continuance of its existence at any moment will be unknown by nature.[69]

There is an order in Ibn Rushd's nature. God endowed things with an ability to move without cessation or weariness. Therefore, there is no need to fear that things in nature might collapse like "ceilings and lofty edifices." And the natural order is manifest in "numbers, shapes, positions and motions."[70]

The Maturidi position on causality is usually interpreted as differing from that of the Ashari school. While some scholars argue that the Maturidi adopts a soft Occasionalism "not exactly the same as that of the Ash'aris,"[71] other scholars argue that Occasionalism has played no role in the development of Maturidi theology.[72] Focusing on al-Maturidi's emphasis on natures (*taba'i*) in *Kitab al-Tawhid*, Richard Frank argues that the Maturidi system does include a causal model similar to those elaborated by the rationalist schools in Islam.[73] Accordingly, al-Maturidi recognizes that events in nature are ordered by established rules that originate in the natures (*taba'i*) of things.[74]

Reading *Kitab al-Tawhid*, one concludes that al-Maturidi's position has some similarities to that of Ibn Rushd. Like Ibn Rushd, al-Maturidi distinguishes between the visible and the divine worlds.[75] Al-Maturidi's understanding of the visible world differs significantly from that of al-Ghazali. By distinguishing between the visible and the invisible worlds, al-Maturidi recognizes that nature may have its own agents. For example, he recognizes that the *natures* of things cause regular movements. In explaining the argument, he gives the example of combustible burning objects.[76] In contrast to al-Ghazali, al-Maturidi accepts that the structure of things may cause burning, indicating his divergence from occasionalism. Thus, like Ibn Rushd, al-Maturidi sees no problem with recognizing that natural laws have causal efficacy: God's agency is not contradicted, since God created the laws, that is, the structure of nature, in the first place.[77] Thus, al-Maturidi advises that a person who wants to succeed at any task in this world needs knowledge of the natures of the pertinent things.[78] However, the Maturidi brand of causation is limited: for example, natures are not able to initiate motion at a high level, such as the motion of stars.[79]

3.1.2   The Theory of Knowledge

As I explained in Chap. 2, the concept of inner knowledge is one of al-Ghazali's major legacies in Sunni theology; however, it derives from his interpretation of the Ash'ari occasionalism. The repudiation of natural laws required alternative methods to know the real mechanism behind natural events, which resulted in the incorporation of inner knowledge into Sunni theology. Al-Ghazali explains the major characteristics of inner knowledge as follows:

This did not come about by systematic demonstration or marshalled argument, but by a light which God most high cast into my breast. That light is the key to the greater part of knowledge. Whoever thinks that the understanding of things Divine rests upon strict proofs has in his thought narrowed down the wideness of God's mercy.[80]

Transmitted through direct contact with God, inner knowledge is not mediated by human senses or reasoning. The knowledge acquired in this way is sublime and incomparable with rational knowledge, which al-Ghazali deemed unreliable.[81] However, the recognition of inner knowledge did not entail a complete rejection of reason. Instead, al-Ghazali reframes reason as a subservient faculty that has no autonomous ability to find out truth; rather, *subservient reason* requires guidance from inner knowledge.[82]

Al-Ghazali holds that inner knowledge is infallible and cannot be doubted.[83] Unlike the knowledge that comes from sensation and reasoning, inner knowledge depends on a "mystical state, which is realized in immediate experience by those who walk in the way leading to it."[84] Inner knowledge, therefore: (i) depends for its acquisition on direct contact with God, and that contact has no intermediaries; (ii) personal spiritual quality is the element that grants access to that contact; the path to inner knowledge is linked to the purity of the soul.[85]

Al-Ghazali's concept of "inner knowledge" is rooted in Occasionalism. If there is a double causality and the divine one is superior (to the natural one), a method that is able to reach to that divine causality is logically the more important one.[86] Like in Neoplatonism, in Islamic inner knowledge, the proposal is to go beyond what we see in this world.[87]

The deficiencies of human sensation and reasoning are usually invoked as reasons for the necessity of inner knowledge. We can trace the logic of defending and explaining inner knowledge based on the limits of human sensation and reasoning back to al-Ghazali.[88] He frequently emphasizes the limits of the human senses:

Again, it looks at the heavenly body (i.e. the sun) and sees it small, the size of a shilling; yet geometrical computations show that it is greater than the earth in size.[89]

The purpose here is to attack the very foundation of the rational knowledge: human senses. However, al-Ghazali's attack is not limited to sensation but took on reasoning too.[90] There are some fields, al-Ghazali argues, like the medical sciences and astronomy, where obtaining knowledge by reason alone is inconceivable; even experts in those fields know that their knowledge is "attained only by Divine inspiration and by assistance from God most high. It cannot be reached by observation."[91] In so doing, he lays siege to the two pillars of rational knowledge: sensation and reasoning.

This is a radical perspective, as it attempted to bring inner knowledge even into the realm of the natural sciences such as the medical sciences and astronomy. Indeed, to do this is to reject any border between religion and science. When al-Ghazali says that he cannot trust sense perception, his distrust also holds in scientific fields. (As I discussed in the Chap. 1, al-Ghazali based his conditional tolerance of science on its not intruding into the territory of religion. Furthermore, he insisted upon the propriety of religious inquiry into all sciences that come up with philosophical arguments that might be at odds with religious ones.) This is not inconsistent for al-Ghazali, since his claiming that reason has limits entails the need to concede that it has limits in all relevant fields.[92]

A section of al-Ghazali's *Ihya* is the blueprint of his explanation of how people are able to connect with inner knowledge through piety and mystical purification. He defines the heart not as the blood-pumping organ but as the locus of a mystical nature that is able to connect with absolute knowledge. It is the seat of knowledge and an organ that "uses all the other faculties as its instruments."[93] Al-Ghazali gives a special role to Sufis, who are in theory the best actors to perform the method: to act and communicate in the visible world (*'alam al-mulk wa'l-shahadah*) with the higher spiritual world (*'alam al-ghayb wa'l-malakat*). The former is observable with the human senses. The latter, the world of higher truth, is not observable with human sense but can be known by an inner spiritual eye.[94] As with causality, al-Ghazali again constructs his concept of inner knowledge based on a model where it is possible to communicate between the visible and the visible worlds.[95] Al-Ghazali's nature is not a closed system that operates according to laws; rather, it is an open system that is affected by the interventions from the invisible world.

Those who obtain inner knowledge learn how "the invisible government of the world is carried out."[96] Al-Ghazali named these knowers the "elite of the elite" (*khass al-khawass*)[97] and defined their knowledge as superior to rational knowledge.[98] For al-Ghazali, such privilege enhanced their social legitimacy and prestige, since they are the agents of communication between man and God.[99]

The incorporation of inner knowledge, as systematized by al-Ghazali, into Sunni theology reinstituted direct contact between man and God through inner knowledge. It is ironic that al-Ghazali, who rejected the notion of the esoteric knowledge of the Fatimid imams, advanced and systematized the theory of inner knowledge. His theory amounts to the assertion "that after the Prophet's death the Muslim community was still in need of divine inspiration, to be found among God's friends."[100] These "friends" are agents endowed with quasi-prophetic powers.[101] The incorporation of inner knowledge into Sunni Islam was a watershed in Islamic history.

The Mu'tazili and the Maturidi schools each hold a different position on knowledge. Any religious interpretation in line with the classical Mu'tazili or Maturidi theology is expected to be incompatible with the concept of inner knowledge. To begin with, for the Mu'tazila, it is possible to develop a successful rational method to understand nature, and even to know good and evil solely through human reason.[102] Thus, we do not detect in Mu'tazili thought a criticism of human senses and reasoning. Instead, the Mu'tazila had a rationalist view and accepted reason as a foundational element of their theology. Unlike the Ash'ari school, the Mu'tazila believe that man lives in a world where things can be known. In this order, the human intellect is of greater value than revelation.[103]

The Mu'tazili scholar, 'Abd al-Jabbar, defined speculative reasoning as the first duty of man, and rational argument (*hujjat al-'aql*) as the first evidence.[104] On all accounts, the Mu'tazila believed that confidence in the rational and knowable nature of reality is required; otherwise, the idea of human responsibility would be baseless. In other words, Mu'tazila rationalism emerges from a moral requirement: man's responsibility requires that he develop his ability to explain nature.

Maturidi theologians also emphasize reason, as it would be responsible for acquiring knowledge even if God had sent no prophet for this purpose.[105] This point is a major difference with Ash'ari theology, which did not hold that reason was qualified to lead man without the aid of revelation. Maturidi theology is rationalist in many respects. In *Kitab al-Tawhid*, al-Maturidi renounces those who claim that the only available method of acquiring knowledge is God-given intuition.

Thus, Maturidi rationalism is persistent on the central role of sensation and reasoning.[106] Accordingly, rational knowledge with its pillars of reasoning and observation is the highest human faculty. Al-Maturidi even insists on the authority of reason over *hadith* (traditions). Reminding the reader that narrators are fallible people who can err, he suggests that human reason is the best means of verification.[107] His message through *hadith* is to underline that rational knowledge is the highest authority when it comes to verifying any type of knowledge. By contrast, al-Ash'ari wrote in *al-Ibanah* that "we accept all the traditions for which the traditionists vouch."[108]

In al-Maturidi's methodology, relying on reasoning is not a matter of choice but a necessity. Al-Maturidi writes that denying reason is also an act of reasoning. He therefore had no doubt that rational knowledge based on senses and reasoning is the only available method for acquiring knowledge.[109] For him, knowledge that comes from sense perceptions is the origin of true knowledge, and one should have no doubt about its validity.[110]

Al-Maturidi was not unaware of the limits of human senses and reasoning. As he wrote, the knowledge acquired by sensation is subject to change as a result of environmental factors such as insufficient light. As we saw above, it was on the basis of this point that al-Ghazali would later develop his theory of inner knowledge. By contrast, al-Maturidi sees the limits or weaknesses of sensation and reasoning as a natural part of rational knowledge and does not think that they disprove its validity[111]

3.1.3   Free Will

The issue of free will is another point of entry for an analysis of the Islamic idea of nature.[112] On free will, Ash'ari theologians again follow a God-first approach, where the prime motive is to affirm God's omnipotence. Logically, such an approach compromises or even denies man's free will. In Ash'ari theology, the concept of cocreator with God (even in the limited sense, according to which man claims full agency in determining his actions) amounts to polytheism and contradicts God's absolute power. If there were in the world something unwilled by God, wrote al-Ash'ari, it would be something to the existence of which God would be averse. God's authority leaves no space for anything God does not will.[113] Since no person shares with him in his creative activity, attributing agency to man is simply wrong.[114]

Ash'ari discourse on free will focuses on preserving God's complete control over his creation.[115] Al-Ash'ari left his arguments on human will only as postulates, with no further attempt to demonstrate them.[116] God's creation, which includes all things, even intentions, leaves no space for a man with an autonomous capacity to act, nor even to will.[117] Thus, God is not only the only creator but also the only agent, as al-Ash'ari wrote in *Kitab al-Luma'*.[118] If Islam's maxim is *La ilaha illallah* (There is no god but God), the maxim of Ash'ari theology on free will is "There is no agent but God." The Ash'ari view allows for almost no distinction between creation and agency. Thus, unlike Ibn Rushd, al-Ash'ari does not differentiate agencies, which makes it impossible to attribute any kind of autonomous agency to man. As a result, in the Ash'ari view, man wills only what God willed man to will.[119] Since there is no will in the sense of an autonomy that belongs to the agent, each act of willing or volition of man is a discrete event or accident that God creates.[120]

However, the Ash'ari view of free will is not strict absolutism. Ash'ari theologians have deployed the concept *kasb* carefully, mindful of avoiding inconsistency in their discourse on morality, which includes the teaching that a man's freedom is the essential prerequisite of his being responsible for his actions. The verb *kasb* (to acquire) presents the Arab ethical view that actions are possessed by the acting person.[121] The term was transferred to the theological context with the meaning of man's *will* to do an action. And the term was interpreted to fill the gap between man's responsibility and God's agency. Accordingly, man's acquisition of an action occurs simultaneously with that action.[122] Thus, theologians elaborated the concept of *kasb* to prove that man's actions occur without contradicting either God's absolute sovereignty or man's responsibility.[123]

Reading the Ash'ari explanation of *kasb*, one concludes that not only its role but also its nature is vague. It is defined as a discrete thing created immediately with the act of willing and at the very same moment when man acts and God's creation occurs.[124] Inspired also by Atomist philosophy, the model suggests that God instantaneously creates in the human a power of causality at the very moment of the realization of the act, and this transforms man into the efficacious cause.[125] Thus, God remains the creator of the choice and the thing chosen, and *kasb* secures both human freedom and responsibility.[126] However, the Ash'ari theory of *kasb* has gaps, as Binyamin Abrahamov points out:

> [It] does not tell us to whom the power to will belongs, to man himself or to God, whether God creates it for man at the moment the action takes place or before the occurrence of the action, or whether it is an inherent element in man. However, since, according to al-Ash'ari, God wills and creates all things, one may conclude that He wills and creates man's power to will as well as the will itself. Although al-Ash'ari does not mention the power to will, it is evident that according to *al-Luma'* man cannot will unless God wills.[127]

The crux of the theory is the question of to whom acquisition belongs, and the answer is yet to be clarified. For example, in *Al-Ibanah*, al-Ash'ari wrote that there is no acquisition on the part of human beings that God does not will.[128] Thus, Ash'ari theology, as Georges F. Hourani summarizes it, succeeds at dismissing the problem but not at solving it.[129]

Even some Ash'ari theologians recognize the logical gaps in the Ash'ari account of free will. For example, Mahmud Isfahani (d. 1279), a scholar at the Revahiyye Madrasa, argued that the man's acts are God's creations. Aware of the contradictory content of the theory, Isfahani ended his part in the debate, noting that the best thing to do with this topic is to follow the method of the early scholars, which was to cease arguing about it and to be satisfied with the fact that God understood how there was no contradiction, even if humans did not.[130] The ambitious Ash'ari attempt to harmonize man's will and God's sovereignty has repeatedly resulted in theological analogies. However, none of them has resolved the logical problems. As Ibn Rushd warned, analogies are convincing until they are investigated, when their deficiency becomes evident.[131]

The Mu'tazili perspective on free will is a man-first approach, unlike the God-first approach of the Ash'ari school. Accordingly, man not only has power over his good and bad deeds but also creates them.[132] As 'Abd al-Jabbar (d. 1024) succinctly puts it, the Mu'tazila thesis has a simple logic: "If God were the agent of our acts then they would not have happened according to our purposes and motivation."[133] Pointing out that two different actors cannot do an act as one, for they may disagree sometimes, the Mu'tazila argued that God delegated real power to man to freely make his own choices to act on them. Not giving any credit to theological analogies or contrived concepts like *kasb*, they simply accept that man has the ability to determine his action according to his will.[134]

While summarizing the Mu'tazila's five general principles, Abu'l-Qasim al-Balkhi (d. 931) made the point that God does not create the acts of human beings, as God created human beings with the capacity for action (*qudra*).[135] Looking at such arguments today against the backdrop of Sunni theology, they appear so divergent from mainstream views as to be utterly incapable of acquiring any legitimacy. Thus, the typical criticism of the Mu'tazila view of human freedom, a criticism that is also relevant for the Maturidi, is the problem of harmonizing man's choice and God's will. In challenging the Mu'tazila, many have asked the same question that was posed by 'Abd Allah al-Baydawi (d. 1286), a leading Ash'ari theologian: What if man makes a choice, and his will is contrary to the will of God?[136]

To overcome such questions, the Mu'tazila developed a concept of God that rejects divine attributes.[137] Lacking divine attributes, this God is impersonal and does not know the particulars of or create man's actions. This conception of God is compatible with the Mu'tazila's view of free will, where man has absolute autonomy in his actions.

The Maturidi concept of free will is also a man-first approach, though within a reserved framework. Al-Maturidi tried to develop a theology where human beings are really doers of their actions and are free.[138] However, al-Maturidi rejected the notion that man is the creator of his acts.[139]

Maturidi developed his idea of man's autonomy in a balanced way, careful not to imply anything that resonates with Mu'tazila's arguments. As we saw, leading Maturidi scholars like al-Nasafi (1067–1142) aimed to develop a theological interpretation where man chooses his actions.[140] Al-Hakim al-Samarqandi (d. 925), an early representative of the school, similarly insisted that man has the capacity for action but that capacity exists contemporaneously with the action.[141] The Maturidi account focuses on man's autonomy over his deeds. In the Maturidi view, man is truly free and thus is the doer of his actions.[142] Like the Mu'tazila, Maturidi theologians gave priority to prove the autonomy of man, leaving the God-linked side of the debate in abeyance. Thus, on this account, the Maturidi's view differs substantially from the God-first Ash'ari theology of free will.

The Maturidi concept of *kasb* is straightforward: Man is the doer of action (*fa'il*) and a free one (*mukhtar*), and thus he is an acquirer, *kasib*.[143] Unlike the Ash'ari position, which qualifies man's acquisition, the Maturidi position accepts that God has no impact on man's action in terms of acquisition.[144] In this model, God gives man freedom to act, and man's acts emerge as a result of cooperation between God and man.[145] The cooperation occurs with a kind of division of labor: God is the creator and man is the doer.[146] Man is able to freely act without requiring God's intervention as creator.[147]

But, how is this possible? The answer lies in al-Maturidi's concept of agency, which is reminiscent of that of Ibn Rushd. In contrast to al-Ash'ari and his followers, al-Maturidi suggests that although agency belongs to God in terms of creating man's action, man does have agency when it comes to doing his own actions, and such agency does not contradict God's sovereignty. In this conception, every human action has two segments; the first belongs to God, and the second belongs to man.[148]

Al-Maturidi's conception of human will is located to the left of the Ash'ari position on the spectrum of Islamic theology. At the same time, al-Maturidi saw the Mu'tazila position as red line that could not be legitimately crossed. Thus, it is consistent to argue that Maturidi's analysis of human action involves elements of both Mu'tazila and Ash'ari theology.[149]

3.1.4   The Idea of God

The final issue that constitutes part of the Islamic idea of nature is the concept of God: how God is described, and the implications of that description for the explanation of natural events.

The Diyanet's *The Encyclopedia of Islam* defines Allah as the supreme being that created and governs the universe.[150] According to this definition, one crucial information about God is that he governs the universe. If God governs the universe, what is the proper attitude toward God with regard to the functioning of things in the universe?

On this issue, the Qur'an can be interpreted to support both personal and impersonal conceptions of God.[151] It declares God to be unique: "There is nothing whatever like unto Him."[152] The doctrine of uniqueness and difference (*mukhalafa*) is underscored. However, the Qur'an also speaks of certain attributes of God that present him as having a personality that knows, speaks, and even sits on a throne. Furthermore, the Qur'an uses anthropomorphic terms like God's eyes and hands. Throughout history Islamic thought has oscillated between the personal and impersonal conceptions of God. In *Kitab al-Luma'*, al-Ash'ari warns that it is not proper to refer to God using those names about whose meaning is no consensus among Muslims, indicating how the conception of God is also a social construction.[153]

We can plot various Islamic groups' conceptions of God on a spectrum. On one pole, there is *ta'til*, where God is depicted as essentially an impersonal power. On the opposite pole lies *tashbih*, where God is endowed with attributes that make him a personal deity.[154] Throughout Islamic history, Muslims have given credit to both approaches when interpreting this pillar of their faith.[155]

The theological debates about the nature of God certainly have their dilemmas: While God's divine essence requires a very abstract conceptualization of him, understandings of God in Muslim daily life can lead to anthropomorphization. Contending conceptions of God have appeared between the two poles of the spectrum, as displayed in Table 3.2. Ibn

Table 3.2 The spectrum of the concept of God in Islam

Ta'til	*Tashbih*
Non-personal God	Personal God

Miskawayh (d. 1030) summarized the dilemma thus: any conception of God is always incomplete.[156] The problem therefore is how this incompleteness might be observed in the various conceptions of God. For example, reflecting a sort of utilitarian view, he states that religion requires a personal God replete with attributes understandable to people, who could then fear and love him: the popular demand is for a God who is the personal target of worship and prayer.

However, bringing God into the realm of daily life generates a complex concern: It must be done without contradicting God's absolute unity.[157] Ibn Miskawayh's warning was important. Putting God into any context, be it theological one or natural causality, is likely to end in the erosion of his absolute and divine unity, that is, in some kind of incompleteness.[158] At the same time, philosophers' abstract conception of God is also affected by incompleteness for failing to be meaningful to the people. Aware of the same problem, Ibn Rushd also warned that for average people, it is difficult to accept the idea of God that is not linked with something imaginable.[159]

On the other hand, a concept of God is usually the outcome of how an Islamic school of thought defines its position in regard of causality, inner knowledge, and free will. Logically, less emphasis on the role of secondary agents would result in a more personal conception of God. Such a relationship is also observed between other elements of the Islamic idea of nature. For example, more emphasis on causality usually results in less emphasis on inner knowledge. Repudiating secondary causes, for instance, Ash'ari theology is already inclined toward an active and personal God. Similarly, inner knowledge consolidated the personal concept of God by allowing for direct contact between man and God.

Sunni scholars usually try to locate their conception of God at the center of the spectrum of Islamic theology (Table 3.2), avoiding both extremes of *ta'til* and *tashbih*. For example, al-Ghazali deemed anthropomorphism and the philosophical idea of an impersonal God to be equally dangerous. For him, God is unique: divine, so unlike any created thing. He has no face, body, or form, nor size, manner, or quality, for he resembles nothing and is resembled by nothing.[160] In *Moderation in Belief*, he explained that God is not a body, for all bodies are composed of more than one element and have a specific magnitude. But he also added that God is not a mode or substance.[161]

Therefore, not thinking of God as body or substance, al-Ghazali refrains from giving an incorporeal image of God that resembles the philosophers' God, who is a cosmic entity or an abstract intellect. Remembering Ibn Miskawayh's dilemma, al-Ghazali wanted to fix his concept of God on exactly the right point, which is supposed to satisfy both social-utilitarian and theological requirements. For example, exhibiting a typical social-utilitarian concern in his conception of God, al-Ghazali argued that seeing is more perfect than the one who does not see, and that thus it is illogical to attribute seeing to man but not to God.[162]

Sunni scholars have generally accepted that presenting the Islamic idea of God in a well-balanced, populist discourse is necessary for teaching the general Muslim population about God. Thus, whoever listens to his creatures, helps them, and accepts or rejects their prayers becomes the popular idea of God. This discourse led to the integration of God into the daily life of Muslims. To rephrase Erwin I.J. Rosenthal: this God is like the Abrahamic God who declares "I am" with a defined personality, who actively fills the soul and heart of people. He is unlike the Greek notion of God, who is the author of mathematical truths, or the order of the elements.[163] However, such a strategy naturally resulted in a theology where God is defined with various attributes. Accordingly, a personal God whose agency is defined as the origin of all events in nature required attributes.[164] However, defining God with attributes carries the risk of anthropomorphism, and both the Ash'ari and the Maturidi schools developed complex arguments to prove that attributes are neither identical to nor other than God.[165] Thus, both in Ash'ari and Maturidi theology, we frequently observe the warning "but not in the way humans do...." This is the typical assurance for the proponents of the personal conception of God that God is not like a human. For instance, al-Ghazali wrote that the name is different than the act of naming and the thing named, and thus God's names and attributes should be understood within their idiosyncrasy.[166] Similarly, on God's attributes, al-Maturidi wrote that they are neither the same as God's personality nor they different from his personality.[167] Probably the most eloquent formulation of this point is again available in al-Ghazali's *Alchemy of Happiness*, where he wrote that no one can understand a king but a king.[168]

One way of guarding against anthropomorphizing God ironically involved borrowing notion of *hal* from the Mu'tazila and linking it with concept of attributes. Briefly, *hal* (pl. *ahwal*) is a metaphysical entity that is neither existent nor non-existent and that informs us of how God acts through his self. *Hal* theory claims that God's acts as grounded in his self are like being knowing or being hearing.[169] The theory explains God's continuous agency in nature without giving way to anthropomorphism. Thus, it could be seen as an attempt within Ash'ari theology to correct an overly personal conception of God. Abu Bakr al-Baqillani (d. 1013) introduced the notion of *hal* to Ash'ari thought, and later other key scholars like al-Juwayni and al-Razi adopted it.[170]

However, al-Ghazali did not approve of *hal* theory and even his discussions on the concept of God were critical of such an approach.[171] Thus, al-Ghazali played an important role in sustaining the traditional Ash'ari conception of a personal God with anthropomorphic features. In *Kitab al-Luma'*, there are various passages where al-Ash'ari proposes some opinions that clearly contradict *hal* theory. For example, he writes that God cannot be knowing by himself. Basically, he was against any theological interpretation that might mean rejecting divine attributes. For him, God's knowledge is divine and eternal but separate from God.[172] Similarly, in *Al-Ibanah*, he wrote that whoever says that God is a knower but does not have knowledge is wrong.[173] The result of such principles is a personal conception of God whose agency operates through divine attributes such as seeing, hearing, and even the use of hands. Even, al-Ash'ari proposes a personal conception of God, with a face, two hands, and eyes.[174] He believed that rejecting the divine attributes would result in a passive God with no hearing and no sight.[175] One major reason for al-Ash'ari's opposition toward abstract conceptions of God and for his support for a personal conception is his linguistic method in interpreting the Qur'anic passages about God. In his explications of the Qur'anic statements about concepts like God's hands, throne, and eyes, al-Ash'ari proposes that God addressed the Arabs only in their classical language and that "we have recourse to what we find understood in their speech and comprehended in their address."[176] For al-Ash'ari, since, "their language does not allow what the innovators claim," abstract speculations about the concept of God are improper; thus, a literal interpretation of the related parts of Qur'an is correct as the Arab understood them.[177] A logical result of this method is an anthropomorphic interpretation of the relevant Qur'anic verses.

In contrast, God according to al-Farabi—whom al-Ghazali declared a heretic—is an impersonal, abstract, thinking, and acting power, like the Greek notion of God.[178] For al-Farabi, existence and thought are almost indivisible in the case of God, which makes God nothing but an immaterial intellect that exists only in or through its thinking.[179] Depicting God as only intellect is indeed beyond what Ash'ari theologians could have accepted. Though they suggest that God has no body and form, they are of the opinion that God is never the fuzzy or nebulous existence that philosophers like al-Farabi postulate. The typical Sunni view maintains that God has a divine personality that humans cannot comprehend.[180]

The Mu'tazila conception of God presents another striking contrast: their priority was to formulate a theology where God is an intellect.[181] Thus, their God is a kind of pure actuality of thought that requires no differentiation between essence and attribute.[182] It is more like a pure abstraction, a cipher, as 'Abdus-Subhan explained it.[183] There is nothing that separates God's nature and his attributes or actions, and thus anything other than God's nature, attributes, and actions is created and has no divine essence.[184] Logically, this view leads to the rejection of the divine attributes of God that are not part of his essence, in order to maintain God's unity.[185] Rejecting coeternal and separate attributes, God is said to act by virtue of his self (*ahwal*).[186] By rejecting attributes, the Mu'tazila also conclude that God knows only through universals. Loyal to an abstract conception of God, the Mu'tazila accepted that God is not seeable in the afterlife, for to be seeable, God would have to exist in a dimension that people can observe through their senses.[187]

The question of whether God is seen in the afterlife was a key difference between the two conceptions of God. Undoubtedly, the possibility of seeing God in the hereafter was helpful in the consolidation among Muslims of the personal idea of God. Thus, the possibility of seeing God in the afterlife became a pillar of the Ash'ari and the Maturidi schools. Al-Ash'ari holds that God will be seen in the next world by sight.[188] Al-Maturidi also accepts the visibility of God, however his explanation is qualified: people will see God in way that it is incomprehensible to humans in this life and is not like the normal sight that we use to sense light and distance.[189] Al-Ghazali promised that people would enjoy "the pleasure of looking on God's noble face."[190] Both Ash'ari and Maturidi theologians approach this issue as an argument against the philosophical conception of the immaterial God. Despite its various negative theological implications, it drew a red line between their conception and that of the philosophers', for seeing

God in the afterlife requires a personal God.[191] As Aaron Huges wrote, the desire to visualize the divine mediates the fundamental tension between "God's incorporeality and the need to apprehend Him as a personal divinity with continuous involvement in human affairs."[192] In fact, al-Ash'ari wrote almost the same point in *Al-Ibanah* and argued that those who reject the visibility of God through sight have in mind only *ta'til*.[193]

Another pertinent question that further distinguished the personal and impersonal conceptions of God is that of how God knows things in nature. The Mu'tazila, as well as several philosophers like Ibn Sina, argued that God knows only universals, and thus his knowledge of particulars is possible only through those universals. Otherwise, they argued, God's knowing particular things would require a change in him, which would contradict his divinity. Since the eternal cannot change in anyway, as Ibn Rushd reasoned, rationalist scholars proposed God's knowing through universals.[194]

The idea that God knows through universals coheres with the view that man possessed an absolute ability to act in a world governed by natural laws. In his *The Incoherence of the Philosophers*, al-Ghazali condemns such opinions as heresy on the grounds that they entail change in God's essence. This is so because if knowledge changes, the knower must also change. And therein lies the fallacy, as al-Ghazali wrote, for this argument leads to equating God with the dead, where God is able to have only self-knowledge, in a state of "ignorance of everything else."[195] As in the case of seeing God, al-Ghazali warns that God's knowing is unlike man's, for otherwise, knowing for God would mean a change in him, and that is not compatible with his divinity.[196] Thus, al-Ghazali criticized rationalists for negating everything in God's greatness that serves to magnify God.[197] Al-Ghazali's God knows every detail: "the sands of the deserts, the leaves of the trees, the palpitations of the human heart."[198] More critically, in Ash'ari theology, the fact that God knows particulars entails that God is a personal deity with separate attributes who governs the universe and responds to prayers.[199]

As we observed in related discussions on the concept of God, the major difference among scholars was a reflection of personal and non-personal concepts of God. Following a non-personal concept of God, the Mu'tazila do not engage in obscurantism, but they do have their own problems: The highly abstract concept of God that they propose was never popular, nor understandable for the average Muslim. Despite the risk of anthropomorphism, the personal concept of God of both Ash'ari and Maturidi branches of Sunni orthodoxy was appealing to ordinary believers and meaningful in the daily life of the average Muslim. The cost of such a theology is the classical problem of anthropomorphism, a topic of philosophy since Xenophanes (570–480 BCE). On this account, all attributes of God are understandable in terms of comparisons with human beings, be those comparisons of a negative or positive kind. For instance, "God is eternal but man is not" is negative comparison. However, when it is said that man knows but God's knowledge is limitless, it is a positive comparison. Thus, the point of comparison (*vahid-i qiyas*) is man. This might be logical, but even so, it can lead to a man-oriented understanding of God, or even, as Ibn Rushd puts it, turning God into (merely) an eternal man.[200]

The debate over the conception of God also reflects the same divergences when it comes to whether a moral inquiry about God's actions is relevant or not. For the Mu'tazila, the moral framework of human reason can be applied even to God's actions.[201] They argued that God's actions have a moral framework that is understandable by human reason. For instance, Qadi 'Abd al-Jabbar wrote that God's acts are morally good, and he describes them as morally good as understood from the human perspective.[202] The logical conclusion of the Mu'tazila argument is a moral conclusion about God: God also has a moral obligation, for example, to reward people who fulfill their moral obligations.[203]

The Ash'ari commitment to preserving God's absolute divinity leads to a different interpretation of God's actions and morality.[204] God's acts cannot be fully grasped by human minds. Thus, human being cannot propose a moral framework to evaluate his actions. Right and wrong are merely human categories that cannot be applied to God's acts. The Ash'ari perspective categorically rejects even the idea of evaluating the logic of God's actions according to human rationality.[205] Al-Ashari holds that God is not bound to do anything.[206] He wrote that one who is unjust is not unjust because he makes injustice as another's injustice[207] Thus, what we see as injustices are created by God for people and prove the injustice of those people not rather than of God.[208]

Al-Ghazali also argues that it is not obligatory for God even to care about the wellbeing of his servants, for he may do "whatever he wills and decree whatever he wants."[209] To clarify how God's actions are perfectly arbitrary, al-Ghazali gives a compelling example: "God is able to bring suffering upon an animal that is innocent of any crime, and he is not required to reward it."[210] This example derives from al-Ash'ari's *Kitab al-Luma*, where it is written that God can inflict pain on infants in the next life or can punish believers while rewarding unbelievers in paradise.[211] The message that Ash'ari theologians want to convey is that there is no moral determinism that can explain God's actions.[212] God is simply not obligated to reward even obedient people,[213] and it up to God to assign his servants' obligations, whether within their ability or beyond their ability.[214] The Ash'ari position on this topic is similar to the schools' view of causality. There are no autonomous natural laws, and thus what we see in nature is his customs; likewise, there are no autonomous moral principles, and thus what God does is good.

On the evaluation of the morality of God's actions, the Maturidi position is located somewhere between the Ash'ari emphasis on God's sovereignty and the Mu'tazila emphasis on God's justice. Not accepting the Ash'ari repudiation of moral inquiry,[215] Maturidi theology holds that while God is the absolute sovereign, his creatures are not subjects of arbitrariness, for they have their own characteristics and their own rights.[216] Thus, while Maturidi theology accepts that God cannot be obligated to perform to a specific act, there is no injustice or folly in his actions.[217]

Without imposing a binding morality on God's actions, al-Maturidi insists that God's acts are always wise and just. God never acts arbitrarily; he puts everything in its right place.[218] Thus, for al-Maturidi, it is inconceivable that the cosmos is based on anything other than wisdom, and it is equally inconceivable that God deviates from wisdom.[219] Though Maturidi does not follow the Mu'tazila, he is very clear that God's actions are necessarily wise, as any other possibility would diminish his divinity.[220] Though sharing with al-Ash'ari the principle that God is not bound to any kind of principle, al-Maturidi insists that God's actions must be wise, even if he does not formulate this as a binding norm.[221]

3.2   Conclusion

In this chapter I have plotted on a spectrum the contending arguments about four subjects that together constitute the Islamic idea of nature. We can identify both rationalist interpretations that emphasize man's autonomy and traditionalist interpretations that emphasize God's omnipotence. Another key point that this chapter has demonstrated is that the Islamic idea of nature is composed of interconnected subjects. Thus, how one explains one subject, for example causality or the concept of God, informs how one explains the other three.

The Islamic idea of nature has been a key component of the interplay between Islam and Muslims. It has affected Muslims' understanding of nature, morality, freedom, and many other important issues. Understanding different groups' interpretations of the Islamic idea of nature is thus critical for understanding how Islam relates to and may help explain various situations and problems in the Muslim world.

Having summarized the formation of Sunni orthodoxy and the Islamic idea of nature within the Sunni theology, the following chapters will study how these ideas are relevant in the Turkish case and how Muslims in contemporary Turkey are taught Islamic theology with regard to the four subjects of the Islamic idea of nature.

NOTES

1. Ak, *Selçuklular Döneminde Maturidilik*, 54.
2. Ormsby, *Ghazali*, 27. The Nishapur Madrasa was founded by the Seljuqs in al-Juwayni's name. al-Jawzi, *Mir'at al-zaman*, 135.
3. Arjomand, "The Law, Agency, and Policy," 269–270. Berkey, "Madrasas Medieval and Modern," 43.
4. Khalidi, *Arabic Historical Thought in the Classical Period*, 192.
5. Miura, *Dynamism in the Urban Society of Damascus*, 13
6. Strange, *Baghdad During the Abbasid Caliphate*, 298–299.
7. Brown, *The Canonization of Al Bukhari and Muslim*, 4. Also see: al-Athir, *The Annals of the Saljuq Turks*, 257.
8. Safi, *The Politics of Knowledge in Premodern Islam*, xxiii–xxv.
9. Makdisi, "Muslim Institutions of Learning," 3. And see: Makdisi, "Madrasa and University in the Middle Ages," 263.
10. Hourani, *Reason and Tradition in Islamic Ethics*, 57.
11. Elder, "Introduction," ix.
12. Makdisi, "Ash'ari and the Ash'arites in Islamic Religious History I," 80.
13. Schacht, "New Sources for the History of Muhammadan Theology," 35.
14. Kaminski, *The Contemporary Islamic Governed State*, 40.
15. Goodman, "Ghazali's Argument from Creation. (I)," 69.
16. al-Ash'ari, *Kitab al-Luma'*, 33–34.
17. Frank, *Creation and the Cosmic System*, 22.
18. al-Ash'ari, *Kitab al-Luma'*, 35.
19. al-Ghazali, *The Incoherence of the Philosophers*, 226.
20. al-Ghazali, *Deliverance From Error*, 37.
21. al-Ghazali, *The Incoherence of the Philosophers*, 58.
22. Nasr, *An Introduction to Islamic Cosmological Doctrines*, 9.
23. Ali, "Al-Ghazali and Schopenhauer," 410.

24. al-Ghazali, *The Alchemy of Happiness*, 38.
25. Ibn Rushd, *The Incoherence of the Incoherence*, 38.
26. al-Ghazali, *The Incoherence of Philosophers*, 22–35.
27. Pyle, *Atomism and Its Critics*, 210.
28. Sorabji. *Time, Creation and the Continuum*, 297.
29. Frank, *Creation and the Cosmic System*, 23.
30. Post, "The Problem of Atomism," 19.
31. Glasner, *Averroes' Physics*, 66, 172.
32. Frede, "Stoic Determinism," 187.
33. Meyer, "Chain of Causes," 80–84. Also see: Strange, "The Stoics on the Voluntariness of the Passions," 38.
34. Bergh, "Ghazali on "Gratitude Towards God"," 77.
35. Ibn Rushd, *The Incoherence of the Incoherence*, 291.
36. Fakhry, *A History of Islamic Philosophy*, 217.
37. Murdoch, "Beyond Aristotle," 19–25.
38. Fakhry, *Islamic Occasionalism and Its Critique*, 9.
39. Ibrahim, "Faḫr ad-Din ar-Razi, Ibn al-Haytam and Aristotelian Science," 381–382.
40. Fakhry, *Al-Farabi*, 220.
41. Moad, "Al-Ghazali's Occasionalism," 1. Giacaman and Bahlul, "Ghazali on Miracles," 41–42.
42. al-Ghazali, *Moderation in Belief*, 279–315. al-Razi, *Ilm al-Akhlaq*, 69.
43. al-Ghazali, *The Incoherence of Philosophers*, 166.
44. Remes, *Neoplatonism*, 46. Also see: Daiber, "God versus Causality," 12.
45. Dillon and Gerson, *Neoplatonic Philosophy*, 269.
46. al-Ghazali, *The Incoherence of Philosophers*, 167.
47. Ibid., 166.
48. Ibid., 146–147.
49. Ibid., 167.
50. Fakhry, *A History of Islamic Philosophy*, 235.
51. Rahman, *Major Themes of the Qur'an*, 46.
52. Fakhry, *A History of Islamic Philosophy*, 167.
53. There is a revisionist literature on Al-Ghazali. Revisionist views include that: (i) al-Ghazali "combined contingent causality and Occasionalism" (Daiber); (ii) al-Ghazali was in favor of causality and implied quantum physics (Harding); (iii) al-Ghazali was not against the idea of causality (Goodman); and (iv) al-Ghazali held a neutral position on Occasionalism (Moad). See: Daiber, "God versus Causality," 12. Harding, "Causality Then and Now," 167. Moad, "Al-Ghazali on Power, Causation, and Acquisition", 1. Goodman, "Did Al-Ghazali Deny Causality?" 83–120. Alon, "Al-Ghazali on Causality," 397. Abrahamov, "Al-Ghazali's Theory of Causality," 98.

54. Ibn Rushd, *The Incoherence of the Incoherence*, 88. Goodman, "Ghazali's Argument from Creation (II)," 171.

55. Ibn Rushd, *The Distinguished Jurist's Primer*.

56. Glasner, *Averroes' Physics*, 172.

57. Ibn Rushd, *The Incoherence of the Incoherence*, 88.

58. Ibid., 90–91.

59. Ibid., 93–95.

60. Ibid., 318, 133–134.

61. Ibn Rushd, *Ibn Rushd's Metaphysics*, 61.

62. Ibid., 89.

63. Ibn Rushd, *The Incoherence of the Incoherence*, 90.

64. al-Ghazali, *The Incoherence of Philosophers*, 56.

65. Ibn Rushd, *The Incoherence of the Incoherence*, 29.

66. Ibid., 289.

67. Ibid., 131.

68. Ibid., 291.

69. Ibid., 325.

70. Ibn Rushd, *Faith and Reason*, 80. Other Muslim Aristotelian scholars had similar ideas on causality. For example, Ibn Bajjah accepted that the general principle of physics could explain nature. A similar position is observable in the work of al-Tusi, who accepted that every motion has a principle. He was very critical even of the idea that God suspended the natural order. Ibn Bajja, *'Ilm al-Nafs*, 19. al-Tusi, *Nasir al-Din Tusi's Memoir on Astronomy*, 100.

71. Muhtaroglu, "Al-Maturidi's View of Causality," 4.

72. Rudolph, *Al-Maturidi and the Development of Sunni Theology in Samarqand*, 260.

73. Frank, "Notes and Remarks on the *taba'i*," 138. Also see: Yavuz, "İmam Maturidi'nin Tabiat ve İlliyete Bakışı," 57.

74. Bernand, "La critique de la notion de nature (*Tab'*) par le Kalam," 73–74. Dhanani, "Al-Maturidi and Al-Nasafi," 65–76.

75. al-Maturidi, *Kitab al-Tawhid*, 100–101.

76. Ibid., 207, 244, 251.

77. Ibid., 311.

78. Ibid., 305. al-Maturidi, *Te'vilatul-Kur'an Tercümesi I*, 288, 296.

79. al-Maturidi, *Kitab al-Tawhid*, 313.

80. al-Ghazali, *Deliverance From Error*, 25.

81. Ibid., 22.

82. Makdisi, "Ash'ari and the Ash'arites in Islamic Religious History II," 22. Moad, "Comparing Phases of Skepticism," 89–90. Wohlman, *Al-Ghazali, Averroës and the Interpretation of the Qur'an*, 33. Also see: Burrell, "The Unknowability of God in Al-Ghazali," 175.

83. al-Ghazali, *Deliverance From Error*, 21–22.
84. Ibid., 60–62.
85. Kukkonen, "Al-Ghazali on Error," 7. Albertini, "Crisis and Certainty of Knowledge," 4. Davis, "Living in Negligent Ease," 102–103.
86. We see here a strong Neoplatonist impact. In Neoplatonism, the idea of visible and invisible worlds is significant in defining other major issues such as knowledge and causality, see: Wisknovsky, "Towards a History of Avicenna's Distinction," 58. Frank, *Creation and Cosmic*, 43. Also see: Bigg, *Neoplatonism*, 191. Here Bigg wrote: "Plotinus drew a very sharp distinction between the World of Sense and the World of Intelligence". Also on 194, he wrote that in Neoplatonism, "we are led to believe in the existence of another world higher and better than the world of sense".
87. Remes, *Neoplatonism*, viii, 3.
88. Alwahaib, "Al-Ghazali and Descartes," 26.
89. al-Ghazali, *Deliverance From Error*, 23.
90. In *The Just Balance*, al-Ghazali wrote: "May God protect me from the rules of personal opinion (*ra'y*) and analogy (*qiyas*)! These are the rules of the Devil! If one of my friends claims that they are the rules of knowledge, I pray God that He will eliminate evil from his religion, for this is the religion of an ignorant friend, and worse than an intelligent enemy's". al-Ghazali, *The Just Balance*, 2.
91. al-Ghazali, *Deliverance From Error*, 65.
92. Ibid., 23.
93. al-Ghazali, *The Alchemy of Happiness*, 37, 21.
94. Nakamura, "Imam Ghazali's Cosmology Reconsidered," 32.
95. Similarly, in Neoplatonism, there are limits to rational knowledge so one should go beyond it to get the absolute truth. Rappe, "Self-Knowledge and Subjectivity," 258. Oosthout, *Modes of Knowledge*, 28.
96. Grunebaum, *Medieval Islam*, 141.
97. Brown, "The Last Days of Al-Ghazzali," 104.
98. Smith, "A-Risalat Al-Laduniyya," 359.
99. Lapidus, *A History of Islamic Societies*, 94. Karamustafa, "Walaya According to al-Junayd," 66–68.
100. Fierro, "The Almohads and the Hafsids," 69.
101. Treiger, "Al-Ghazali's Classification of the Sciences," 31. As a result of his stance on inner knowledge, al-Ghazali is criticized for being some sort of esoteric. This criticism was echoed even as early as Ibn Tufayl in the twelfth century. Geirdner, "Al-Ghazali's Mishkat al-Anwar," 121–153.
102. Schmidtke, "Theological Rationalism," 17.
103. Ghani, "The Concept of Sunna," 60.
104. Martin and Woodward with Atmaja, *Defenders of Reason in Islam*, 90–91.

105. Yaman, "Small Theological Differences Profound Philosophical Implications," 181.

106. Al-Maturidi, *Kitab al-Tawhid*, 57–58.

107. Ibid., 61.

108. al-Ash'ari, *Al-Ibanah*, 53.

109. al-Maturidi, *Kitab al-Tawhid*, 64.

110. Al-Galli, *The Place of Reason*, 7. Taftazani, *A Commentary on the Creed of Islam*, 15.

111. al-Maturidi, *Kitab al-Tawhid*, 309–310. al-Subki, *Al-Sayf Al-Mashur*, 4.

112. Bouamrane, *Le problème De La liberté Humaine*, 10.

113. al-Ash'ari, *Kitab al-Luma'*, 36. al-Ash'ari, *Al-Ibanah*, 102.

114. al-Ghazali, *Council for Kings*, 10. Though their views exhibit some nuances, other key names in Ash'ari thought like Juwayni and Razi also share the classical reserved position on free will. See: Bisar, "Al-Juwani and Al-Ghazali," 161. Haywood, "Fakhr al-Din al-Razi's Contribution," 281. Ceylan, "Theology and Tafsir in the Major Works of Fakhr al-Din al-Razi," 209.

115. Griffel, *Al-Ghazali's Philosophical Theology*, 125.

116. Abrahamov, "A Re-Examination of al-Ash'arī's Theory of "Kasb"," 220.

117. al-Ash'ari, *Maqalat al-Islamiyyin*, 542.

118. al-Ash'ari, *Kitab al-Luma'*, 56.

119. Ibid., 43. al-Ash'ari, *Al-Ibanah*, 102.

120. Frank, *Creation and Cosmic*, 32. al-Ghazali, *Revival of Religious Learnings Vol. 3*, 11–12.

121. Bravmann quoted in Pessagno, "Irada, Ikhtihayar, Qutra," 178.

122. Cillis, *Free Will and Predestination in Islamic Thought*, 14.

123. al-Ash'ari, *Kitab al-Luma'*, 57.

124. Martin and Woodward with Atmaja, *Defenders of Reason in Islam*, 25.

125. Frank, "The Structure of Created Causality," 30.

126. Frank, *Creation and Cosmic*, 36.

127. Abrahamov, "A Re-Examination of al-Ash'ari," 215.

128. Ibid., 103.

129. Hourani, *Reason and Tradition in Islamic Ethics*, 8.

130. Calverley and Pollock, *Nature, Man and God in Medieval Islam*, 931.

131. Ibn Rushd, *The Incoherence of the Incoherence*, 256.

132. Shahrastani, *Muslim Sects and Divisions*, 42.

133. Martin and Woodward with Atmaja, *Defenders of Reason in Islam*, 97. Heemskerk, *Suffering in the Mu'tazilite Theology*, 36–56.

134. Cillis, *Free Will and Predestination*, 11.

135. Vasalau, *Moral Agents and Their Deserts*, 2. Dhanani, *The Physical Theory of Kalam*, 146.

136. Calverley and Pollock, *Nature, Man and God in Medieval Islam*, 915.

137. Fakhry, "Some Paradoxical Implications of the Mu'tazilite View of Free Will," 96.

138. al-Maturidi, *Kitab al-Tawhid*, 458–461.

139. Rudolph, *Al-Maturidi and the Development of Sunni Theology in Samarqand*, 305. Pessagno, "The Uses of Evil in Maturidian Thought," 66.

140. al-Taftazani, *A Commentary on the Creed of Islam*, 80.

141. al-'Omar, *The Doctrines of the Maturidite School*, 77.

142. al-Maturidi, *Kitab al-Tawhid*, 64. Also see: Esen, "Maturidi'nin Bilgi Kuramı," 55.

143. Pessagno, "On Al Maturidi's Notion of Human Acts," 61–64.

144. al-Maturidi, *Kitab al-Tawhid*, 439.

145. Işık, *Maturidi'nin Kelam Sisteminde İman*, 91.

146. Pessagno, "On Al Maturidi's Notion of Human Acts," 62.

147. al-Maturidi, *Kitab al-Tawhid*, 444.

148. Ibid., 455–463.

149. Muhtaroglu, "Al-Maturidi's View of Causality," 14.

150. Topaloğlu, "Allah," 471.

151. Shehadi, *Ghazali's Unique Unknowable God*, 11.

152. *Qur'an*: Shura, 11.

153. al-Ash'ari, *Kitab al-Luma'*, 12.

154. Several anthropomorphists like Muqatil ibn Suleiman (d. 767) attributed God a place; others, like Ahmad ibn Ata, even argued that it was possible to meet God and shake hands with him. Üzüm, "Mücessime," 50.

155. Williams, "Aspects of the Creed of Imam Ahmad ibn Hanbal," 455.

156. Adamson and Pormann, "More than Heat and Light," 484.

157. Ansari, *The Ethical Philosophy of Ibn Miskawaih*, 52.

158. Bakar, "Some Aspects of Ibn Miskawayh's Thought," 117.

159. Ibn Rushd, *The Book of the Decisive Treatise*, 22. The style and discourse have always played a role in the dissemination of Islamic theological opinions. A typical rationalist text is usually abstract, unlike the stylish texts of popular scholars like al-Ghazali who employed poetic discourse, a key difference in terms of public outreach. Like other rationalists, Ibn Rushd was critical of the use of poetic discourse in argumentation. See: Averroes, *Three Short Commentaries*, 35.

160. al-Ghazali, *Council for Kings*, 7.

161. al-Ghazali, *Moderation in Belief*, 46–48.

162. Zayd, *Al-Ghazali on Divine Predicates*, 42.

163. Rosenthal, *Political Thought in Medieval Islam*, 17–18.

164. al-Maturidi, *Kitab al-Tawhid*, 99.

165. al-Ash'ari, *Kitab al-Luma'*, 46. al-Maturidi, *Kitab al-Tawhid*. 99. Thiele, "Abu Hashim al-Jubba'i's (d. 321/933) Theory of 'States'," 374–379.

166. al-Ghazali, *Ninety-Nine Beautiful Names of God*, 5.

167. al-Subki, *Al-Sayf Al-Mashur*, 66–70.
168. al-Ghazali, *The Alchemy of Happiness*, 59.
169. Benevich, "The Classical Ash'ari Theory of *Ahwal*," 142–174. Koloğlu, "Ebu Haşim el-Cübbai'nin Ahval Teorisi," 208.
170. Thiele, "Abu Hashim al-Jubba'i's (d. 321/933) Theory of 'States', 374–379. Memiş, "Eş'ariliğe Yaptığı Katkılar Bakımından Ebu'l-Meali El-Cüveyni," 100.
171. Frank, *Al-Ghazali and the Ash'arite School*, 109.
172. al-Ash'ari, *Kitab al-Luma'*, 19.
173. al-Ash'ari, *Al-Ibanah*, 95.
174. Ibid., 48, 50.
175. Ibid., 88.
176. Ibid., 59.
177. Ibid., 90.
178. Fakhry, *Al-Farabi, Founder of Islamic Neoplatonism*, 79.
179. Janos, *Method, Structure, and Development in al-Farabi's Cosmology*, 182.
180. al-Ghazali, *Moderation in Belief*, 110–126.
181. Al-Jubouri, *History of Islamic Philosophy*, 181.
182. Fakhry, *A History of Islamic Philosophy*, 59.
183. Subhan, "The Relation of God to time and space," 234.
184. Ibn Rushd has a similar opinion about the attributes. He writes: "Ash'arites allow a plurality in God, regarding Him as an essence with attributes". Ibn Rushd, *The Incoherence of the Incoherence*, 175.
185. Adamson, "Al-Kindi and the Mu'tazila," 50.
186. Belo, "Mu'tazilites, Al-Ash'ari and Maimonides," 120.
187. Subhan, "Mu'tazilite View on Beatific Vision," 422–428.
188. al-Ash'ari, *Al-Ibanah*, 51.
189. al-Maturidi, *Kitab al-Tawhid*, 178, 184–185, 193.
190. al-Ghazali, *Moderation in Belief*, 63–70. Though believing in the visibility of God, Razi was more moderate as he maintained that the vision of God couldn't be demonstrated through rational arguments. Ceylan, "Theology and Tafsir in the Major Works of Fakhr al-Din al-Razi," 196.
191. The Hanbali tactic against the Mu'tazila conception of God differed from that of Ash'ari and Maturidi schools. Alarmed by their encounter with the Mu'tazila, Hanbalis promoted anthropomorphic ideas about God. See Blankinship, "The early creed," 52. Listening to a Friday sermon of Ibn Taymiyya in 1326, Ibn Battuta narrated that, in the midst of his speech, he said "Verily God descends to the sky over our world in the same bodily fashion I make this decent". Ibn Battuta, *Travels in Asia and Africa*, 67–68.
192. Hughes, "Imagining the Divine," 33.

193. al-Ash'ari, *Al-Ibanah*, 62.
194. Ibn Rushd, *The Incoherence of the Incoherence*, 3.
195. al-Ghazali, *The Incoherence*, 107, 130, 135.
196. Another debate about God's actions led to the crisis of the *Mihna*. The origin of the crisis was the question: Is God's speech created or divine? Not recognizing any other thing as divine, the Mu'tazila declared the Qur'an to be created. The traditionalist camp, led by Ahmad bin Hanbal, rebutted this. See: Al-Tabari, *The History of Al-Tabari Vol. 32*, 199–214. Walter M. Patton argued that the defeat of the Mu'tazila view of the Quran impeded the rise of "the principle of free thought, without recognition of authority" in the Muslim world. Patton, *Ahmet ibn Hanbal and the Mihna*, 2.
197. al-Ghazali, *The Incoherence of Philosophers*, 70–71.
198. al-Ghazali, *The Alchemy of Happiness*, 146.
199. Abrahamov, "Fakhr al-Din al-Razi on God's Knowledge," 154.
200. Ibn Rushd, *The Incoherence of the Incoherence*, 285.
201. Hourani, "Islamic and Non-Islamic Origins of Mu'tazilite Ethical Rationalism," 59.
202. Martin and Woodward with Atmaja, *Defenders of Reason in Islam*, 92.
203. Frank, "Moral Obligation in Classical Muslim Theology," 207.
204. Syed, *Coercion and Responsibility in Islam*, 25–28.
205. El-Rouayheb, "Must God Tell Us the Truth?" 412.
206. al-Ash'ari, *Al-Ibanah*, 28.
207. al-Ash'ari, *Kitab al-Luma'*, 63.
208. Ibid., 64.
209. al-Ghazali, *Moderation in Belief*, 178. al-Ash'ari, *Kitab al-Luma'*, 99.
210. al-Ghazali, *Moderation in Belief*, 177.
211. Ibid., 99.
212. Hourani, "Ghazali on the Ethics of Action," 96.
213. al-Ash'ari, *Kitab al-Luma'*, 180.
214. Ibid., 172.
215. Çakmak, "Analogies between al-Maturidi's and Duns Scotus," 473–475.
216. Rudolph, "Al-Maturidi's Concept of God's Wisdom," 48, 53.
217. Karaman, Çağrıcı, Dönmez and Gümüş, *Kur'an Yolu Türkçe Meal ve Tefsiri II*, 400–401.
218. Rudolph, "Hanafi Theological Tradition and Maturidism," 289.
219. Pessagno, "The Uses of Evil in Maturidian Thought," 423.
220. al-Maturidi, *Kitab al-Tawhid*, 192.
221. Ibid., 430.

REFERENCES

Abrahamov, Binyamin. 1988. Al-Ghazali's Theory of Causality. *Studia Islamica* 67 (1): 75–98.

———. 1989. A Re-Examination of al-Ash'arī's Theory of "Kasb" According to "Kitāb al-Luma". *The Journal of the Royal Asiatic Society of Great Britain and Ireland* 2 (1): 210–221.

———. 1992. Fakhr al-Din al-Razi on God's Knowledge of the Particulars. *Oriens* 33 (1): 133–155.

Abu Bakar, Ibrahim. 1989. Some Aspects of Ibn Miskawayh's Thought. *Islamiyyat* 10 (1): 115–123.

Abu Zayd, Abdu-r-rahman. 1990. *Al-Ghazali on Divine Predicates and Their Property*. Lahore: S. M. Ashraf.

Adamson, Peter. 2003. Al-Kindi and the Mu'tazila: Divine Attributes, Creation and Freedom. *Arabic Sciences and Philosophy* 13 (1): 45–77.

Adamson, Peter, and Peter E. Pormann. 2012. More than Heat and Light: Miskawayh's Epistle on Soul and Intellect. *The Muslim World* 102 (3/4): 478–524.

Ak, Ahmet. 2009. *Selçuklular Döneminde Maturidilik*. Ankara: Yayın Evi.

al-Ash'ari. 1940. *Al-Ibanah 'An Usul Ad-Diyanah [The Elucidation of Islam's Foundation]*. Translated by Walter C. Klein. New Haven: American Oriental Society.

———. 1953. *Kitab al-Luma' [The Luminous Book]*. Translated by Richard J. McCarthy. Beirut: Imprimerie Catholique.

———. 1963. *Maqalat al-Islamiyyin wa Ikhtilaf al-Musallin*. Edited by H. Ritter. Wiesbaden: Franz Steiner.

al-Athir, 'Ali Ibn. 2002. *The Annals of the Saljuq Turks: Selections from al-Kamil fi'l-Ta'rikh of 'Izz al-Din Ibn al-Athir*. New York: Routledge-Curzon.

Al-Galli, Ahmad Mohamad Ahmad. 1976. The Place of Reason in the Theology of al-Maturidi and Al-Ash'ari. PhD diss., University of Edinburgh.

al-Ghazali. 1963. *Deliverance From Error [Al Munkidh min Ad Dallal]*. Translated by W.M. Watt. Lahore: Sh. Muhammad Ashraf.

———. 1964. *Council for Kings [Nasihat al-Muluk]*. Translated by F.R.C. Bagley. London: Oxford University Press.

———. 1978. *The Just Balance [Al-Qistas Al-Mustaqim]*. Translated by D.P. Brewster. Lahore: Sh. M. Ashraf.

———. 1991. *The Alchemy of Happiness [Kimiya-yi Sa'adat]*. Translated by Claud Field. Lahore: Sh. M. Ashraf.

———. 1993. *Revival of Religious Learnings Vol. 3 [Ihya Ulum Al-din]*. Translated by Fazl-ul-Karim. Karachi: Darul Ishaat.

———. 2000. *The Incoherence of the Philosophers [Tahafut al-falasifa]*. Translated by Michael E. Marmura. Utah: Brigham Young University Press.

———. 2007. *Ninety-Nine Beautiful Names of God [Al-Maqsad al-asna fi sharh asma'Allah al-husna]*. Translated by David B. Burrel and Nazih Daher. Cambridge: The Islamic Text Society.

———. 2013. *Al-Ghazali's Moderation in Belief [Al-Iqtisad Fi Al-I'tiqad]*. Translated by Alaaddin M. Yaqub. Chicago: The University of Chicago Press.

al-Jawzi, Sibt ibn. 1968. *Mir'at al-zaman fi ta'rikh al-a'yan*. Ankara: A. Sevim.

Al-Jubouri, I.M.N. 2004. *History of Islamic Philosophy With View of Greek Philosophy and Early History of Islam*. Hertford: Bright Pen.

al-Maturidi. 2017. *Te'vilatul-Kur'an Tercümesi I [Kitab Ta'wilat al-Qur'an]*. Translated by Bekir Topaloğlu. Istanbul: Ensar.

———. 2018. *Kitabü't-Tevhid Açıklamalı Tercüme [Kitab al-Tawhid]*. Translated by Bekir Topaloğlu. Ankara: İSAM.

al-'Omar, Farouq 'Omar 'Abd-Allah. 1974. The Doctrines of the Maturidite School With Special Reference to As-Sawad Al-A'azam of Al-Hakim As-Samarqandi. PhD diss., University of Edinburgh.

al-Razi, Fakhr. 1992. *Ilm al-Akhlaq [Kitab Al-Nafs Wa'l-Ruh Wa Sharh Quwahuma]*. Translated by M. Saghir H. Ma'sumi. New Delhi: Bhavan.

al-Shahrastani, Muhammad b. 'Abd al-Karim. 2014. *Muslim Sects and Divisions: The Section on Muslim Sects in Kitab al-Milal wa'l-Nihal*. Translated and Edited by A. Kazi and J.G. Flynn. London and New York: Routledge.

al-Subki, Tac al-Din. 2015. *Al-Sayf Al-Mashur fi Sarh 'aqida Abu Mansur*. Ankara: TDV.

al-Tabari. 1987. *The History of al-Tabari Vol. 32*. New York: The State University of New York Press.

al-Taftazani, Mas'ud ibn 'Umar. 1950. *A Commentary on the Creed of Islam Sa'd al-Din al-Taftazani on the Creed of Najm al-Din al-Nasafi [Sharh al-Aqaid]*. Translated and Edited by Earl E. Elder. New York: Columbia University Press.

al-Tusi, Nasir al-Din. 1993. *Nasir al-Din Tusi's Memoir on Astronomy Vol. 1 [al-Tadhkira fi 'ilm al-hay'a]*. Translated by F.J. Ragep. New York: Springer Verlag.

Albertini, Tamara. 2005. Crisis and Certainty of Knowledge in Al-Ghazali (1058–1111) and Descartes (1596–1650). *Philosophy East and West* 55 (1): 1–14.

Ali, Zain Imtiaz. 2007. Al-Ghazali and Schopenhauer on Knowledge and Suffering. *Philosophy East and West* 57 (4): 409–419.

Alon, Ilai. 1980. Al-Ghazali on Causality. *Journal of the American Oriental Society* 100 (4): 397–405.

Alwahaib, Mohammad. 2017. Al-Ghazali and Descartes From Doubt to Certainty: A Phenomenological Approach. *Discusiones Filosóficas* 18 (31): 15–40.

Ansari, M. Abdul Haq. 1964. *The Ethical Philosophy of Ibn Miskawaih*. Aligarh: The Aligarh Muslim University Press.

Arjomand, Said Amir. 1999. The Law, Agency, and Policy in Medieval Islamic Society: Development of the Institutions of Learning from the Tenth to the Fifteenth Century. *Comparative Studies in Society and History* 41 (2): 269–293.

Averroes. 1977. *Three Short Commentaries on Aristotle's "Topics", "Rhetoric" and "Poetics"*. Translated by Charles E. Butterworth. Albany: State University of New York Press.

Belo, Catarina. 2007, September. Mu'tazilites, Al-Ash'ari and Maimonides on Divine Attributes. *Veritas* 52 (3): 117–131.

Benevich, Fedor. 2016. The Classical Ash'ari Theory of *Ahwal*: Juwayni and His Opponents. *Journal of Islamic Studies* 27 (2): 142–174.

Bergh, Simon van den. 1957. Ghazali on "Gratitude Towards God" and Its Greek. *Studia Islamica* 7 (1): 77–98.

Berkey, Jonathan P. 2007. Madrasas Medieval and Modern: Politics, Education, and the Problem of Muslim Identity. In *Schooling Islam: The Culture and Politics of Modern Muslim Education*, ed. Robert W. Hefner and Muhammad Qasim Zaman, 40–60. Princeton: Princeton University Press.

Bernand, Marie. 1980. La critique de la notion de nature (*Tab'*) par le Kalam. *Studia Islamica* 51 (1): 59–101.

Bigg, C. 1895. *Neoplatonism*. New York: E and J. B. Young.

Bisar, M.A. Al-Juwani and Al-Ghazali As Theologians With Special Reference to Al-Irshad and Al-Iqtisad. PhD diss., University of Edinburgh, 1953.

Blankinship, Khalid. 2008. The Early Creed. In *The Cambridge Companion to Classical Islamic Theology*, ed. Tim Winter, 33–54. Cambridge: Cambridge University Press.

Bouamrane, Chikh. 1978. *Le problème De La liberté Humaine Dans La Pensée Musulmane*. Paris: Librairie Philosophique J. Vrin.

Brown, Jonathan. 2006. The Last Days of Al-Ghazzali and the Tripartite Division of the Sufi World Abu Hamid Al-Ghazali's Letter to the Seljuq Vizier and Commentary. *The Muslim World* 96 (1): 89–113.

———. 2007. *The Canonization of Al Bukhari and Muslim: The Formation and Function of the Sunni Hadith Canon*. Brill: Leiden and Boston.

Burrell, David B. 1987. The Unknowability of God in Al-Ghazali. *Religious Studies* 23 (2): 171–182.

Çakmak, Mustafa. 2017. Analogies between al-Maturidi's and Duns Scotus's Ethical Perspectives. *Islam and Christian-Muslim Relations* 28 (4): 473–491.

Calverley, Edwin E., and James W. Pollock. 2002. *Nature, Man and God in Medieval Islam: 'Abd Allah Baydawi's Text Tawali' al-Anwar min Matali' al-Anzar Along With Mahmud Isfahani's Commentary Matali' al-Anzar, Sharh Tawali' al-Anwar*. Leiden: Brill.

Ceylan, Yasin. 1980. Theology and Tafsir in the Major Works of Fakhr al-Din al-Razi. PhD diss., University of Edinburgh.

Cillis, Maria De. 2014. *Free Will and Predestination in Islamic Thought: Theoretical Compromises in Islamic Thought Theoretical Compromises in the Works of Avicenna, al-Ghazali and Ibn-'Arabi*. London and New York: Routledge.

Daiber, Hans. 2015. God Versus Causality Al-Ghazali's Solution and Its Historical Background. In *Islam and Rationality: The Impact of Ghazali Papers Collected on His 900th Anniversary*, ed. Georges Tamer, 1–22. Leiden and Boston: Brill.

Davis, D. Morgan. 2012. Living in Negligent Ease: Evidence for Al-Ghazali's Crisis of Conscience in His *Iqtisad fi al-I'tiqad*. In *Bountiful Harvest: Essays in Honor of S. Kent Brown*, ed. Andrew C. Skinner, D. Morgan Davis, and Carl Griffin, 99–111. Provo, UT: Brigham Young University.

Dhanani, Alnoor. 1984. *The Physical Theory of Kalam: Atoms, Space, and Void in Basrian Mu'tazili Cosmology*. Leiden: E. J. Brill.

———. 2009. Al-Maturidi and Al-Nasafi on Atomism and the Taba'i. In *Büyük Türk Bilgini Imam Maturidi ve Maturidilik*, ed. İlyas Çelebi, 65–76. Istanbul: Marmara İlahiyat.

Dillon, John, and Lloyd P. Gerson. 2004. *Neoplatonic Philosophy: Introductory Readings*. Indianapolis: Hackett.

El-Rouayheb, Khaled. 2015. Must God Tell Us the Truth? A Problem in Ash'arī Theology. In *Islamic Cultures, Islamic Contexts Essays in Honor of Professor Patricia Crone*, ed. Behnam Sadeghi, Asad Q. Ahmed, Adam Silverstein, and Robert Hoylandp, 411–429. Leiden: Brill.

Elder, E. Edgar. 1950. Introduction. In S'ad al-Din Taftazani, *A Commentary on the Creed of Islam: Sa'd al-Din al-Taftazani on the Creed of Najm al-Din al-Nasafi*, i–xxxii. Translated by Elder E. Edgar. New York: Columbia University Press.

Esen, Muammer. 2008. Maturidi'nin Bilgi Kuramı ve Bu Bağlamda Onun Alem, Allah ve Kader Konusundaki Görüşlerinin Kısa Bir Tahlili. *Ankara Üniversitesi İlahiyat Fakültesi Dergisi* 49 (1): 45–56.

Fakhry, Majid. 1953. Some Paradoxical Implications of the Mu'tazilite View of Free Will. *The Muslim World* 43 (2): 95–109.

———. 1958. *Islamic Occasionalism and Its Critique by Averroes and Aquinas*. London: G. Allen and Unwin.

———. 2002. *Al-Farabi: Founder of Islamic Neoplatonism: His Life, Works and Influence*. London: Oneworld.

———. 2004. *A History of Islamic Philosophy*. New York: Columbia University Press.

Fierro, Maribel. 2011. The Almohads and the Hafsids. In *The New Cambridge History of Islam Vol. 2 The Western Islamic World From Eleventh to Eighteenth Centuries*, ed. Maribel Fierro, 66–105. Cambridge: Cambridge University Press.

Frank, Richard M. 1966. The Structure of Created Causality According to Al-Ash'ari: An Analysis of the Kitab al Luma. *Studia Islamica* 25 (1): 13–75.

———. 1974. Notes and Remarks on the *taba'i* in the Teaching of al-Maturidi. In *Melanges d'islamologie a la memoire d'Armand*, ed. P. Salmon, 137–149. Leiden: Brill.

———. 1983. Moral Obligation in Classical Muslim Theology. *The Journal of Religious Ethics* 11 (2): 204–223.

———. 1992. *Creation and the Cosmic System: Al Ghazali and Avicenna*. Heidelberg: Carl Winter.

———. 1994. *Al-Ghazali and the Ash'arite School*. London: Duke University Press.

Frede, Dorothea. 2003. Stoic Determinism. In *The Cambridge Companion to Stoics*, ed. Brad Inwood, 179–205. Cambridge: Cambridge University Press.

Geirdner, W.H.T. 1914. Al-Ghazali's Mishkat al-Anwar and the Ghazali Problem. *Der Islam* 5 (1): 121–153.

Ghani, Usman. 2015. The Concept of Sunna in Mu'tazilite Thought. In *The Sunna and Its Status in Islamic Law*, ed. Adis Duderija, 59–73. New York: Palgrave Macmillan.

Giacaman, George, and Raja Bahlul. 2000. Ghazali on Miracles and Necessary Connection. *Medieval Philosophy and Theology* 9 (1): 39–50.

Glasner, Ruth. 2009. *Averroes' Physics: A Turning Point in Medieval Natural Philosophy*. Oxford: Oxford University Press.

Goodman, Lenn E. 1971a. Ghazali's Argument from Creation (I). *International Journal of Middle East Studies* 2 (1): 67–85.

———. 1971b. Ghazali's Argument from Creation (II). *International Journal of Middle East Studies* 2 (2): 168–188.

———. 1978. Did Al-Ghazali Deny Causality? *Studia Islamica* 47 (1): 83–120.

Griffel, Frank. 2009. *Al-Ghazali's Philosophical Theology*. Oxford: Oxford University Press.

Grunebaum, Gustave E.von. 1954. *Medieval Islam: A Study in Cultural Orientation*. Chicago: The University of Chicago Press.

Harding, Karen. 1993. Causality Then and Now: Al Ghazali and Quantum Theory. *The American Journal of Islamic Social Sciences* 10 (2): 165–177.

Haywood, John A. 1979. Fakhr al-Din al-Razi's Contribution to Ideas of Ultimate Reality and Meaning. *Ultimate Reality and Meaning* 2 (1): 264–291.

Heemskerk, Margaretha T. 2000. *Suffering in the Mu'tazilite Theology: 'Abd Al-Jabbar's Teaching on Pain and Divine Justice*. Leiden: Brill.

Hourani, George F. 1976a. Ghazali on the Ethics of Action. *Journal of the American Oriental Society* 96 (1): 69–88.

———. 1976b. Islamic and Non-Islamic Origins of Mu'tazilite Ethical Rationalism. *International Journal of Middle East Studies* 7 (1): 59–87.

———. 1985. *Reason and Tradition in Islamic Ethics*. Cambridge: Cambridge University Press.

Hughes, Aaron. 2002. Imagining the Divine: Ghazali on Imagination, Dreams, and Dreaming. *Journal of the American Academy of Religion* 70 (1): 33–53.

Ibn Bajja. 1999. *'Ilm al-Nafs.* Translated by M.S. Hasan Ma'sumi. Frankfurt: J. W. Goethe University Press.

Ibn Battuta. 1953. *Travels in Asia and Africa 1325–54.* London: Routledge and Kegan.

Ibn Rushd. 1986. *Ibn Rushd's Metaphysics: A Translation With Introduction of Ibn Rushd's Commentary on Aristotle's Metaphysics, Book Lam.* Translated by Charles Genequand. Leiden: E. J. Brill.

———. 1987. *The Incoherence of the Incoherence [Tahafut al-Tahafut].* Translated by Simon Van Den Bergh. Cambridge: EJW Gibb Memorial Trust.

———. 2000. *The Distinguished Jurist's Primer [Bidayat al Mujtahid wa Nihayat al-Muqtasid].* Translated by Imran A. Khan Nyazee. Reading: Garnet.

———. 2001a. *Faith and Reason in Islam Averroes' Exposition of Religious Arguments [Al Kashf 'an Manahij Al-Adilla].* Translated by Ibrahim Najjar. London: Oneworld.

———. 2001b. *The Book of the Decisive Treatise [Kitab fasl al-maqal].* Translated by Charles E. Butterworth. Utah: The Birmingham Young University.

Ibrahim, Bilal. 2013. Fahr ad-Din ar-Razi, Ibn al-Haytam and Aristotelian Science: Essentialism versus Phenomenalism in Post-Classical Islamic Thought. *Oriens* 41 (3/4): 379–431.

Işık, Kemal. 1980. *Maturidi'nin Kelam Sisteminde İman Allah ve Peygamberlik İlişkisi.* Ankara: Fütüvvet.

Janos, Damien. 2012. *Method, Structure, and Development in al-Farabi's Cosmology.* Leiden and Boston: Brill.

Kaminski, Joseph J. 2017. *The Contemporary Islamic Governed State: A Reconceptualization.* New York: Palgrave Macmillan.

Karaman, Hayreddin, Mustafa Çağrıcı, Kafi Dönmez, and Sadrettin Gümüş. 2012. *Kur'an Yolu: Türkçe Meal ve Tefsiri II.* Ankara: Diyanet İşleri Başkanlığı.

Karamustafa, Ahmet T. 2005. Walaya According to al-Junayd (d. 298/910). In *Reason and Inspiration in Islam: Theology, Philosophy and Mysticism in Muslim Thought,* ed. Todd Lawson, 64–70. London: I. B. Tauris.

Khalidi, Tarif. 1994. *Arabic Historical Thought in the Classical Period.* Cambridge: Cambridge University Press.

Koloğlu, Orhan Ş. 2007. Ebû Haşim el-Cübbaî'nin Ahval Teorisi Üzerine Bazı Mülahazalar. *Uludağ Üniversitesi İlahiyat Fakültesi Dergisi* 16 (2): 195–214.

Kukkonen, Taneli. 2016. Al-Ghazali on Error. In *Islam and Rationality The Impact of al-Ghazali Papers Collected on His 900th Anniversary 2,* ed. Frank Griffel, 3–31. Leiden: Brill.

Lapidus, Ira. 2002. *A History of Islamic Societies.* Cambridge: Cambridge University Press.

Makdisi, George. 1961. Muslim Institutions of Learning in Eleventh-Century Baghdad. *Bulletin of the School of Oriental and African Studies* 24 (1): 1–56.

————. 1962. Ash'ari and the Ash'arites in Islamic Religious History I. *Studia Islamica* 17 (1): 37–80.

————. 1963. Ash'ari and the Ash'arites in Islamic Religious History II. *Studia Islamica* 18 (1): 19–39.

————. 1970. Madrasa and University in the Middle Ages. *Studia Islamica* 32 (1): 255–264.

Martin, Richard C., and Mark R. Woodward with Dwi S. Atmaja. 2003. *Defenders of Reason in Islam: Mu'tazilism from Medieval School to Modern Symbol.* Oxford: Oneworld.

Memiş, Murat. 2009. Eş'ariliğe Yaptığı Katkılar Bakımından Ebu'l-Meali El-Cüveyni. *Kelam Araştırmaları* 7 (1): 100–111.

Meyer, Susan Sauve. 2009. Chain of Causes: What Is Stoic Fate? In *God and Cosmos in Stoicism*, ed. Ricardo Salles, 71–90. Oxford: Oxford University Press.

Miura, Toru. 2016. *Dynamism in the Urban Society of Damascus: The Salihiyya Quarter from the Twelfth to the Twentieth Centuries.* Leiden and Boston: Brill.

Moad, Omar Edward. 2005. Al-Ghazali's Occasionalism and the Nature of Creatures. *Philosophy of Religion* 58 (1): 1–8.

————. 2009. Comparing Phases of Scepticism in Al-Ghazali and Descartes: Some First Meditations on Deliverance from Error. *Philosophy East and West* 59 (1): 88–101.

Muhtaroglu, Nazif. 2017. Al-Maturidi's View of Causality. In *Occasionalism Revisited: New Essays from the Islamic and Western Tradition*, ed. Nazif Muhtaroglu, 3–21. Abu Dhabi: Kalam Research and Media.

Murdoch, John E. 2009. Beyond Aristotle: Indivisibles and Infinite Divisibility in the Later Middle Ages. In *Atomism in Late Medieval Philosophy and Theology*, ed. Christophe Grellard and Robert Auraelien, 15–38. Leiden: Brill.

Nakamura, Kojiro. 1994. Imam Ghazali's Cosmology Reconsidered with Special Reference to the Concept of Jabarut. *Studia Islamica* 80 (1): 29–46.

Nasr, S.H. 1978. *An Introduction to Islamic Cosmological Doctrines.* London: Thames and Hudson.

Oosthout, Henri. 1991. *Modes of Knowledge and the Transcendental: An Introduction to Plotinus Ennead 5.3.* Amsterdam: B. R. Grüner.

Ormsby, Eric. 2000. *Ghazali.* London: Oneworld.

Patton, Walter M. 1897. *Ahmet Ibn Hanbal and the Mihna.* Leiden: Brill.

Pessagno, J. Meric. 1982. On Al Maturidi's Notion of Human Acts. In *Islamic Thought and Culture*, ed. Ismail al Faruqi, 61–64. Maryland: IIIT.

————. 1984a. The Uses of Evil in Maturidian Thought. *Studia Islamica* 60 (1): 59–82.

————. 1984b. Irada, Ikhtiyar, Qudra, Kasb The View of Abu Mansur Al-Maturidi. *Journal of the American Oriental Society* 104 (1): 177–191.

Post, Heinz. 1975. The Problem of Atomism. *The British Journal for the Philosophy of Science* 26 (1): 19–26.

Pyle, Andrew. 1997. *Atomism and Its Critics*. Bristol: Thoemmes.

Rahman, Fazlur. 1989. *Major Themes of the Qur'an*. Chicago and London: The University of Chicago Press.

Rappe, Sara. 1996. Self-Knowledge and Subjectivity in the *Enneads*. In *The Cambridge Companion to Plotinus*, ed. Lloyd P. Gerson, 150–274. Cambridge: Cambridge University Press.

Remes, Paulina. 2008. *Neoplatonism*. Stocksfi: Acumen.

Rosenthal, Erwin I.J. 2009. *Political Thought in Medieval Islam: An Introductory Outline*. Cambridge: Cambridge University Press.

Rudolph, Ulrich. 2009. Al-Maturidi's Concept of God's Wisdom. In *Büyük Türk Bilgini Imam Maturidi ve Maturidilik*, ed. İlyas Çelebi, 45–53. Istanbul: Marmara İlahiyat.

———. 2015. *Al-Maturidi and the Development of Sunni Theology in Samarqand*. Leiden: Brill.

———. 2016. Hanafi Theological Tradition and Maturidism. In *The Oxford Handbook of Islamic Theology*, ed. Sabine Schmidtke, 280–296. Oxford: Oxford University Press.

Safi, Omid. 2006. *The Politics of Knowledge in Premodern Islam: Negotiating Ideology and Religious Inquiry*. Chapel Hill: The University of North Caroline Press.

Schacht, Joseph. 1953. New Sources for the History of Muhammadan Theology. *Studia Islamica* 1 (1): 29–33.

Schmidtke, Sabine. 2008. Theological Rationalism in the Medieval World of Islam. *Al-'Usur al Wusta* 20 (1): 17–22.

Shehadi, Fadlou. 1964. *Ghazali's Unique Unknowable God*. Leiden: Brill.

Shihadeh, Ayman. 2006. *The Teleological Ethics of Fakhr al-Din Al-Razi*. Leiden: Brill.

Smith, Margaret. 1938. A-Risalat Al-Laduniyya. By Abu Ḥamid Muhammad Al-Ghazali (450/1059-505/1111). *The Journal of the Royal Asiatic Society of Great Britain and Ireland* 3 (1): 177–200, 353–374.

Sorabji, Richard. 1983. *Creation and the Continuum: Theories in Antiquity and the Early Middle Ages*. New York: Cornell University Press.

Strange, Guy Le. 1900. *Baghdad During the Abbasid Caliphate: From Contemporary Arabic and Persian Resources*. Oxford: Clarendon.

Strange, Steven K. 2004. The Stoics on the Voluntariness of the Passions. In *Stoicism Traditions and Transformations*, ed. Steven K. Strange and Jack Zupco, 32–51. Cambridge: Cambridge University Press.

Subhan, 'Abdus. 1941. Mu'tazilite View on Beatific Vision. *Islamic Culture* 15 (1): 422–428.

———. 2000. The Relation of God to Time and Space as Seen by the Mu'tazilities. In *Islamic Philosophy 116: The Teachings of the Mu'tazila Texts and Studies II*, ed. Fuat Sezgin, 228–241. Frankfurt: Institute for the History of Arabic-Islamic Science.

Syed, Mairaj U. 2016. *Coercion and Responsibility in Islam: A Study in Ethics and Law*. Oxford: Oxford University Press.

Thiele, Jan. 2016. Abu Hashim al-Jubbaʾiʾs (d. 321/933) Theory of 'States' (*aḥwal*) and its Adaption by Ashʿarite Theologians. In *The Oxford Handbook of Islamic Theology*, ed. Sabine Schmidtke, 225–242. Oxford: Oxford University Press.

Topaloğlu, Bekir. 2006. Allah. In *İslam Ansiklopedisi Vol. 2*, ed. Türkiye Diyanet Vakfi, 471–198. Istanbul: TDV ISAM.

Treiger, Alexander. 2011. Al-Ghazali's Classification of the Sciences and Descriptions of the Highest Theoretical Science. *Divan* 16 (30): 1–32.

Üzüm, İlyas. 2006. Mücessime. In *İslam Ansiklopedisi*, ed. Türkiye Diyanet Vakfi, 449–450. Istanbul: TDV ISAM.

Vasalau, Sophia. 2008. *Moral Agents and Their Deserts: The Character of Muʾtazilite Ethics*. Princeton: Princeton University Press.

Williams, Wesley. 2002. Aspects of the Creed of Imam Ahmad ibn Hanbal: A Study of Anthropomorphism in Early Islamic Discourse. *International Journal of Middle East Studies* 34 (3): 441–463.

Wisknovsky, Robert. 2013. Towards a History of Avicenna's Distinction between Immanent and Transcendent Causes. In *Before and After Avicenna*, ed. David C. Riesman, 49–68. London and Boston: Brill.

Wohlman, Avital. 2010. *Averroes and the Interpretation of the Qurʾan: Common Sense and Philosophy in Islam*. London: Routledge.

Yaman, Hikmet. 2010. Small Theological Differences Profound Philosophical Implications: Notes on Some of the Chief Differences between the Ashʿaris and Maturidis. *Ankara Üniversitesi İlahiyat Fakültesi Dergisi* 51 (1): 177–194.

Yavuz, Yusuf Şevki. 2009. İmam Maturidi'nin Tabiat ve İlliyete Bakışı. In *Büyük Türk Bilgini İmam Maturidi ve Maturidilik*, ed. İlyas Çelebi, 54–64. Istanbul: Marmara İlahiyat.

CHAPTER 4

The Contested Boundaries of Turkish Islam

The ninth-grade religious course textbook emphasizes that al-Maturidi's opinions have deeply influenced Turks' understanding of religion and faith.[1] A popular remark presents Turks as followers of Abu Hanifa in religious practice and of al-Maturidi in creed: "*Amelde mezhebim Ebu Hanife, itikatta mezhebim İmam Maturidi.*" This formulation suggests that the Maturidi interpretation of Islamic theology—including the Islamic idea of nature—is one among multiple interpretations and implicitly distinguishes Turkey from parts of the Muslim world where Ash'ari theology is dominant. But how distinctive is Turkish Maturidism? Does religious socialization and education in Turkey teach a concept of causality different from that of Ash'ari occasionalism?

I will answer these questions in the following chapters by directly analyzing how selected cases interpret and transmit the Islamic idea of nature in contemporary Turkey. In this chapter, I inquire into Turks' views of Ash'ari and Maturidi theology. In the previous chapters, I discussed how the Ash'ari theology emerged as mainstream Islamic idea of nature in the post-Abbasid era, and how Maturidism has stayed as a legitimate contender school with full legitimacy within the Sunni orthodoxy. Since Islamic theological schools are the historical carriers of theological interpretations from one generation to the next, the contemporary interpretation of the Islamic idea of nature in Turkey cannot be explained without some reference to that background. Therefore, we need to identify first where and how theology in Turkey has been positioned between the Ash'ari and the Maturidi schools.

© The Author(s) 2020
G. Bacik, *Islam and Muslim Resistance to Modernity in Turkey*,
https://doi.org/10.1007/978-3-030-25901-3_4

4.1   THE PRIMARY RELIGIOUS IDENTITY: HANAFISM

A large majority of Muslims in Turkey follows the Hanafi school, while smaller groups have shown interest in Shafi'i, Hanbali, and Maliki.[2] Since the early-Ottoman period, the state has maintained the Hanafism as the dominant school of law. The early-Ottoman elites shared a commitment to the Hanafi School,[3] which enjoyed an exclusive official recognition in the Ottoman Empire.[4] In a typical court ruling, the process usually required "a faithful and convenient rendering of the classical Hanafi version of the sharia."[5]

The Hanafi interpretation of Islam remained dominant into the republican period too, despite that new regime's commitment to secularization. The republican elites tried to confine Islam to the private realm, but within that realm Hanafi law remained influential. Inspired by Atatürk, the Turkish parliament asked Elmalılı Hamdi Yazır to write an exegesis of the Qur'an in 1925. Yazır was an Islamist scholar who became famous during the second Constitutional Period (1908–1920).[6] Reflecting the continuing interest of officialdom in Hanafism, the assignment specified that the exegesis should be written in accordance with the Hanafi School.[7] Yazır noted in the Preface to the exegesis that he followed the Hanafi approach.[8] This case demonstrates how the secular republic continued to recognize Hanafism as the official religion.

Hanafism has also informed Turks' understanding of Maturidi theology. Accordingly, Maturidi theology is usually regarded as a subbranch of Hanafism.[9] However, the primacy that Hanafism enjoyed in the Ottoman interpretation of Islamic law was never conferred upon Maturidism in theology. The Hanafi identity of the Ottomans and today's Turks was and is affirmed by the state, which is not the case with regard to Maturidi theology. Instead, the boundary of Ottoman Maturidism was blurred, due to its continuous receptions from the Ash'ari. Thus, whereas the Turks are staunchly Hanafi, their doctrinal identity has been syncretic. Recognizing this syncretism is essential to understanding the Turkish case with regard to Islamic theology as well as the Islamic idea of nature.

Scholarship generally offers two reasons for Ottoman official interest in Hanafism. The first is the ruling elite's historical affinity with Hanafism, which has its origins in Central Asia, when the first contacts of Turks with Hanafi circles were believed to have been made. In this narrative, the centrality of Hanafism in Turkish Islam is very old and embedded in Turkish culture. The second reason is political pragmatism: It is argued that Hanafism suited Turkish social structure and governance because of its rational and flexible nature.[10] Accordingly, the Ottoman state and elites maintained their support for Hanafism because it offered them flexibility in interpreting the Islamic law.[11]

This explanation brings to mind the Seljuqs' interest in religion, described in Chap. 2 as patronage. As a matter of fact, as Rudolph Peters has argued, a distinctive Ottoman Hanafism emerged, "one that accordingly was well suited to the requirements of the bureaucratic set-up of the Ottoman state."[12] Hanafism was gradually transformed into a legal doctrine for the state with a more uniform and predictable nature, crafted to suit to the state's policies.[13]

The discursive function of Hanafism was also important. Hanafism buttressed the political legitimacy of the dynasty. Classical texts like *Şemaʿilname*—written in the early 1590s by an imperial historian specifically "to demonstrate the Ottoman dynasty's fitness to rule"—attributed the Ottoman dynasty's legitimacy to its adherence to Sunni Islam and the Hanafi school of law.[14] Hanafism offered a legitimizing religious narrative to the Ottomans, rulers of a rising state in the Western Islamic world. Thus, as Colin Imber explains, Hanafi law was symbolically important even in determining the structure of the Ottoman dynasty.[15] For Ottomans, Hanafism was a legitimizing religious discourse that could also accommodate their politico-religious aspirations.

On the other hand, the Ottoman case was another version of the hierarchical-society model that had its roots in the Turco-Sassanid tradition: it reflected the standard features of that model, such as the state's control of economic groups by its imposed bureaucratic rationality.[16] As Suraiya Faroqhi has written, it was a system "where everybody was supposed to know his or her place and, ideally, remain in it."[17] Like the economy, religion was also subordinated within this hierarchy. Ottoman Hanafism depended on a closed alliance of state and religion. The Ottoman "circle of equity," drafted by Kınalizade Ali Çelebi (d. 1571), which Norman Itzkowitz summarized as a "formulation that embodied the ethical, political, and social values of the Ottomans," reflected this state-dominated hierarchy: there can be no royal authority without the military, the state's prop is the religious law, and there is no support for the religious law without royal authority.[18]

The land regime also reflected this hierarchy, as well as the alliance between state and religion in the Ottoman system. The Ottomans declared all cultivated lands to be state property in principle and introduced a strictly controlled land regime.[19] According to Halil İnalcık, it was the militaristic character of the state that led to this policy, reminiscent of the Seljuqi *iqta*. The scarcity of silver, as İnalcık explains, forced the Ottomans to adopt a direct goods-based system of remuneration.[20] This sate-centered system benefited the state treasury, as it secured a predictable amount of revenue from land, but harmed the interests of the peasantry, who had fixed tax burdens independent of agricultural output. For İnalcık, such problems were typical of the economic model in place since the Sassanid period.[21]

With respect to the land regime, the Ottomans expected Hanafi jurists to offer an accommodating framework. Their expectation was satisfied. As Baber Johansen has shown, in its early period, Hanafi law protected peasant ownership of land against state claims.[22] Hanafi law included a principle somewhat resembling individual ownership of property. However, the classical Hanafi view of land regime gradually changed to the detriment of individual rights. As of the fifteenth century, we see a new interpretation of land tenure, in which ownership of agricultural land is understood "not as arising from possession by individuals but as vested in the treasury and delegated in different forms to intermediate and cultivators."[23]

This new interpretation was clear: Land was state property merely leased to a temporary proprietor until it reverted to the state upon the death of the proprietor. Various groups including the notables opposed the new land regime.[24] That was the typical response of autonomy-seeking actors witnessing the erosion of their domain. But what we observe is the transformation of Hanafi law according to the Ottoman *raison d'etat*. We can see this development in the example of the change in the land regime (in Iraq and elsewhere) through jurists' new interpretations, which went beyond the previous Hanafi rulings to justify Ottoman policies. Advancing new interpretations on the pretext of the public interest or necessity, jurists developed pro-government approaches to displace the original Hanafi views, which included a principle resembling individually owned property.[25]

The harmony between the Ottoman state and Hanafi law cannot be interpreted solely in terms of the latter's readiness to meet the former's practical needs. It was also a reflection of the alliance between religion and state legitimized and reinforced by Sunni orthodoxy. The state was able to intervene in the formulation of religious law. As Guy Burak has observed, state interest in regulating the doctrine of the Hanafi school of law produced a hierarchy of state-supported scholars whose purpose was to bring religious law in line with state interests.[26] Baki Tezcan's findings—though in a different context—also support the view that it was mainly the state, rather than the characteristics of the particular (Hanafi) school, that determined the interpretation of Islamic law.[27]

The harmony between the state and Hanafism generated an administrative culture among Ottoman bureaucrats that defined Hanafism as the dominant school. Accordingly, the best solution for an Ottoman administrator was to handle a case according to the Hanafi School. However, they were not completely closed to other schools of law, so long as those schools remained below Hanafism on the legal hierarchy. Hanafi law was the rule, and others were tolerated in particular cases. Recep Cici has shown the Hanafi dominance among major texts of the Ottoman religious circles of the classical period (1300–1600), despite the lack of objection to referring to other schools.[28]

The close relationship with the state tied religion to political developments. In the sixteenth century, Ottoman rule extended over territories of Muslim populations where other schools were followed. The Ottomans became less tolerant of other interpretations in courts than they had before.[29] The Ottoman judge became a dispenser of Hanafi-law justice in most parts of the Balkans and Anatolia, "no matter what the religion or legal school of the parties concerned."[30] Adherence to the Hanafi interpretation of Islamic law was now an obligation of judges.[31] The exception was places where people observed other schools of law, like those of the newly gained Arab lands. The Ottoman's reaction to the new demographic composition of the empire resulted in the rise of Hanafism as an official school of law.[32]

At times the Ottomans promoted Hanafism in Arab lands. For example, sustained state support for Hanafi scholars in Damascus led the profile of jurists and scholars in the city to become more Hanafi-oriented by the seventeenth and eighteenth centuries. This happened despite the Shafi'i dominance of Damascus in the previous century.[33] Similarly, the Ottomans restricted judges to Hanafi jurisprudence during the reorganization of the Sharia courts in nineteenth-century Egypt as part of an administrative reform aimed at uniformity in law.[34]

The Ottoman approach to the Hanafi School created a model where the state brought Hanafism in line with its agenda. The Hanafi jurists did not refuse to accommodate the ebbs and flows of Ottoman politics because of the power relations that linked them to the state in the usual logic of the Sunni orthodoxy. The model worked similarly in later periods of the Empire. When the Ottomans initiated reforms with the Tanzimat Decree (1839),

Hanafism helped determine the boundaries between Sunni Muslims and the state since new administrative reforms introduced many rights for non-Muslims as well as for non-Hanafi ethnic groups. The Ottoman support for Hanafism ended in what Selim Deringil defines as Hamidian Hanafism, epitomized in the Islamist policies of Abdulhamid II.[35] Hanafism had become the framework of an accommodative ideology.

Finally, the Hanafi School also accommodated the Ottoman reforms of the late period of the Empire by supplying a legitimizing discourse for the reforms. The ambitious Ottoman agenda of law reform, which required codification and unification, was based on Hanafi law.[36] The *Majalla*, the first Sharia-based Ottoman civil code of law, intended to standardize the law across the Empire, came into force in 1877, and was based on Hanafi jurisprudence.[37] Emerging out of the existing legal tradition of Hanafi interpretations and practices, the *Majalla* was the zenith of Ottoman Hanafism in a modern text.[38] Despite its secular nature, Republican Turkey would inherit the late Ottoman practice of collaborating modern structures and religion. Though the Republic would purge religion from the legal codes, Islam would remain within the modern structure of government in its peculiar institutional form.

4.2   THE OTTOMANS AND THE MATURIDI SCHOOL

In theological matters, Ottomans did not hesitate to pick and choose arguments from different schools.[39] They followed a quite dynamic, if irregular, path between the Maturidi and the Ash'ari schools, despite the former's having been recognized as the confessional creed. In certain periods of Ottoman rule, it even appears as though the Ash'ari school dominated. The state's relationship with both schools gives an impression that the Ottomans aimed to synthesize the two. Thus, the Ottoman case provides an example of the consolidation of the Ash'ari school even among Turks, whose confessional identity is Maturidi. On the other hand, such an ambitious synthesizing strategy should be thought of, within its historical and geographical contexts, as the journey of Maturidism from Transoxiana to the heartland of Islamic societies, mainly via the Turks, leading to Maturidism's encounter and engagement with Ash'arism.[40]

Ash'arism exerted strong influence over Ottoman madrasas, at times enjoying the status of the primary theological school. Experts like Süleyman Uludağ have even argued that in the Ottoman system it was Ash'ari more than Maturidi theology that held sway.[41] The studies of

Yahya R. Haidar of the Ottoman classical period support Uludağ's argument. Accordingly, as far as doctrinal affiliation is concerned, the classical Ottoman Hanafi theologians' attitude to the issues between Ash'arism and Maturidism was marked by: (i) infrequent subscription to the Maturidi position; and (ii) the hegemony of Ash'arism, manifested in the common inclination to the Ash'ari position on conventional points of dispute with Maturidism.[42] Haidar also notes that Ash'arism occupied a central place in the classical Ottoman theological texts written in Anatolia and the Balkans.[43] Ironically, Anatolia and the Balkans were the backbone of Ottoman Hanafism, which would normally lead us to expect a Maturidi dominance. Haidar concludes that the leading names of Ottoman theological scholarship showed no hesitation in affirming al-Ash'ari as the foremost *mutakallim* (theologian) of Islam, even superior to al-Maturidi.[44]

Ali İhsan Karataş's study of popular books based on the sixteenth-century *tereke* records—lists of the movable and immovable items inherited after people's death—of Bursa, a former Ottoman capital, confirms Haidar's and Uludağ's arguments. The list includes only the books owned by individuals in their households. The records display that the most popular book on theology was al-Nasafi's (1067–1115) *Aqaid al-Nasafi*, nearly all of which were al-Taftazani (1322–1390) editions known as *Sharh al-Aqaid*. The second most common was Adududdin al-İci's (1281–1355) *el-Mawaqif fi 'Ilm al-kalam*.[45]

The *tereke* records reflect the Ottoman syncretic approach to theology in the case of Bursa. Al-Ici was an Ash'ari scholar of great renown in the Ottoman intellectual milieu. Al-Nasafi was dubbed the "second founder of Maturidi" theology. However, al-Nasafi was read through the commentary of al-Taftazani, who was an Ash'ari.[46] Similarly, the most popular commentary of al-Ici's book was *Sharh al-Mawaqif* by al-Sharif al-Jurjani (d. 1413), who was an Ash'ari scholar.

The sixteenth-century Bursa *tereke* records reflect a strong Ash'ari influence. The key theology book had a Maturidi framework; however, it was presented to the Ottomans through the lens of an Ash'ari scholar. As the Bursa records demonstrate, despite an affiliation with the Hanafi School, the Ottoman elite, particularly that of the urban religious milieu, had a syncretic relationship with the Maturidi and the Ash'ari but recognized the latter as the dominant school.

The particular case of al-Taftazani is itself an important one for understanding how the Ottomans approached theological schools. He was one of the most influential scholars in Ottoman theology. He was also among the most read scholars in the madrasas.[47] Along with those of al-Nasafi, al-Taftazani's works dominated madrasa curricula in the fifteenth and sixteenth centuries.[48] His fame endured *via* his *Sharh al Aqaʿid*, an authoritative compendium on theology that remained a standard textbook in Ottoman schools.[49] The book is a commentary on al-Nasafi's treatise, in which al-Nasafi systematized Hanafi-Maturidi theology. However, al-Taftazani adopted an Ashʿari perspective in his commentary.

Al-Taftazani was born in the heavily Shiʿite region of Khorasan. Spending time in cities where different theological schools dominated, like the Muʾtazila in Khawarazm and the Maturidi in Samarkand, he personally developed an accommodative approach to theological schools. However, he was by definition an Ashʿari scholar, which is also apparent in his *Sharh al Aqaʿid*.[50] He started the book by praising Ashʿari after criticizing the Muʾtazila.[51] On various issues like free will, al-Taftazani intervenes as an Ashʿari scholar.[52] Though his commentary in parts reflects an Ashʿari-Maturidi synthesis, the main framework was Ashʿari theology.

Another example of the complicated state of theology in Ottoman society is found in the case of Ekmelüddin al-Baberti (1310–1384). Al-Baberti was a renowned defender of Maturidi theology and a critic of the Shafiʿi School of law.[53] He lived in the first century of the Ottoman state, which made him influential among the emerging religious elites. However, he was mostly a Maturidi scholar in an Ashʿari-dominated environment.[54] One observes the complicated relations between the Maturidi and the Ashʿari schools in the case of al-Baberti. For example, the first Sheikh-al-Islam of the Ottoman State, Fenari (d. 1431), was a student of al-Baberti. However, despite his teacher's Maturidism, Fenari later adopted the Ashʿari school. The Ashʿari affiliation of the first Ottoman Sheikh-al-Islam is illustrative of the complex relations of the Maturidi and the Ashʿari in the Ottomans.

Another case related to al-Baberti is that of al-Jurjani. Like Fenari, al-Jurjani was a disciple of al-Baberti, who gave him *ijazah* in Cairo.[55] Al-Jurjani was another towering figure whose impact on Ottoman society is comparable with that of al-Taftazani. As we discussed above, al-Jurjani was a popular scholar and a household name. But unlike his tutor al-Baberti, al-Jurjani was Ashʿari, even if he was critical of that school on particular points.[56] Reading his *Sharh al-Mawaqif*, we see that he was a follower of Ashʿari on key issues like free will[57] and God's attributes.[58]

The young Ottoman state felt the impact of many dynamics, producing a new society like a "new amalgam."[59] In this complex and ever-shifting environment, Ottomans saw in Ash'arism an advanced, dynamic theology while they saw in Maturidism a stagnant and therefore less attractive system of thought. As a matter of fact, Ottomans in the early period sent their scholars to abroad for education, which become another conduit of Ash'ari influence.[60] For example, Davud Kayseri (d. 1351), a leading scholar of the early-Ottoman madrasa, was educated in Cairo, where Ash'arism dominated. Similarly, the first Sheikh al-Islam of the Ottomans, Fenari, traveled to Egypt to study religious sciences.[61]

Simply put, Maturidism did not have the intellectual grandeur of Ash'arism in Ottoman society. Even several Ottoman-era theologians who identified with Maturidi, as Philip Dorrol has written, were not exposed to Maturidi's ideas from that scholar's own texts. Instead, they mostly engaged with Maturidi theology through alternative resources.[62] By contrast, Khojazada (d. 1488) wrote one of the earliest commentaries on al-Ghazali's *The Incoherence of The Philosophers*, even expanding the latter's criticism of philosophy.[63] Thus, the choice of a syncretic path between Ash'arism and Maturidism was a result of necessity rather than a primarily ideological choice.[64]

Until the sixteenth century, the Ottomans drew on Ash'arism when interpreting certain topics of Islamic theology. Ash'arism determined the interpretation of theological matters. As Mustafa Akman has observed in his analysis of a commentary on al-Nasafi written by Ramazan Efendi (d. 1571), Ottoman Maturidism ironically survived through the Ash'ari-oriented scholarship of the Ottoman madrasas.[65]

However, the Ottomans gave signals of change in their understanding of Islamic theology after the sixteenth century. They were no longer a small state confined to Western Anatolia. Transformed into a leading power with sophisticated institutions, and ruling Arab-Islamic centers including Cairo, the Ottoman state required ideological and intellectual legitimacy. Official interest in Maturidism changed, letting it emerge as an alternate intellectual framework for the nascent imperial religious narrative. The Ottomans reinvented Maturidism as part of their political venture in the sixteenth century.[66] Though they did not end their syncretic approach to Ash'arism, they began to emphasize Maturidism, particularly in the education in the Balkans and Anatolia.[67]

At the same time, rivalry with the Safavids spurred greater Ottoman interest in Maturidi theology. As a Shi'ite state, the Safavids were not only a political rival; they were also ideological competitors. The Ottoman administration needed a politico-theological narrative that would both distinguish their subjects and mitigate Safavid influence. The Ottomans developed new methods, not only in the political realm but also in their interpretation of Islam, which resulted in an emphasis on the Sunni characteristics of the empire on the basis of Hanafism. For example, as the Safavid state waged an asymmetrical war by infiltrating the Turkmen tribes in adjacent Ottoman lands, the Ottomans responded by supporting Sunni-Hanafi religious orders like the Khalwatiyya and the Naqshbandiyya within Safavid lands.

The general strategy of supporting Hanafism to counterbalance the Safavid threat consolidated Maturidism in Ottoman society. The Ottomans did not radically break with their previous syncretic approach to the Ash'arism, but they reinterpreted Maturidism as the major theological school to complement the Hanafism.[68]

The new narrative represented Maturidism as an independent theological school. In a widely circulated book that reflects the trends of the age, Kemalpaşazade Şemseddin Ahmed (d. 1534) compared Ash'ari and Maturidi theologies, treating the latter as a distinct school.[69] Maturidism was no longer a subbranch of Hanafism but an independent school comparable to Ash'arism. The book reflects the change in the status of Maturidism in Ottoman society. The last popular book on the same subject before Kemalpaşazade's, written by Taceddin al-Subki (d. 1370), had reflected the old superiority of Ash'arism.[70] Unlike Kemalpaşazade, al-Subki compared al-Ash'ari and Abu Hanifa rather than al-Ash'ari and al-Maturidi.

However, notwithstanding the interest in Maturidi, the Ottomans upheld their traditional conciliatory approach that granted Ash'arism some space in officially sanctioned theology. For example, major texts written in the eighteenth century display the enduring syncretism of the Ottoman approach to theology. Sheikh al-Islam Mehmed Esad Efendi (1684–1753) wrote a treatise comparing the differences between the Ash'ari and the Maturidi schools.[71] Esad Efendi compared Ash'ari and Maturidi theologies on 40 topics. Under each heading, he only summarized the two Schools' arguments, without taking any position on them. As he reveals in last paragraph of the book, his only purpose was to clarify the theological issues on which he was writing.[72] Even under especially important topics such as the seventeenth, on the morality of God's acts, Esad Efendi made no personal judgment; all he did was present a summary of each school's opinion.

The book exemplifies the traditional Ottoman restraint vis-à-vis judging between the theological schools. This is apparent in numerous other Ottoman theological works. For example, Akkirmani (d. 1760), a peer of Esad Efendi, who served as a *qadi* in important regions like Izmir and Egypt, also wrote a treatise on free will, the *İrade-i Cüziyye Risalesi*. Although he judged the Maturidi perspective superior in general, Akkirmani adopted an Ash'ari stance on particular issues like free will.[73] Similarly, another important book of the period, written by Davud-i Karsi (d. 1756), also followed the syncretic approach between Ash'ari and Maturidi theologies.[74] However, like the earlier example of al-Baberti, there were Maturidi scholars though their impact was limited. For example, Beyazızade (d. 1684) had a clearly Maturidi approach.[75]

The syncretic approach continued in the latter centuries of the Empire, even as the state occasionally reinterpreted Hanafism or Maturidism for political purposes. For example, during the reign of Abdulhamid II, as discussed above, state-supported scholars reformulated Hanafism as an accommodating ideology. More generally, the Ottomans adapted Maturidi, into a reform-friendly theological school in the later centuries of the empire. However, the traditional syncretic approach remained unchanged. For instance, Manastırlı İsmail Hakkı (d. 1912) wrote a school textbook with a Maturidi perspective without abandoning the traditional syncretic approach to Ash'arism.[76] Hüseyin Avni (1864–1954), who worked in multiple respected Ottoman schools, also had an Ash'ari perspective.[77] As late as the late nineteenth century, Abdurrahim Fedai Efendi (d. 1885), a lecturer in Skopje Madrasa in Balkans—another historical center of Ottoman Hanafism—wrote a book that harshly criticized the Maturidi view of free will.[78]

To conclude, the Ottomans were Maturidi in their theology. However, they also entertained Ash'ari opinions on multiple issues. Their syncretic approach proves, ironically, both the success of Ash'arism in becoming the dominant school and of Maturidism in remaining the legitimate secondary school. Thus, the standard claim that presents Turks as the followers of Maturidi requires some modification. The Ottoman state gave support to Maturidism, even as it drew on Ash'arism and in so doing reinforced that school's de facto dominance.

An imperial decree from the mid-sixteenth century encapsulates the Ottoman stance on theology. In 1565, during the reign of Suleiman I, the Ottoman administration sent a list of 55 books to the madrasas under its control. This missive constituted an intervention by the state in the determination of the madrasa curriculum. Having analyzed the books cited in the Imperial Decree, I believe that we can find a good summary of the traditional Ottoman approach to theology in Shahab Ahmed's and Nenad Filipovic's response to the critical question, "if anything, what does the 1565 State Decree tell us about the official identity of Ottoman Islam in the reign of Suleiman?"

> The basic text chosen is by a Turkish scholar who belonged to the official legal rite of the Ottoman state—Hanafism—but who was a Mu'tazila. The commentaries thereon are mainly by Shafi Ash'aris, whose presence, as we have noted, is doubtless symptomatic of the gradual coming together of Ash'arism with the Maturidi theology favored by the Ottoman state. But as regards the law—the primary medium in which the graduates of the *medaris-i Haqaniya* [royal madrasas] would eventually serve and represent the state—the identity of the Sultans syllabus is emphatically and exclusively Hanafi. The Ottoman empire had no interest in training its ulema in any other legal madhhab.[79]

The Ottoman's priority was to keep Hanafism as the official school of law and to leave the theological track open to the influence of a continuous dialogue between Ash'arism the Maturidism.

4.3   THE MATURIDI IN CONTEMPORARY TIMES

Despite its staunchly secular policies that almost purged Islam from the public sphere, the Turkish Republic continued the interest in theology exhibited by the Ottoman state. Republican Turkey continued to promote a particular form of Maturidism that had its roots in the Ottoman modernization, in which Maturidism was reinterpreted as a theology that was compatible with modernity.

In this narrative that we observe during the Ottoman reforms, Maturidism was interpreted as a rational school of Islam that suited the historical patterns of Turkish culture. This narrative also insinuated a cultural differentness from Arab Muslims among whom Ash'arism dominated. Nationalism and secularism were also incorporated later: Maturidism evolved into an Islamic school that was secularism-friendly and displayed Turkish cultural motifs. It was coded as a "practical, pragmatic and mundane" school adaptable to new realities.[80] Important names that dominated intellectual life since the late Ottoman period to the early Republican period (like Ahmed Cevdet Pasha, Şemsettin Günaltay, Yahya Kemal, Ahmad Naim, and many others, coming from various ideological backgrounds) contributed to the formation of the new narrative that Maturidism was a Turkish Islam different from Arab Islam and moderate, secular, apolitical, and open to egalitarian interpretations on gender issues.[81] This constituted the reinvention of Maturidism in modern Turkey as "Turkish neo-Maturidism."[82]

Kemalism embraced this Turkish neo-Maturidism. In a speech delivered at the Second Turkish History Congress of 1937—one of a series of conferences in which the Kemalist regime articulated the regime's historical and cultural identity—İsmail Hakkı İzmirli, an Ottoman scholar who later became a supporter of the New Theology Movement (*Yeni İlm-i Kelam*) in the early Republican period, argued that there were substantial links between Islam the Turkish culture.[83] Abu Hanifa had a central role in this narrative, whom İzmirli defined as a rationalist Muslim of Turkish origin.[84] The Kemalist dream was to reinvent the Maturidi and Hanafi traditions so that they accorded with the reformist and modernist policies of the new regime. Writings like İzmirli's *İlm-i Kelam* exemplify the search for a new interpretation of Islamic theology in the early years of the republic.[85]

Though the extremism of early Kemalism later waned, the new narrative of Maturidi has survived. The term "Maturidi" today not only indicates an Islamic school of theology, it also connotes a specific theology that has historical and cultural affinity with Turks.[86] Secular, nationalist, and even religious groups share the new narrative on Maturidism, albeit with slight differences among them. Accordingly, the elements of tolerance in Maturidism are attributed to traditional Turkish culture that even pre-dates the revelation of Islam.[87] Maturidism comes close to being a special religion of Turks: It is called "Turkish Sunnism"[88] or the "national religion."[89] Popular imagination reinforces the connection of Turkish culture and Maturidism. People speak of "Maturidism as an Ottoman Islam," "Maturidism as a Turkish Islam," "Maturidism as a foundation of the secular Turkish state," and "Maturidism as an Anatolian Islam."[90]

However, despite the interest in Maturidi in the Republican period, it is not easy to concede that Islamic socialization takes place under a dominant Maturidi theology. Mustafa Said Yazıcıoğlu, a professor of Islamic studies who also served one term as the Head of Diyanet, contends the general approach to Maturidism among Turks is not clear. Yazıcıoğlu's academic studies on Maturidism, as well as his presidency of Diyanet, are supposed to have equipped him with experience and expertise to make observations on the current status of Maturidism in Turkish society. Yazıcıoğlu points out that the subject tends to be left at that discursive level, without further information about the details of the Maturidi creed being offered. Accordingly, the confession is like a cliché that has ceased to have impact in Turkish society.

Explaining the Turkish society's indifference to the essentials of Maturidism, Yazıcıoğlu argues that it is nothing but a continuation of the Ottoman legacy. He observes that no major book by al-Maturidi, not even his *Kitab al-Tawhid*, was ever part of the Ottoman madrasa curriculum.[91] There are several data confirming his thesis. In 1980, Kemal Işık complained that in Turkey studies of Maturidism have always been fewer in than those of Ash'arism.[92] The case is similar when it comes to academia: The number of doctoral theses written directly on Maturidism between 1958 and 2012 is only 14. Moreover, the first doctoral thesis on al-Maturidi was written as late as 1964.[93] More strikingly, the first reliable Turkish translation of *Kitab al-Tawhid* was published in 2002. As of February 2019, The Diyanet still had not published a biography of al-Maturidi, though it had published one of al-Ash'ari.[94] In a recent study in Denizli, a relatively prosperous western Turkish city, interviewed imams who are supposed to teach a Maturidi interpretation of Islam were found to have almost no idea about al-Maturidi, save his name.[95] Binali Yıldırım, the former Prime Minister, who has played key roles in shaping the Islamist AKP's policies, said that he first heard al-Maturidi's name when he was a university student (*Yeni Şafak*, October 26, 2018). Such evidence supports Ulrich Rudolph's diagnosis of al-Maturidi as "the famous unknown."[96]

A critical issue in this vein is the impact of Maturidism on religious socialization, including education. Are Turks really socialized in a Maturidi framework? If Maturidism is engaged merely on an empty-discourse level (as Yazıcıoğlu argues), then there must be other theological ideas that fill the gap. What are they? For example, do Turks continue the traditional Ottoman syncretic approach that accommodates many Ash'ari ideas? And most critically, with regard to the subject matter of this book, which theological approach dominates the teaching of the Islamic idea of nature? To answer such questions, I shall, rather than refer to general debates, directly analyze the Turkish case in terms of how selected actors interpret Islamic theology. That will be the subject of the following chapters.

4.4   Eastern Religiosity

A relevant subject for our inquiry is eastern religiosity, which has historically reflected itself as an Ash'ari dynamic in Turkey. By eastern religiosity, I refer to the interpretation and practice of Islam in eastern parts of Turkey in line with the Shafi'i and Ash'ari schools. Eastern religiosity has had a huge impact in the reproduction of Islamic knowledge, particularly in matters of theology, even in the parts of Turkey where the Maturidi is the dominant school. Thus, when studying how various actors interpret and teach the Islamic idea of nature, Eastern religiosity also has to be referenced, since there are influential actors and groups (some are covered in the case studies of this book) whose background is in the Ash'ari intellectual setting of Eastern religiosity.

Geographically, there is in Turkey a western Hanafi religious zone mostly concentrated in urban areas, and an eastern Shafi'i zone. According to a 2014 survey by the Diyanet, the ratios for *madhabs* in Turkey are as follows: Hanafi 77.5%, Shafi'i 11.1%, Hanbali 0.2%, and Maliki 0.03.[97] Geographically, the Shafi'i population is concentrated in Eastern Turkey. 35.2% of the population of north-east Anatolia adhere to the Shafi'i school. That proportion is 48.7% in mid-east Anatolia, and 42% in southeast Anatolia.[98] In Istanbul, the Shafi'i population is 10% (note that this city is an immigration hub) and it is lower than 8% in all other regions. Based on the data provided by the survey, one can define a Shafi'i-Ash'ari theological zone in Eastern Anatolia. However, for several reasons examined below, the comparatively small Shafi'i-Ash'ari zone has had disproportionate impact on theological thought across Turkey.

To begin with, the early Kemalist policies increased the impact of eastern religiosity on the rest of the country. Kemalist policies aimed to purge Islam from the public sphere.[99] The Kemalist dream for Turkey was that it becomes a secular country with along Western lines.[100] Therefore, in the early period of the republic, the state wanted to confine religion to the private realm. In line with this goal, the Kemalist regime curtailed the traditional influence of Islam on Turkish society. However, Kemalist reforms were comparatively successful only in Western urban areas, where Maturidism was historically dominant. They failed in rural areas, particularly in the eastern parts of Turkey, where the Shafi'i-Ash'ari school was strong.

Kemalist secularism alarmed many conservative groups in the periphery of the country. These groups developed what Peter L. Berger theorized as the resentment of the elite culture of secularism.[101] The eastern region became an informal front where religious education continued in traditional institutions. The Kemalist regime was unable to penetrate the periphery to prohibit the activities of the traditional and informal centers of religious education, the madrasas.[102] Thus, *Şark Medreseleri* (The Eastern Madrasas) survived despite the regime's official closure of all madrasas in 1924.

After religious education was virtually eliminated in western Turkey, the informal madrasa system in the east became the only available form of religious education in the entire country.[103] This monopoly on institutions of religious education enabled Ash'ari theology to spread throughout the country. The gap in religious education in the west was filled by people from the east, leading to greater influence of Shafi'i-Ash'arism where Maturidism had previously been dominant.

In retrospect, the movement of religious scholars from the eastern to the western part of Turkey, particularly to Istanbul, began at least as early as the nineteenth century. Said Nursi (d. 1960), who would become one of the most influential Islamic figures and inspire many Islamic groups, came to Istanbul in 1907. Nursi was born in Bitlis, an eastern city. He was also affiliated with the famous madrasa in Tillo.[104] There was also Abdülhakim Arvasi (d. 1943), who was born in Van, another eastern Anatolian city. Arvasi, a leading figure of the Naqshbandiyya order who would also become a leader in the Turkish Islamic revival, came to Istanbul in 1919. Muhammad Esed (d. 1931), another charismatic leader of the Naqshbandiyya, came to Istanbul from northern Iraq in 1882.

Nursi, Arvasi, and Esed, known as *şark uleması* (the Eastern scholars), helped transmit Ash'ari theology to western Turkey.[105] They promoted Ash'ari theology in places where Maturidism had previously dominated, particularly among the educated youth, who would become a key demographic in later Islamic movements.

Another factor for the spread of Shafi'i-Ash'ari thought was the Kurdish identity of some informal madrassas. What made the people of the region toward the Kemalist regime were not only its ultra-secular policies but also the nationalist attack on Kurdish culture. Madrasas in the Kurdish provinces were seen as some of the few institutions that could still promote Kurdish language and culture and were therefore supported by the Kurds.[106]

Third, apart from madrasas, various Islamic groups and orders have their origins in the eastern provinces' influence on Islamic socialization in Turkey. For example, the Menzil group, originating in Adıyaman, is one of the biggest Islamic orders in the Naqshbandiyya-Khalidi tradition. The group also has a considerable influence in the Turkish bureaucracy.[107] Some politicians who were socialized in the group have occupied key political posts in ministries such as health and energy, thanks mainly to the groups' cooperation with the AKP.[108] The Menzil is not the only group that has its origins in Eastern Turkey; there are many small branches of Islamic orders in many provinces of eastern and southeastern Turkey. These include the various Qadiri orders around Tillo and the Naqshbandiyya-Haznevi orders in different cities like Mardin and Kilis. All such Islamic movements are sociological transmitters of Ash'ari theology into the western parts of the country.

Finally, in the broader Muslim world, the term madrasa connotes an intensive religious education with no instruction in modern subjects. Thus, the ongoing madrasa tradition is more about the Muslim response to secularism, modern education, and colonialism.[109] As in many countries, from Pakistan to Egypt, the informal madrasas in Turkey can also be seen as the guardians of traditional Islamic education. Turkey still has a dynamic network of informal madrasas in its eastern region. For example, there are ten informal madrasas in Mardin alone. According to a recent study, there are 162 students in these madrasas collectively.[110] Similarly, many other Eastern cities have their own local networks of such informal institutions.[111] As in many other countries, people in search of traditional Islamic education prefer to spend some time in these informal madrasas, thus exposing them to Shafi'i-Ash'ari influence.

The informal madrasas in Turkey are typical institutions to observe Muslims' resistance to modernity. Their curriculum aims to transmit traditional Islamic disciplines, including theology.[112] It is an institution where Islamic knowledge remains out of synchrony with recent developments in social and natural sciences. The madrasas aim to protect and transmit the traditional Islamic *acquis*. Informal Turkish madrasas are thus typical agents in the transmission of Islamic orthodoxy, including the Ash'ari view of nature.

4.5 CONCLUSION

Our survey of the contested boundaries of Turkish theology has identified several patterns. To begin with, Hanafism is the central element. The boundaries of Turkish Islamic identity are clear when it comes to Islamic law. On the other hand, the boundaries of Turkish theological identity are blurry. In the absence of a clear boundary between the Ash'ari and the Maturidi schools, the traditional Turkish approach to theology is a syncretic one that has promoted a dialogue between the two schools. Secondly, Islam, both in terms of law and theology, is always subject to political influence. This politicization of Islam is the result of power relations maintained by Sunni orthodoxy in the Turkish case.

Having analyzed the boundaries of Turkish Islam in this chapter, the next critical question is how Islamic actors interpret the Islamic idea of nature in present-day Turkey. I will answer this question in the following chapters.

NOTES

1. Yılmaz and et al., *Ortaöğretim Din Kültürü*, 115.
2. Ocak, "Social, Cultural and Intellectual Life, 1071–1453," 385.
3. Goffman, *The Ottoman Empire*, 69.
4. Schacht, *An Introduction to Islamic Law*, 65. İnalcık, *Osmanlı İmparatorluğu*, 189.
5. Gerber, *State, Society, And Law*, 30.
6. Oral, "Elmalılı Muhammed Hamdi Yazır," 190. It might be important to remind in this vein that Yazır also followed an Occasionalist view of causality in his exegesis, see: Muhtaroglu and Koca, "Late Ottoman Occasionalists," 83–104.
7. Şeker, "Türk Müslümanlığı Fikriyatı ve Maturidi Algısının Dönüşümü," 58.
8. Yazır, *Hak Dini Kur'an Dili Vol. 1*, 19.
9. Ak, "Maturidiliğin Hanefilik İle İlişkisi," 223–240. Öztürk, "Semarkand'tan Kahire'ye," 412.
10. Ocak, *Türkiye, Türkler ve İslam Yaklaşım*, 38.
11. Goffman, *The Ottoman Empire*, 73.
12. Peters, "What Does it Mean to be an Official Madhhab?" 147.
13. Ibid., 158.
14. Woodhead, "Murad III and the Historians," 93.
15. Imber, *The Ottoman Empire*, 87.
16. Kütükoğlu, *Osmanlılarda Narh Müessesesi*, 3–5.
17. Faroqhi, "The Ottoman Ruling Group and the Religions," 239.
18. Itzkowitz, *Ottoman Empire*, 88.
19. İnalcık, *The Ottoman Empire*, 221.
20. Ibid.
21. İnalcık, *Essays in Ottoman History*, 164.
22. Johansen, *The Islamic Law*, 4.

23. Mundy and Smith, *Law, Administration and Production*, 12.
24. Cuno, "Was the Land of Ottoman Syria Miri or Milk?" 147–151.
25. Mundy and Smith, *Governing Property*, 13–16. Another case to observe the "flexibility of the Ottoman legal interpretation," however with different dynamics, was the Ottoman's legalization of the cash *waqf*. Mandaville, "Usurious Piety," 289–308.
26. Burak, *The Second Formation of Islamic Law*, 207, 66.
27. Tezcan, "Hanafism and the Turks," 67–86.
28. Cici, "Osmanlı Klasik Dönemi Fıkıh Kitapları," 244.
29. Aydın, "İslam Hukuku'nun Osmanlı Devleti'nde Kanun Hukukuna Doğru Geçirdiği Evrim," 13–16.
30. Imber, *The Ottoman Empire*, 233.
31. Repp, "Qanun and Sharia in the Ottoman Context," 125. İnalcık, "Islam in the Ottoman Empire," 22.
32. Cici, "Osmanlı Hanefiliği," 267.
33. Quataert, *The Ottoman Empire*, 105.
34. Cuno, "Reorganization of the Sharia Courts," 97. The Ottomans also invested in the expansion of the Hanafi law in Arabia in this century. See: Ochsenwald, "Ottoman Arabia and the Holy Hicaz, 1516–1918," 28.
35. Deringil, *The Well-Protected Domains*, 46–48.
36. Peters, "From Jurists' Law to Statue Law," 87.
37. Bein, *Ottoman Ulema*, 38.
38. Ayoub, "The Mecelle, Sharia, and the Ottoman State," 129–156.
39. Dorrol, "Maturidi Theology in the Ottoman Empire," 228.
40. Kalaycı, "Eşarilik ve Maturidiliği Uzlaştırma Girişimleri," 127.
41. Uludağ, "Giriş," 33. Also see: Dorrol, "The Turkish Understanding of Religion," 539.
42. Haidar, *The Debates Between Ash'arism and Maturidism*, 138.
43. Ibid., 205.
44. Ibid., 118.
45. Karataş, "16. Yüzyılda Bursa'da Tedavüldeki Kitaplar," 209–230.
46. Yavuz, "Nesefi," 569.
47. Hızlı, "Osmanlı Medreselerinde Okutulan Dersler ve Eserler," 25–46.
48. Yazıcıoğlu, "XV. XVI. Yüzyıllarda Osmanlı Medreselerinde İlm-i Kelam Öğretimi," 274.
49. al-Taftazani, *A Commentary on the Creed of Islam*, viii–xx.
50. Özen, "Teftazani," 299–308.
51. al-Taftazani, *A Commentary on the Creed of Islam*, 8–9.
52. Ibid., 84.
53. Gencer, "Ekmelüddin Baberti," 23–60.
54. Türcan, "Baberti'nin el-Maksad fi İlmi'l-Kelam Başlıklı Risalesi," 141–145.

55. Gölcük, *Kelam Tarihi*, 246.
56. Türcan, "Baberti'nin Kelama Bakışı," 7–20. Süruri, "İslam Düşüncesinde Süreklilik ve Değişim," 147–156.
57. Al-Jurjani, *Şerh'ul Mevakıf II*, 458, 473–478. Also see: al-Jurjani, *Şerh'ul Mevakıf I*, 102.
58. Al-Jurjani, *Şerh'ul Mevakıf III*, 77–80.
59. Lowry, *The Nature of the Early Ottoman State*, 133.
60. Uzunçarşılı, *Osmanli Devletinin Ilmiye Teskilâti*, 227.
61. Adıvar, *Osmanlı Türklerinde İlim*, 16–17. Harman, "Osmanlı Dönemi Eşari Mezhebi," 172.
62. Dorrol, "Maturidi Theology in the Ottoman Empire," 226.
63. Lit, "An Ottoman Commentary Tradition," 368–413
64. Kalaycı, "Osmanlı'da Eş'arilik-Maturidilik İlişkisine Genel Bir Bakış," 399.
65. Akman, "Vizeli Kelamcı Bihişti Ramazan Efendi," 66.
66. Gencer, "Osmanlı İslam Yorumu," 68.
67. Kalaycı, "Şeyhülislam Mehmet Esat Efendi," 102.
68. Gencer, "Osmanlı İslam Yorumu," 69.
69. Kalaycı, "Kemalpaşazade'nin Eşarilik-Maturidilik İhtalafi," 217.
70. Kalaycı, "Eşarilik ve Maturidiliği Uzlaştırma Girişimleri," 122.
71. Kalaycı, "Şeyhülislam Mehmet Esat Efendi," 99–134.
72. "Bu makamda maksud olan ancak mesail-i ma'dudeyi icmalen beyan olmağla…". Ibid., 131.
73. Öçal, "Osmanlı Kelamcıları Eşari miydi?" 225–254.
74. Ergül, "Davud-i Karsi'nin Şerhu'l Kasideti'n-Nuniyye Aslı Eseri," 503. Göregen, " Davud-i Karsi'nin *Risale Fi Beyani Sıfatillahi Teala* Adlı Risalesi," 143–175.
75. Kalaycı, "Bir Osmanlı Kelamcısı Ne Okur?" 146. Mostly based on God's attributes Beyazizade wrote various commentaries in line with the Maturidi. See: al- Bayadi [Beyazızade], *Imam-ı Azam Ebu Hanife'nin İtikadı Görüşleri*, 95–104. Kalaycı, "Osmanlı'da Eş'arilik-Maturidilik İlişkisine Genel Bir Bakış", 405.
76. Aytekin, "Manastırlı İsmail Hakkı," 7–31.
77. Bozkurt, "Arapkirli Hüseyin Avni'de Bilgi," 89–112.
78. Soysal, "Abdürrahim Fedai Efendi'nin *İrade-i Cüziyye Risalesi*," 159.
79. Ahmed and Filipovic, "The Sultan's Syllabus," 218.
80. Ocak, *Türkler, Türkiye ve İslam*, 38.
81. Şeker, "Türk Müslümanlığı Fikriyatı," 47–80. For a counter perspective see: Özdeş, "Maturidi İslam'ın Seküler Yorumuna Temel Olabilir mi?," 40.
82. Dorrol, "The Turkish Understanding of Religion," 542.
83. Duman, "İzmirli İsmail Hakkı," 72.
84. İzmirli, "Peygamberler ve Türkler," 1021.

85. İzmirli defined theology as the highest science. Unlike law-oriented analysis, his approach underlined the critical role of theology in problems pertaining to the contemporary issues of Muslims. İzmirli, *'İlm-i Kelam*, 3.
86. This narrative was encapsulated in the title of a recent international conference on Maturidi, which gathered leading scholars like Ulrich Rudolph: "the Great Turkish Scholar Maturidi and Maturidism". See: Çelebi, *Büyük Türk Bilgini Imam Maturidi*, 1–5.
87. Sarıkaya, "Maturidi'nin Din Anlayışında Hoşgörü," 145–147.
88. Yörükan, *İslam Akaid Sisteminde Gelişmeler*, xxxiv.
89. Ecer, "Büyük Türk Bilgini Mehmet Matüridî ve Türk Kültürünü Destekleyen Görüşleri," 89–106. According to Ecer, Turks' pre-Islamic culture and even faith were largely like Islam, and thus, their adoption of Islam was nothing but a kind of continuation of their culture. Similarly, Sönmez Kutlu, wrote "Turks did not face difficulty in adopting Islam's faith of Allah because they had long been had a monotheist faith". Kutlu, *Türk Müslümanlığı Üzerine Yazılar*, 12. However, not being part of the Turkish cultural perspective, several Turkish scholars admitted the impact of regional conditions upon the formation of Maturidism. Accordingly, Transoxiana was a place where different political, religious, and sectarian groups coexisted, which led to the development of tolerant thinking. See Karadaş, "Semerkand Hanefi Kelam Okulu," 67. For Korkmaz, it was the cultural milieu that enabled Maturidi to adopt a more philosophical approach than Ash'ari, who lived in Baghdad, where such an approach was less likely to emerge. Korkmaz, "Imam Ebu Mansur al-Maturidi'nin Hayatı ve Eserleri," 93.
90. İşcan, "Türk Basınınnda Maturidi ve Maturidilik," 478.
91. Yazıcıoğlu, "Osmanlı Dönemi Türk Kelam Bilginleri," 176–180.
92. Işık, *Maturidi'nin Kelam Sisteminde İman*, 5.
93. Biçer, "Türkiye'de Kelam ve İslam Mezhepleri Çalışmaları," 1.
94. Mavil, *Eş'ari*, 1–15.
95. Vurucu, "Din Görevlilerinin Ebu Hanife ve İmam Maturidi Hakkındaki Bilgi Düzeyleri," 1–5.
96. Rudolph, *Al-Maturidi*, 3.
97. Subaşı, *Türkiye'de Dini Hayat*, xxix.
98. Ibid., 8.
99. White, *Muslim Nationalism*, 28.
100. Ciddi, *Kemalism in Turkish Politics*, 25.
101. Berger, "The desecularization of the World," 11.
102. Öztoprak, *Şark Medreselerinde*, 42.
103. A recent study on various Turkish people including academics who had madrasa education confirms that the dominant approach among them is the Shafi'i perspective. See: Yayla and et all., "Medreselerde Eğitimsel Bir Geçmişi Olan Kişilerin Medrese Eğitimine İlişkin Görüşleri", 490.
104. Nursi, *Tarihçe-i Hayat*, 52–57, 46.

105. In Nursi's autobiography, a dialogue between Nursi and Tahir Pasha, the governor of Van, reveals perceptions of the relationship between the ulema of the eastern provinces and those of Istanbul. Having observed Nursi's charismatic influence among the Eastern ulema, Tahir Pasha challenged Nursi as follows: "You are convincing and silencing the Eastern ulema, but can you go to Istanbul and challenge the big fishes in the sea?" Ibid., 52.

106. Şengül, "Cizre Kırmızı Medrese," 64. Bruinessen, "The Kurds and Islam," 1. Tan, *Kürt Sorunu*, 50–60.

107. Akyüz, "The Basic Dynamics of the Justice and Development Party's Religious Policies", 54.

108. Yavuz, *Erbakan'dan Erdoğan'a Laiklik*, 215.

109. Moosa, *What is a Madrasa?*, 5

110. Işıkdoğan, "Güneydoğu Medreselerinde Eğitim-Öğretim Faaliyetleri," 82–83.

111. Pilatin, "Batman ve Çevresinde Faaliyet Gösteren Geleneksel Eğitim Kurumları," 122. Memduğoğlu, "Geçmişten Günümüze Tillo Medreseleri," 141.

112. Çelik, *Şark Medreselerinin Serencamı*, 169–178.

REFERENCES

Adıvar, Adnan. 1982. *Osmanlı Türklerinde İlim*. Ankara: Remzi.

Ahmed, Shahab, and Nenad Filipovic. 2004. The Sultan's Syllabus: A Curriculum for the Ottoman Imperial medreses Prescribed in a Ferman of Qanuni I Süleyman, Dated 973(1565). *Studia Islamica* 98/99 (1): 183–218.

Ak, Ahmet. 2010. Maturidiliğin Hanefilik İle İlişkisi. *Milel ve Nihal* 7 (2): 223–240.

Akman, Mustafa. 2017. Vizeli Kelamcı Bihişti Ramazan Efendi ve Kelami Dünyası. *Namık Kemal İlahiyat Dergisi* 3 (2): 45–90.

Akyüz, İsmail. 2016. The Basic Dynamics of the Justice and Development Party's Religious Policies. *International Journal of Political Studies* 2 (3): 38–58.

al-Bayadi [Beyazızade], Ahmed Efendi. 2010. *Imam-ı Azam Ebu Hanife'nin İtikadı Görüşleri [al-usul al-Munifa]*. Translated by İlyas Çelebi. İstanbul: MÜİFVAF.

al-Jurjani, Sayyid al-Sharif. 2015a. *Şerh'ul Mevakıf I [Sharh al-Mawaqif]*. Translated by Ö. Türker. İstanbul: Türkiye Yazma Eserler Kurumu.

———. 2015b. *Şerh'ul Mevakıf II [Sharh al-Mawaqif]*. Translated by Ö. Türker. İstanbul: Türkiye Yazma Eserler Kurumu.

———. 2015c. *Şerh'ul Mevakıf III [Sharh al-Mawaqif]*. Translated by Ö. Türker. İstanbul: Türkiye Yazma Eserler Kurumu.

Al-Taftazani, Mas'ud ibn 'Umar. 1950. *A Commentary on the Creed of Islam Sa'd al-Din al-Taftazani on the Creed of Najm al-Din al-Nasafi [Sharh al-Aqaid]*. Translated and edited by Earl Edgar Edler. New York: Columbia University Press.

Aydın, M. Akif. 2006. İslam Hukuku'nun Osmanlı Devleti'nde Kanun Hukukuna Doğru Geçirdiği Evrim. *Türk Hukuk Tarihi Araştırmaları* 1 (1): 11–21.

Ayoub, Samy. 2016. The Mecelle, Sharia, and the Ottoman State: Fashioning and Refashioning of Islamic Law in the Ninetenth and Tweintieth Centuries. In *Law and Legality in the Ottoman Empire and Republic of Turkey*, ed. Kent F. Schull, M. Safa Saraçoğlu, and Robert Zens, 129–156. Bloomington: Indiana University Press.

Aytekin, Arif. 2018. Manastırlı İsmail Hakkı ve *Mevaidü'l-İn'am Fi Berahini Akaidi'l-İslam* Adlı Eseri. *Rumeli Journal of Islamic Studies* 2 (2): 7–31.

Bein, Amit. 2011. *Ottoman Ulema, Turkish Republic: Agents of Change and Guardians of Tradition*. Stanford: Stanford University Press.

Berger, Peter L. 1999. The Desecularization of the World: A Global Overview. In *The Desecularization of the World: Resurgent Religion and World Politics*, ed. Peter L. Berger, 1–18. Washington, DC: Ethics and Public Policy Center.

Biçer, Ramazan. 2012. Türkiye'de Kelam ve İslam Mezhepleri Çalışmaları. *Kelam Araştırmaları* 10 (2): 1–10.

Bozkurt, Mustafa. 2018. Arapkirli Hüseyin Avni'de Bilgi, Bilginin Kaynakları ve Değeri. *Kader* 16 (1): 89–112.

Bruinessen, Martin Van. 1999. The Kurds and Islam. *Islamic Area Studies Project Working Paper 13*. Tokyo.

Burak, Guy. 2015. *The Second Formation of Islamic Law: The Hanafi School in the Early Modern Ottoman Empire*. Cambridge: Cambridge University Press.

Çelebi, İlyas, ed. 2009. *Büyük Türk Bilgini Imam Maturidi ve Maturidilik*. Istanbul: Marmara İlahiyat.

Çelik, Halil. 2009. *Şark Medreselerinin Serencamı*. Istanbul: Beyan.

Cici, Recep. 2005. Osmanlı Klasik Dönemi Fıkıh Kitapları. *Türkiye Literatür Dergisi* 3 (5): 215–248.

———. 2015. Osmanlı Hanefiliği: Hanefi Mezhebi'nin Resmi Mezhep Haline Gelmesi. In *Devirleri Aydınlatan Meş'ale İmam-ı Azam: Ulusal Sempozyum Tebliğler Kitabı*, ed. Ahmet Kartal and Hilmi Özden, 259–271. Eskişehir: Osmangazi Üniversitesi.

Ciddi, Sinan. 2009. *Kemalism in Turkish Politics: The Republican People's Party, Secularism and Nationalism*. New York: Routledge.

Cuno, Kenneth M. 1995. Was the Land of Ottoman Syria Miri or Milk? An Examination of Juridical Differences Within the Hanafi School. *Studia Islamica* 107 (81): 121–152.

———. 2016. Reorganization of the Sharia Courts of Egypt: How Legal Modernization Set Back Women's Rights in the Nineteenth Century. In *Law and Legality in the Ottoman Empire and Republic of Turkey*, ed. Kent F. Schull, M. Safa Saraçoğlu, and Robert Zens, 92–107. Bloomington: Indiana University Press.

Deringil, Selim. 1999. *The Well-Protected Domains: Ideology and the Legitimation of Power in the Ottoman Empire 1876–1909*. London: I. B. Tauris.

Dorrol, Philip. 2016. Maturidi Theology in the Ottoman Empire: Debating Human Choice and Divine Power. In *Osmanlı'da İlm-i Kelam: Alimler, Eserler, Meseleler*, ed. Osman Demir, Veysel Kaya, Kadir Gömbeyaz, and U. Murat Kılavuz, 219–238. Istanbul: İsar.

———. 2018. The Turkish Understanding of Religion: Rediscovering Maturidi in Modern Turkey. In *International Symposium on Maturidism*, ed. Sönmez Kutlu, 539–548. Ankara: A. Yesevi Üniversitesi.

Duman, Ali. 2008. İzmirli İsmail Hakkı: Hayatı, Eserleri ve Fıkhı. *Bilimname* 14 (1): 72–72.

Ecer, A. Vehbi. 2010. Büyük Türk Bilgini Mehmet Matüridî ve Türk Kültürünü Destekleyen Görüşleri. *Hikmet Yurdu* 3 (6): 89–106.

Ergül, Ömer. 2017. Davud-i Karsi'nin Şerhu'l Kasideti'n-Nuniyye Aslı Eseri Çerçevesinde Kelami Görüşleri. *The Journal of Islamic Civilization Studies* 2 (3): 492–517.

Faroqhi, Suraiya. 2010. The Ottoman Ruling Group and the Religions of Its Subjects in the Early Modern Age: A Survey of Current Research. *Journal of Early Modern History* 14 (3): 239–266.

Gencer, Bedri. 2010. Osmanlı İslam Yorumu. *Doğu Batı* 13 (54): 61–95.

———. 2014. Ekmelüddin Baberti İslam Düşüncesi Olarak Fıkhın Yeniden Yapılandırılması. In *Ekmeleddün Baberti'yi Keşif Yolunda*, ed. S. Coşkun, 23–60. Bayburt: Bayburt Üniversitesi.

Gerber, Haim. 1994. *State, Society, and Law in Islam: Ottoman Law in Comparative Perspective*. Albany: State University of New York Press.

Goffman, Daniel. 2004. *The Ottoman Empire and Early Modern Europe*. Cambridge: Cambridge University Press.

Gölcük, Şerafettin. 2016. *Kelam Tarihi*. İstanbul: Kitap Dünyası.

Göregen, Mustafa. "Davud-i Karsi'nin *Risale Fi Beyani Sıfatillahi Teala* Adlı Risalesi Bağlamında Kelamcılığı ve Sıfatlar Konusundaki Görüşleri." *Türkiye İlahiyat Araştırmaları Dergisi* 1, no. 2 (2017): 143–175.

Haidar, Yahya R. 2016. The Debates Between Ash'arism and Maturidism in Ottoman Religious Scholarship: A Historical and Bibliographical Study. PhD diss., Australian National University.

Harman, Vezir. 2015. Osmanlı Dönemi Eşari Mezhebi'nin Güçlü Olmasının Muhtemel Sebepleri. *Kelam* 13 (1): 167–189.

Hızlı, Mefail. 2008. Osmanlı Medreselerinde Okutulan Dersler ve Eserler. *Uludağ İlahiyat Dergisi* 17 (1): 25–46.

Imber, Colin. 2002. *The Ottoman Empire, 1300–1650: The Structure of Power*. New York: Palgrave Macmillan.

İnalcık, Halil. 1968/1970. Islam in the Ottoman Empire. *Cultura Turcica* 5–7 (1): 19–29.

———. 1978. *The Ottoman Empire: Conquest, Organization and Economy*. London: Variorum.

———. 1998. *Essays in Ottoman History*. Istanbul: Eren.

———. 2003. *Osmanlı İmparatorluğu Klasik Çağ (1300–1600)*. Istanbul: YKY.

İşçan, M. Zeki İşcan. 2009. Türk Basınınnda Maturidi ve Maturidilik. In *Büyük Türk Bilgini Imam Maturidi ve Maturidilik*, ed. İlyas Çelebi, 408–494. Istanbul: Marmara İlahiyat.

Işık, Kemal. 1980. *Maturidi'nin Kelam Sisteminde İman Allah ve Peygamberlik İlişkisi*. Ankara: Fütüvvet.

Işıkdoğan, Davut. 2012. Güneydoğu Medreselerinde Eğitim-Öğretim Faaliyetleri: Mardin Örneği. *Ankara Üniversitesi İlahiyat Fakültesi Dergisi* 53 (2): 43–83.

Itzkowitz, Norman. 1972. *Ottoman Empire and Islamic Tradition*. Chicago: The University of Chicago Press.

İzmirli, İsmail Hakkı. 1925. *'İlm-i Kelam Birinci Kitab*. Istanbul Şehzadebaşı: Evkafi İslamiyye Matbaası.

———. 2010. Peygamberler ve Türkler. In *İkinci Türk Tarih Kongresi*, ed. Türk Tarih Kurumu, 1013–1044. Ankara: Türk Tarih Kurumu.

Johansen, Baber. 1988. *The Islamic Law on Land Tax and Rent: The Peasants' Loss of Property Rights as Interpreted in the Hanafite Legal Literature of the Mamluk and Ottoman Periods*. London: Croom Helm.

Kalaycı, Mehmet. 2012a. Eşarilik ve Maturidiliği Uzlaştırma Girişimleri: Taceddin Es-Sübki ve Nuniyye Kasidesi. *Dini Araştırmalar* 14 (40): 112–131.

———. 2012b. Kemalpaşazade'nin Eşarilik-Maturidilik İhtalafi Konusunda Risalesi. *Ankara İlahiyat Dergisi* 53 (2): 211–218.

———. 2012c. Şeyhülislam Mehmet Esat Efendi ve Eşarilik-Maturidilik İhtilafına İlişkin Risale. *Hitit İlahiyat Dergisi* 11 (21): 99–134.

———. 2016. Bir Osmanlı Kelamcısı Ne Okur? Osmanlı İlim Geleneği Çerçevesinde Beyazızade'nin *Mecmua Fi'l-Mesail'il Münteheba* Adlı Eseri. In *Osmanlı'da İlm-i Kelam: Alimler, Eserler, Meseleler*, ed. Osman Demir, Veysel Kaya, Kadir Gömbeyaz, and U. Murat Kılavuz, 53–146. Istanbul: İsar.

———. 2017. Osmanlı'da Eş'arilik-Maturidilik İlişkisine Genel Bir Bakış. *İlahiyat Akademik Dergisi* 5 (1): 113–128.

———. 2018. Osmanlı'da Eş'arilik-Maturidilik İlişkisine Genel Bir Bakış. In *International Symposium on Maturidism*, ed. Sönmez Kutlu, 398–410. Ankara: A. Yesevi Üniversitesi.

Karadaş, Cağfer. 2006. Semerkand Hanefi Kelam Okulu Oluşum Zemini ve Gelişim Süreci. *Usul* 6 (2): 57–100.

Karataş, Ali İhsan. 2001. 16. Yüzyılda Bursa'da Tedaüldeki Kitaplar. *Uludağ İlahiyat Dergisi* 10 (1): 209–230.

Korkmaz, Sıddık. 2001. Imam Ebu Mansur al-Maturidi'nin Hayatı ve Eserleri. *Dini Araştırmalar* 4 (10): 89–119.

Kutlu, Sönmez. 2017. *Türk Müslümanlığı Üzerine Yazılar: Haneflik-Maturidilik-Yesevilik*. Istanbul: Ötüken.

Kütükoğlu, Mübahat. 1983. *Osmanlılarda Narh Müessesesi ve 1640 Tarihli Narh Defteri*. Istanbul: Enderun.

Lit, L.W.C.van. 2015. An Ottoman Commentary Tradition on Ghazali's Tahafut al-Falasifa Preliminary Observations. *Orien* 43 (3/4): 368–413.

Lowry, Heath W. 2003. *The Nature of the Early Ottoman State*. Albany: State University of New York Press.

Mandaville, Jon E. 1979. Usurious Piety: The Cash Waqf Controversy in the Ottoman Empire. *International Journal of Middle East Studies* 10 (3): 289–308.

Mavil, Hikmet Y. 2017. *Eş'ari*. Istanbul: DİB.

Memduğoğlu, Adnan. 2012. Geçmişten Günümüze Tillo Medreseleri. Paper presented at The Conference on Madrasa Tradition and Madrasas in the Process of Modernization, Muş, October 5–7, 2012.

Moosa, Ebrahim. 2015. *What Is a Madrasa?* Chapel Hill: The University of North Caroline Press.

Muhtaroglu, Nazif, and Ozgür Koca. 2016. Late Ottoman Occasionalists on Modern Science. In *Occasionalism East and West*, ed. Nazif Muhtaroglu, 83–104. Abu Dhabi: Kalam Research and Media.

Mundy, Martha, and Richard Saumarez Smith. 2007. *Law, Administration and Production in Ottoman Syria*. London: I. B. Tauris.

Nursi, Said. 1995. *Tarihçe-i Hayat*. Istanbul: Envar.

Ocak, Ahmet Yaşar. 2003. *Türkiye, Türkler ve İslam: Yaklaşım, Yorum ve Yöntem Denemeleri*. Istanbul: İletisim.

———. 2009. Social, Cultural and Intellectual Life, 1071–1453. In *The Cambridge History of Turkey Vol. 1 Byzantium to Turkey, 1071–1453*, ed. Kate Fleet, 353–422. Cambridge: Cambridge University Press.

Öçal, Şamil. 1999. Osmanlı Kelamcıları Eşari miydi? *Dini Arastirmalar* 2 (5): 225–254.

Ochsenwald, William. 2016. Ottoman Arabia and the Holy Hicaz, 1516–1918. *Journal of Global Initiatives* 10 (1): 23–34.

Oral, Özgür. 2005. Elmalılı Muhammed Hamdi Yazır. In *İslamcılık*, ed. Yasin Aktay, Tanıl Bora, and Murat Gültekingil, 184–194. Istanbul: İletişim.

Özdeş, Talip. 2010. Maturidi İslam'ın Seküler Yorumuna Temel Olabilir mi? *Milel ve Nihal* 7 (2): 31–52.

Özen, Şükrü. 2011. Teftazani. In *İslam Ansiklopedisi Vol. 40*, ed. Türkiye Diyanet Vakfi, 299–308. Ankara: TDV İSAM.

Öztoprak, Sadrettin. 2017. *Şark Medreselerinde Bir Ömür*. Istanbul: Beyan.

Öztürk, Yunus. 2016. Semarkand'tan Kahire'ye Hanefi Kültürünün İzleri. *İslami Araştırmalar* 27 (3): 404–413.

Peters, Rudolph. 2003. From Jurists' Law to Statue Law or What Happens When the Shari'a Is Codified. In *Shaping the Current Islamic Reformation*, ed. B.A. Roberson, 82–95. London: Frank Cass.

———. 2005. What Does It Mean to Be an Official Madhhab? Hanafism and the Ottoman Empire. In *The Islamic School of Law: Evolution, Devolution, and Progress*, ed. P. Bearman, R. Peters, and F.E. Vogel, 147–158. Cambridge, MA: Harvard University Press.

Pilatin, Übeydullah. 2012. Batman ve Çevresinde Faaliyet Gösteren Geleneksel Eğitim Kurumları. *Batman Üniversitesi Yaşam ve Bilim Dergisi* 1 (1): 1217–1228.

Quataert, Donald. 2005. *The Ottoman Empire, 1700–1922*. Cambridge: Cambridge University Press.

Repp, Richard C. 1998. Qanun and Sharia in the Ottoman Context. In *Islamic Law: Social and Historical Contexts*, ed. Aziz al-Azmeh, 124–145. London and New York: Routledge.

Rudolph, Ulrich. 2015. *Al-Maturidi and the Development of Sunni Theology in Samarqand*. London and Boston: Brill.

Sarıkaya, Mehmet Saffet. 2010. Maturidi'nin Din Anlayışında Hoşgörü. *e-makalat Mezhep Araştırmaları* 3 (2): 145–165.

Schacht, Joseph. 1982. *An Introduction to Islamic Law*. Oxford: Oxford University Press.

Şeker, Fatih. 2010. Türk Müslümanlığı Fikriyatı ve Maturidi Algısının Dönüşümü. *Marmara İlahiyat Dergisi* 38 (1): 47–80.

Şengül, Serdar. 2014. Cizre Kırmızı Medrese Bağlamında Tarih Kimlik Hafıza Oluşumu. *Kebikeç* 19 (34): 57–78.

Soysal, M. Fatih. 2017. Abdürrahim Fedai Efendi'nin *İsrade-i Cüziyye Risalesi:* Tahlil, Tercüme ve Tahkik. *Ankara Üniversitesi İlahiyat Fakültesi Dergisi* 9 (1): 133–163.

Subaşı, Nejdet. 2014. *Türkiye'de Dini Hayat Araştırması*. Ankara: DİB.

Süruri, Ahmet. 2015. İslam Düşüncesinde Süreklilik ve Değişim: Seyyid Şerif Cürcani Örneği. *İslam Araştırmaları Dergisi* 33: 147–156.

Tan, Altan. 2015. *Kürt Sorunu: Ya Tam Kardeşlik Ya Hep Birlikte Kölelik*. İstanbul: Timaş.

Tezcan, Baki. 2011. Hanafism and the Turks in al-Ṭarasūsī's Gift for the Turks (1352). *Mamluk Studies Review* 15 (1): 67–86.

Türcan, Galip. 2006. Baberti'nin el-Maksad fi İlmi'l-Kelam Başlıklı Risalesi: Tanıtım ve Tahkik. *Review of the Faculty Divinity* 2 (17): 141–166.

———. 2010. Baberti'nin Kelama Bakışı Ebu Hanife'nin Etkisi Bağlamında Bir Değerlendirme. *SUIFD* 30 (1): 7–20.

Uludağ, Süleyman. 1991. *Taftazâni, Kelam İlmi ve İslam Akaidi Şerhu'l-Akâid*. İstanbul: Dergah.

Uzunçarşılı, İsmail Hakkı. 1988. *Osmanli Devletinin Ilmiye Teskilâti*. Ankara: TTK.

Vurucu, İkbal. 2014. Din Görevlilerinin Ebu Hanife ve İmam Maturidi Hakkındaki Bilgi Düzeyleri. *A Paper Presented at the International Conference on Maturidi*, Eskişehir, April 28–30, 2014.

White, Jenny. 2013. *Muslim Nationalism and the New Turks.* Princeton and Oxford: Princeton University Press.

Woodhead, Christine. 2005. Murad III and the Historians: Representations of Ottoman Imperial Authority in Late 16th-Century Historiography. In *Legitimizing the Order: The Ottoman Rhetoric of State Order*, ed. Hakan T. Karateke and Maurus Reinkowski, 85–98. Leiden and Boston: Brill.

Yavuz, Hakan. 2011. *Erbakan'dan Erdoğan'a Laiklik, Demokrasi, Kürt Sorunu ve İslam.* Istanbul: Kitap.

Yavuz, Yusuf Şevki. 2006. Nesefi. In *İslam Ansiklopedisi Vol 32*, ed. Türkiye Diyanet Vakfı, 568–570. Ankara: TDV ISAM.

Yayla, Ahmet, Özlem Alav, Esra Kazancı, Mehmet Şirin Demir, and Mehmet Emin Usta. 2017. Medreselerde Eğitimsel Bir Geçmişi Olan Kişilerin Medrese Eğitimine İlişkin Görüşleri. *Mustafa Kemal Üniversitesi Sosyal Bilimler Dergisi* 14 (39): 486–503.

Yazıcıoğlu, M. Said. 1980. XV. XVI. Yüzyıllarda Osmanlı Medreselerinde İlm-i Kelam Öğretimi ve Genel Eğitim İçindeki Yeri. *İslam İlimleri Enstitüsü Dergisi* 4 (1): 273–283.

———. 1999. Osmanlı Dönemi Türk Kelam Bilginleri. *Yeni Türkiye* 33 (8): 176–186.

Yazır, Elmalılı Hamdi. 1971. *Hak Dini Kur'an Dili Vol. 1.* Istanbul: Eser.

Yılmaz, Mustafa, Firdevs Arı, Veli Karataş, Tuğba Kevser Uysal, Ahmet Yasin Okudan, Ayşe Macit, Dilek Menküç, Sabahattin Nayir, Emine Öğülmüş Doğa, Sümeyye Kırman, and Elif Köroğlu. 2017. *Ortaöğretim Din Kültürü ve Ahlak Bilgisi Ders Kitabı 9. Sınıf.* Ankara: MEB.

Yörükan, Yusuf Ziya, and Turhan Yörükan. 2001. *İslam Akaid Sisteminde Gelişmeler: Imam-ı Azam Ebu Hanife ve Imam Ebu Mansur-i Maturidi.* Ankara: Kültür Bakanlığı.

CHAPTER 5

Mapping the Cases: Official Islam and Islamic Movements

In a weekly radio broadcast, Esad Coşan, the late leader of an Islamic movement, raised the issue of nature with his audience:

> What is nature? Is it stone, tree or water? What is nature? It is the sum-total of all these things. But, each of these things is different from the other. Nature is like a scene. It is not a unitary being to cause something. It is the collection of things. So, referring to nature as a cause is illogical, as nothing exists as a unitary thing called nature.[1]

By introducing this argument, Coşan communicated the Ghazalian theory of movement. It might seem strange to see an Islamic leader citing al-Ghazali's ideas on nature in a radio program. However, what we observe is in fact a typical example of the reproduction and transmission of the Islamic idea of nature in a daily context. Muslims learn Islamic ideas concerning nature during their religious socialization and education. As Coşan's radio broadcast displays, any kind of Islamic activity may include engagement with the Islamic idea of nature. Therefore, such cases are the best evidence for an empirical inquiry into the interpretation and transmission of the Islamic idea of nature.

© The Author(s) 2020
G. Bacik, *Islam and Muslim Resistance to Modernity in Turkey*,
https://doi.org/10.1007/978-3-030-25901-3_5

5.1   Socialization and Ingroup Socialization

When selecting a case for this inquiry, we should consider two major dynamics in the study of Islam in the Turkish context. First, Turkey is predominantly a Muslim society. Second, its Islamic characteristics have become more visible since the early 2000s. Islamization reveals itself in a new religiously inspired political and sociological configuration, now dubbed "the new Turkey," where Islamic actors along with Islamic political and social norms have emerged to replace the previous secular ones.[2] Considering those two dynamics together, it becomes evident that in the Turkish case, religion as a social and political phenomenon should be analyzed on the levels of both *socialization* and *ingroup socialization.*

In this discussion, while socialization refers to the procedure through which people learn and internalize Islamic norms and values, ingroup socialization refers to a different type of Islamization that takes place within Islamic movements through intensive religious activism. Historically speaking, ingroup socialization has played an important role in the transmission of Islamic knowledge to the public, as well as in the Islamization of society and politics. Islamic movements have been the standard form of conducting an Islamic activism in Turkey. Ingroup socialization is different from standard socialization; the former is an intensive and enduring boundary-maintenance process.[3] Both can be effective process for transmitting knowledge. Below, I examine cases from each process—socialization and ingroup socialization—to observe how the Islamic idea of nature is reproduced and transmitted.

5.1.1   Socialization in Official Islam: The Diyanet and Compulsory Religious Courses

Socialization is the sociologically customary way by which people come to learn their religion in Turkey, a predominantly Muslim country. The socialization of the average Muslim individual, or a person who has already learned something about Islam as part of the at-home socialization process, takes place at school and in the neighborhood.

In this book, we are interested in the epistemic framework of socialization. I use "epistemic framework" to refer to the sets of ideas that a person learns in the course of socialization, which then form that person's knowledge base. If we imagine socialization within family and the narrow neighborhood as the primary socialization, then the epistemic framework is linked to secondary socialization, through which individuals acquire knowledge.[4] In Turkey, authoritative agents guide people's acquisition of religious knowledge and development of an epistemic framework. This brings us to the Diyanet and compulsory religious courses.

The Diyanet is the major organization in religious socialization. It has many opportunities to transmit its interpretation of religion as official Islam. Law 633, which sets out the legal framework of the Diyanet, provides that the institution is responsible for implementing relevant procedures and works pertaining to faith, worship, and morality. It also governs places of worship.[5] Effectively, the Diyanet enjoys a monopoly over control of officially sanctioned religion, including the formulation of faith. Over the course of time, the Diyanet has become a massive network controlling many segments of religious life. No authority other than the Diyanet is authorized to appoint an imam to a mosque, nor to any other religious office.[6]

The Diyanet is also a major agent of the reproduction and transmission of Islamic faith in Turkey. It directs Islamic socialization through religious courses where people acquire basic religious knowledge. According to official data, 745,000 students—mostly elementary and secondary schools—enrolled in Diyanet-run religious summer courses in 2014 (*Habertürk*, March 7, 2015). A survey reports that 43% of Turks participated in Diyanet courses several times during childhood. There is another large group of 25% who participated in those courses at least once.[7] The Diyanet's influence on early religious socialization is especially clear, given that 77.5% Turks get their most of religious knowledge before 13 years old.[8]

Thus, the Diyanet is the main institution shaping Islam for people across social groups.[9] There is a consensus in Turkish society that the Diyanet is the second source of religious socialization and learning after the family.[10] Even secular people who are critical of Islamic movements encounter the Diyanet's teachings. A survey demonstrated that 43% of Turks believe that Diyanet imams are the origin of their religious knowledge.[11] Thus, notwithstanding some reservations from various groups, the Diyanet holds the social legitimacy to construct religious interpretations that are widely recognized as the orthodox Sunni Islam in Turkish society. Almost 60% of people prefer to consult Diyanet's imams to get clarification on religious matters.[12]

The Diyanet constructs an Islamic episteme for Turks through its books, journals, imams, muftis, sermons, radio, and TV broadcasts. Each of these conduits has its peculiar impact. An average of 15 million people hear a Diyanet-prepared sermon each Friday at mosque (*Habertürk*, March 7, 2015). Its massive bureaucracy is important in this vein: There is one *mufti* (chief religious official) in each city. Its employees total more than 112,000.[13] A comparison of the Diyanet's budget with other institutions may give a sense of its institutional capacity; its budget for 2019 is bigger than those of several ministries, including the Ministry of Foreign Affairs and the Ministry of the Interior (*Cumhuriyet*, October 11, 2018).

The Diyanet enjoys not only social legitimacy but also bureaucratic legitimacy. All its employees are civil servants and therefore unique agents who exercise both religious and state authority. To put this in historical context: it is a continuation of the Ottoman-Turkish state tradition of defining religious orthodoxy and preserving its cooperation with religious authorities.[14] Islam as interpreted and propagated by the Diyanet is a modern incarnation of Sunni orthodoxy as promoted by the Ottoman state, a reflection of power relations governing society and religion-state relations.[15] The state expects the Diyanet is to support its agenda on any issues. For example, when the Turkish government sent troops to Syria to prevent the Kurds' from consolidating power there, the Diyanet supported the move through a Friday sermon (*Cumhuriyet*, February 16, 2018). Given such a relationship, the modern Turkish model of religion-state relations is very much like the model that Nizam al-Mulk proposed in *Siyasatnamah*.

The second case to study concerning the construction of the Islam epistemic framework in Turkey is the compulsory religious courses, where most students first encounter the Islamic idea of nature. Compulsory religious courses form a significant portion of early Islamic socialization in Turkey. Starting as early as the last year of elementary school, students receive religious education. On that account, religious courses are a formal and systematic socialization, in the classic Durkheimian sense.[16]

Religious courses are compulsory, pursuant to the 24th article of the constitution, which provides that religious education shall be conducted under state supervision. The courses fall under the purview of the Ministry of Education (not the Diyanet). The constitution also provides that religious instruction shall be included in the curricula of primary and secondary schools. As a consequence, students have religious courses from the fourth through the twelfth grade. Primary education in Turkey consists of four years of elementary school (1–4) and four years of middle school (5–8). It is followed by secondary education (high school) of 4 years (9–12). Compulsory religious courses indicate the state's interest in teaching what it deems to be the true interpretation of Islam.[17] Thus, like the Diyanet, the Ministry of Education and more broadly the Turkish State can be seen as a modern incarnation of the Ottoman system, where state plays role in interpreting and propagating religion.

5.1.2   Ingroup Socialization

Ingroup socialization happens within Islamic movements, which have their own process of alternate religious socialization. A typical Islamic movement in Turkey seeks to proselytize Islam among the people. Practically, this amounts to an agenda of Islamizing society, and even politics. Unlike the standard Islamic socialization described above, this model requires the cultivation of intense and devoted religious activism. Though the Islamic movement disseminates its religious message to the public *via* journals and radio stations, and methods such as religious gatherings, the ideal method is the expansion of group boundary by gaining new members. Accepting a movement's identity, individuals become subject to an intensive and continuous religious indoctrination as well as a perpetual engagement with the Islamic message as interpreted by the movement's leaders. Naturally, as a result of ingroup socialization, individuals self-differentiate from ordinarily socialized people as adherents of a new Islamic framework. The movement itself becomes a framing mechanism, for members interpret events to resonate with the interpretations of the other members.[18] In addition, ingroup socialization expects its members to become part of a continuous Islamic activism. Activism occurs in different ways, such as new member recruitment, financial support to the movement, or involvement in other activities deemed useful by the movement.[19] Most critically, activism for movement members is a process of both learning and transmitting the Islamic message. Thus, activism and indoctrination/knowledge are never completely separated in an Islamic movement.[20]

Turkey is a hub of many Islamic movements organized in different forms, such as movements and religious orders. In this book, I examine ingroup socialization in three movements: Işıkçılar, İskenderpaşa, and Erenköy. The main selection rationale is that these movements are typical examples of ingroup socialization with a comparatively long history reaching back to the nineteenth century origin. Each movement plays an important role in shaping the religious thinking of members. These cases can shed light on the main subject of this book: the interpretation of the Islamic idea of nature.

I have selected these cases for a number of other reasons as well.

1. These movements' impact on their followers, as well as on the public at large, has played a decisive role in the recent Islamization of Turkey. All three movements have been involved in the promotion of ideology of "new Turkey." Thus, when examining their experience, one should bear in mind that their interpretation of Islam has had practical outcomes. An analysis of their trajectories will help us understand Turkish politics, religion, and society today.

2. These movements have also been associated with many prominent and influential public figures. For instance, President R. Tayyip Erdoğan was socialized in the lodge of İskenderpaşa. Similarly, Mustafa Şentop, the speaker of the Turkish parliament, was an active member of the lodge when he was a university student.

3. Despite their substantial and enduring influence on Turkish society, these groups have not been extensively studied. Studies of Islamization in Turkey have focused on the Gülen movement or the Justice and Development Party (AKP). By including less-studied cases in the framework, it is possible to check our hypotheses from different angles, which would enhance the theoretical consistency of work in this field.

4. Finally, after the Gülen movement was declared illegal, thousands of Gülen schools and institutions were closed down, and their property was seized. These measures left a large gap to be filled by other Islamic movements.[21] Thus, the study of other cases is also timely, to get some early insights into the new dynamics of ingroup religious socialization in the post-Gülen period.

Işıkçılar, İskenderpaşa, and Erenköy operate through complex sociological and historical dynamics that they have developed since the nineteenth century. Methodologically, such dynamics are important in understanding the inner mechanisms of each group in terms of religious activism, as well as in terms of transmitting Islamic knowledge. The following section therefore reviews the history, leadership, and main ideas of each group.

5.2   İskenderpaşa

The İskenderpaşa Community (*İskenderpaşa Cemaati*) is a group affiliated with the Khalidi branch of the Naqshbandiyya. The Khalidi branch is historically been influential in Eastern Turkey, Iraq, Syria, and in the Kurd-inhabited parts of Iran. The Khalidi branch reached its height of influence in the nineteenth century, having succeeded to recruit members even among the Ottoman elites.

The founder of the Khalidi branch was Khalid al-Baghdadi (1799–1827). Al-Baghdadi elaborated a concept of political activism inspired by Ahmad al-Sirhindi (1564–1624), who is widely held to be the reviver (*mujaddid*) of the second millennium. Al-Sirhindi is credited for reviving the Naqshbandiyya by pushing the Sufis into daily life and transforming them into men of action rather than of the spirit alone.[22] Al-Sirhindi's revivalism also affected politics.[23] As a matter of fact, it was al-Sirhindi's fight against the Moghul Emperor Akbar Shah's newly designed religion that raised him to fame as the reviver of Islam.[24] Al-Sirhindi's interest in political affairs continued. Jahangir, who succeeded Akbar, appreciated al-Sirhindi's friendship. Al-Sirhindi met with the king regularly and even accompanied him on several campaigns.[25] The Naqshbandiyya's enthusiastic interest and participation in political affairs is a legacy of al-Sirhindi and al-Khalidi.

İskenderpaşa gave birth to the Islamist political movement in Turkey and thus exemplifies the Sirhindi-Khalidi tradition. The emergence of İskenderpaşa as a distinct Islamic movement started with the rise of Mehmed Zahid Kotku (1897–1980), an aspiring Islamic leader in the Naqshbandiyya. His allegiance to the Gümüşhanevi order, founded and led by Ahmed Ziyaüddin (1813–1893), marked a turning point in the history of İskenderpaşa. Like Sirhindi, Ziyaüddin was a leading figure in the major political events of his age.[26] For example, he organized influential protests against the economic regulations introduced by the 1838 Anglo-Ottoman Trade Agreement.

Naqshbandiyya protest against the Ottoman government was a rare event. Ziyaüddin believed that the agreement would open Ottoman lands to Western exploitation. Ziyaüddin incorporated economic elements into his Islamic political discourse. Later, he supported Abdulhamid II's pan-Islamist policies, again based on a religio-political narrative. His thought and activism deeply influenced later generations of Naqshibandis, including Mehmed Zahid Kotku.

Kotku first distinguished himself as a preacher in İstanbul in the 1950s. His religious activism around the İskenderpaşa Mosque gradually constructed a new group identity. In 1952, when Abdülaziz Bekkine (who led the group) passed away, Kotku became the new leader. As a charismatic figure, Kotku first strengthened the cohesion among members. His main strategy was to develop a strong network with the urban and middle class. Gradually, İskenderpaşa became popular among the newly urban, educated young Muslims, as well as with the representatives of the Muslim middle class.[27]

Religion, politics, and economy are the key concepts in Kotku's activism. As a follower of the Sirhindi-Ziyaüddin tradition, Kotku urged his followers to hold posts in all sectors of life, including politics. He formulated a new religious thinking that addressed, among other issues, political economy. As part of this thinking, Kotku defined Western economic dominance as a form of colonialism. Thus, for Kotku, Islamic activism should also focus on economic issues, mainly by developing effective links with local economic actors.[28] Beyond preaching Islamic morality, Kotku was calling for a new type of Islamic activism aimed at transforming Turkey *via* political and economic revival.

In 1969, inspired by Kotku's activism, Necmettin Erbakan established the National Order Party (NOP), the first Turkish Islamist party.[29] The NOP reflected the contemporary Naqshbandiyya's interest in politics. Sirhindi did not refrain from having close contact with Jahangir. The Khalidi order had had followers in the Ottoman bureaucracy.[30] İskenderpaşa developed the Khalidi tradition of political activism with a political party. The creation of the NOP was indeed a turning point, for İskenderpaşa became the major institution through which Turkish Islamists could gain political expertise. It was the origin of modern Turkish political Islam, out of which the AKP later evolved.

In 1971, the Constitutional Court dissolved the NOP for its antisecular activities. The National Salvation Party (NSP) was founded as the successor to the NOP in 1972. In 1974, the party joined the coalition government, and Necmettin Erbakan became the deputy prime minister. In the 1970s, the party shaped the patterns and narrative of Islamist politics.

Meanwhile, the consolidation of the Islamist party's corporate identity created a friction with İskenderpaşa, especially in the late 1970s. At its core, the rift was about the power-sharing problem between the party and the movement.[31] Kotku was unhappy about some results of the Erbakan-led political activism under the banner of an Islamic party.[32] The party was a colossal organization that communicated with the larger public, defining its own pros and cons. Thus, the İskenderpaşa movement gradually became vulnerable to risks caused by the political activism of the party itself. However, the growing rift between İskenderpaşa and the NSP was interrupted by unexpected developments: Kotku died in 1980, and the Turkish army seized control of the government in the same year. The junta dissolved the NSP. Erbakan was banned from politics.

Mahmud Esad Coşan, son-in-law of Kotku, became leader of the movement after the latter's death. Meanwhile, the Welfare Party (WP) was founded in 1983 as a follow-up of the NSP. Banned from politics, Erbakan led the WP through proxies till 1987. However, the rift between İskenderpaşa and Erbakan resumed and grew apace. This time, Erbakan demanded that religious authority follow political authority.[33] Coşan preferred a controlled separation with the WP, though he kept supporting it in elections.[34] Meanwhile, the WP was expanding beyond the boundaries of the İskenderpaşa movement. The party won the local elections in Ankara and Istanbul in 1994. R. Tayyip Erdoğan became the first Islamist mayor of Istanbul. In 1995, the WP won the parliamentary elections, and Erbakan was appointed Prime Minister.

Esad Coşan, the new leader, was an influential name within the İskenderpaşa movement even before the death of Kotku. He quickly initiated a new strategy for a balanced disengagement from politics and put more emphasis on civil society. Under his leadership, İskenderpaşa initiated new projects, such as printing journals and establishing foundations in different fields, like education, trade, and civil society activities. Coşan's priority was to reorganize İskenderpaşa at the grassroots level by transforming the movement into an urban network of civil society. *İslam*—a journal initiated under Coşan's leadership—became influential among a large group of Islamists. Its monthly circulation reached 150,000, an impressive figure by Turkish standards. İskenderpaşa also created a new journal for women, *Kadın ve Aile*, which focused on the Islamic life of urban women.

Coşan's purpose was to transform İskenderpaşa into an intellectual center where urban and educated individuals would be socialized as contributors to Turkish society. Not satisfied with the traditional narrative, he declared professionalism, expertise, and knowledge as the new principles of religious activism. It was an ambitious strategy to redefine İskenderpaşa's mission in politics and the civil services.[35] He was convinced that political activism was not conducive to generating a modern Islamic generation equipped with professional abilities. Coşan was also alert to the danger of too much engagement with a political party and worried that it would alienate his movement and inhibit good relations with different groups.

In his first article in *İslam*, Coşan wrote that education is the most important task of their mission and warned that traditional activist methods like preaching were no longer sufficient.[36] Itzchak Weisman summarized Coşan's impact on İskenderpaşa as follows:

> He turned the Iskenderpaşa mosque into the hub of educational, economic, and communications networks, while advocating peaceful adjustment to the modern state and the capitalist market. Coşan attracted wealthy businessmen and merchants, and with their help developed economic enterprises and religious endowments for the benefit of the community. His moral economic vision was propagated through his own magazines and radio station, and later also through the Internet.[37]

Coşan's educational background helps account for his civil-society oriented Islamic activism. Coşan graduated from the Department of Arabic and Persian Philology of Istanbul University in 1960. He also enrolled in a double-degree program in History of the Middle Ages and Turkish Islamic Arts. Interaction with several key scholars of the period was also decisive in Coşan's intellectual formation. Z. Velidi Togan, who played formative role in the development of the modern historical discipline in Turkey, was his professor. Another professor was Helmut Ritter, a German scholar whose studies introduced modern philology to Turkish academia. Coşan would bring up anecdotes from Ritter's classes even 40 years later.[38] Coşan also enrolled in several courses given by Muhammad Hamidullah, the renowned scholar of Islamic studies who was then teaching at Istanbul University.

After graduation, Coşan worked as a research assistant at Istanbul University. He later moved to Ankara, where he taught humanities courses at Department of Turkish Islamic Literature of the Divinity School.[39] As his biography demonstrates, Coşan had a modern education, and his interest in religious studies was developed mainly through literature, rather than Islamic sciences. His academic background informed the discourse he developed about Islamic activism, which drew heavily from multiple modern pedagogical approaches.

However, Coşan's reformist agenda was arrested by the dynamics of Turkish politics. In 1997, after the military again seized power from the Erbakan government, Coşan left Turkey and settled in Australia.[40] Out of Turkey, İskenderpaşa's activism diminished. Meanwhile, the Constitutional Court dissolved the WP in 1998, and a new group of young Islamists began its own political career under the leadership of R. Tayyip Erdoğan with a new party: the JDP. The JDP attracted huge public interest and heralded a new era in Turkish politics defined by the dominated by Islamist politics. Having observed the success of the JDP in monopolizing political power, İskenderpaşa reluctantly adopted a low profile, with the strategy of protecting its autonomy, lest the new party absorb it.

Esad Coşan died in a traffic accident in 2001, and his son, Nureddin Coşan, succeeded him as leader of İskenderpaşa. Leadership succession in Islamic groups is decided by both formal and informal dynamics. Two parameters are important in this vein: family-friendship networks and financial structure. Customarily, a person who has a central position in the family-friendship network becomes the new leader, who then takes control of the companies affiliated with the movement. Usually, Islamic movements have their own companies. The rationale is to convert the groups' social network into financial power by creating various companies in different fields. The control of companies is critical in the succession, since whoever controls the companies controls the group's economic power. In the case of İskenderpaşa, Nureddin Coşan—who had the advantage of being the son of Esad Coşan—claimed leadership and successfully took control of the financial conglomerate affiliated with the movement, that is, Server Holdings.

Though İskenderpaşa has lost its previous splendor, its historical impact upon Turkish political Islam remains crucial. It has a living legacy through many prominent Islamists who were socialized within İskenderpaşa.[41] Any inquiry into the theological foundations of Turkish Islamism requires an analysis of İskenderpaşa. Furthermore, it is an ongoing movement that keeps promoting its interpretation of Islam among the wider public. İskenderpaşa is a significant social movement where people are taught a certain brand of Islamic knowledge. A study of the epistemic framework in İskenderpaşa's interpretation of Islam will help in revealing how the Islamic idea of nature is interpreted in Turkey.

5.3   Işıkçılar

Işıkçılar is another group that follows the Naqshbandiyya order. The group traces its modern origin to Abdülhakim Arvasi (1865–1943), who joined the Naqshbandiyya in 1879. According to Işıkçılar, Arvasi was the chief representative of the Naqshbandiyya in his time. Like many other eastern scholars, Arvasi also came to İstanbul. In İstanbul, he was appointed as faculty member to *Medresetü'l-mütehassısın*, a short-lived Ottoman madrasa, which was created in 1914 as part of the last Ottoman education reforms.

After Arvasi's death, Hüseyin Hilmi Işık (1911–2001), one of his disciples, succeeded him as leader. Işık was the most critical figure in the history of the movement and even gave the group its name—"Işıkçılar" is derived from his surname and means "those of Işık" or "the Işık-ites." The group asserts continuity with the Naqshbandiyya line through the succession of Arvasi by Işık.

After graduating from military high school, Işık enrolled in the Chemistry Department of Istanbul University, graduating in 1936. Işık also met some leading German scientists who had escaped from Nazi oppression. Işık was promoted to the rank of captain in 1938. After serving in various military units, he was appointed as a teacher to Kuleli Military High School (İstanbul) in 1951. He taught chemistry there until a forced retirement after the 1960 *coup d'etat*.

Işık remained a follower of Arvasi after the two met in 1929. After Arvasi's death, Işık continued his religious education with Arvasi's son Ahmet Mekki Üçışık. Işık was later given an *ijazah* (a certificate of religious authority) by Üçışık in 1953.[42] In the late fifties, Işık wrote his first books, where he developed his method of Islamic revivalism. Işık called for a Sunni revival against several perceived threats including Communism, positivism, and the various "heretical" interpretations of Islam like Wahhabism, Shi'ism, reformism, and Islamism (including the works of Sayyid Qutb and Maududi). Arguing that all these approaches are wrong, Işık proposed a revival of Sunnism as defined in previous books of distinguished Muslim scholars. In other words, revivalism for Işık was to return to the authentic Sunni interpretation of Islam. From this perspective, alternative attempts at Islamic revival through new interpretations of Islam became unacceptable.

Işık believed that Islam needs no new interpretations and that existing opinions and books were excellent.[43] His loyalty to the previous scholars transformed his group into a conduit for the transmission of previous interpretations of Islam. Işık's books are mostly translations of previous books, but they include his comments in a confusing way, such that the reader is hard pressed to distinguish his comments from those of the original author. Since the purpose is to reconnect with the previous Islamic scholars' teachings, the result is a staunch stance against any kind of innovation in Islam.[44]

Işık was the undisputed ideologue of Işıkçılar. However, he tolerated his son-in-law Enver Ören (1939–2013), to become the de factor leader in the late 1970s. Ören was Işık's student from Kuleli Military School. After Kuleli, Ören attended the Zoology and Botany Department at Istanbul University. After graduation, he spent a year in Italy on a NATO scholarship and then returned to Istanbul University to pursue an academic career. However, in 1970, Ören resigned from the university to devote himself entirely to the activities of Işıkçılar. Ören's rise as the de facto leader introduced a new model to Işıkçılar, in which Işık was the group's spiritual tutor, and Ören was the group's executive leader. Accordingly, Ören assumed control of all group-linked companies.

The cooperation of Işık and Ören was more than a division of labor; it also symbolized the movement's transformation into a community, thus divesting its traditional appearance as an Islamic order. Now a community in appearance, Ören's suitably executive style of leadership introduced various strategies to reach the larger public. For example, the television channel controlled by Ören distinguished itself as a highly popular channel with magazine programs, which was a quite radical change, if one remembers that Işık had previously disavowed even listening music.[45]

Işıkçılar started its first newspaper, *Hakikat*, in 1970. The newspaper was renamed *Türkiye* in 1972. *Türkiye* deserves attention as an example of an Islamic group's venture into print: Its main strategy was to follow a nationalist line with a populist narrative that includes Islamic messages. Its populist approach generated broad interest, and it became the most widely circulated newspaper in Turkey in the late 1980s. In 1989, *Türkiye* put out 1.5 million daily copies, still one of the highest circulation rates in national history.[46] It was the first time that a newspaper owned by an Islamic movement became popular nationwide, having gone beyond the boundaries of the movement. Işıkçılar's expertise in media increased its ability to take its Islamic message beyond its base.

In 1993, all group-linked units were organized under the İhlas Holding, a conglomeration that has investments in a variety of fields such as education, energy, media, construction, and health.[47] In the same year, the group acquired its TV channel, where Islamic messages were broadcasted. Işıkçılar founded a bank, İhlas Finans, in 1995, marking the zenith of its financial power. At the same time, the group's transformation into a community with many financial interests strengthened its already pro-government stance. As a matter of fact, nationalism has always been a component of Işıkçılar's brand of Islamic activism. The group adopted a religio-nationalistic outlook, which is publicly recognized as the Turkish Islamic synthesis. Işık developed a peculiar narrative where the destinies of Islam and Turks are uniquely linked.

I previously offered the works of İsmail Hakkı İzmirli as an example of how Islam and Turkish culture may be linked. Like that of İzmirli, the Işık-Ören tradition defines the Turkish nation as having a special mission in the history of Islam. Işık believed that the Turks are the protectors of the Sunnism.[48] Concomitant to this Turkish Islamic synthesis is a typical feature of groups inspired by Arvasi. For instance, Necip Fazıl Kısakürek, an influential poet who popularized the Turkish Islamic synthesis, was a follower of Arvasi.[49] While commenting on the nationalistic overtones in Işıkçılar messaging, the military backgrounds of Işık and Ören are also relevant. In fact, the case of Işıkçılar is itself a rare example of an army officer acting as an ideologue of an Islamic movement.

In 2001, İhlas Finans went bankrupt, causing an unprecedented crisis of prestige for the group. Hüseyin Hilmi Işık died in the same year. The group partially recovered, thanks to the government-backed projects, at the expense of losing its autonomy from the AKP government. When Enver Ören died in 2013, Işıkçılar was still in a deep crisis, despite its support by government-backed projects. Mücahid Ören quickly took over his father's official posts within the economic conglomerates of the group, despite serious debate within the group regarding his qualifications as a religious leader. That he eventually assumed leadership reflects the decisive importance of control of the affiliated companies in the Işıkçılar succession process.

Mücahid Ören was able to consolidate power in the group for Işıkçılar had already developed a more CEO-style group leadership with Enver Ören, while Işık's books continued to provide the group's ideological framework. Enver Ören did not exert significant influence over the ideology of the group. Işıkçılar defined the reading and distributing of Işık's books as the most critical Islamic service. Furthermore, such activity was consistent with Işık's views, which held that Islam needs no new interpretation, since books by previous Islamic scholars hold all answers. Işık's books did not include any new interpretation but summarized previous scholars' books. Mücahid Ören could assume leadership of the group on account of his economic skill and CEO-style leadership in part because he did not attempt to alter the ideology of the group and continued to uphold the works of the late Işık as basis for its activities.

5.4 ERENKÖY

Erenköy, known as "Erenköy Cemaati" in Turkish, is another Islamic group that follows the Naqshbandiyya order. The group takes its name from Erenköy, a neighborhood in İstanbul where the key names of the movement have lived. The group traces its origins back to Muhammad Esed (1847–1931). Esed, who was born in Erbil, is the leader through whom Erenköy connects itself to the greater Naqshbandiyya network.

Esed came to Istanbul in 1876, and he quickly became a popular figure, developing connections with the higher Ottoman bureaucracy. He was subsequently appointed to the *Meclis-i Meşayih*, the council responsible for supervising religious orders across the empire. The Ottoman administration extended stricter control over religious orders in the nineteenth century as part of its modernization program.[50] The council was created in 1866, symbolizing increasing state control over the religious orders.[51] However, since the council was composed of members from various Islamic orders, such as the Qadiriyya and the Naqshbandiyya, it was more like a self-disciplining mechanism than an external imposition of direct state authority.

In 1883, despite his allegiance to the Khalidi order, Esed was appointed to a Qadiriyya lodge in İstanbul, since he also had a Qadiri *ijazah*. Reflecting typical Khalidi characteristics, Esed had been interested in politics since his first days in Istanbul. He supported the Young Turks against Abdulhamid II, who exiled him to his hometown, Erbil.[52] However, Esed continued political activism there by organizing local networks against the increasing British influence in the region.[53] Esed died in 1931, leaving behind a legacy of strong political activism.

Mahmud Sami Ramazanoğlu (1892–1984), a graduate of the School of Law at Istanbul University, emerged as the new leader of the movement in the 50s. Ramazanoğlu worked as an accountant in various Anatolian cities, where he developed contacts with merchants. In 1954, he returned to İstanbul and stayed there till 1979, when he moved to Medina, where he lived until his death in 1984. Ramazanoğlu's leadership marked the crystallization of Erenköy as a differentiated group within the Naqshbandiyya tradition. Ramazanoğlu emphasized the spiritual development of the group's followers. Unlike Esed, Ramazanoğlu preferred a quiet life and was not interested in political affairs.[54] However, his close contacts, particularly with merchants, gave Erenköy a sophisticated network of economic actors across the country. Under Ramazanoğlu, the group advanced a distinctive brand of Islamic activism targeting the merchant class.

After Ramazanoğlu's death, Musa Topbaş (1916–1999) became the new leader. Topbaş had no university education. Instead, his father arranged for him to study informally under a series of famous intellectuals. For example, he studied under Elmalılı H. Yazır, who wrote the Qur'anic exegesis at the request of Turkish parliament (and upon Atatürk's initiative). Another prominent name among his private tutors was Hamid Aytaç, who was dubbed the greatest calligrapher of the period. The private courses included also French, taught by a local Jewish instructor.

Musa Topbaş continued the merchant-oriented mentality of Islamic activism. Under his leadership, Erenköy established many, as did other Islamic groups like İskenderpaşa and Işıkçılar. In the 1980s, Erenköy also created various new institutions, such as its journal, schools, and a publishing house. After Ramazanoğlu, who had focused on the crystallization of the group's message, Musa Topbaş achieved the institutional consolidation of Erenköy.

When Musa Topbaş passed away, his son Osman Nuri Topbaş emerged as the new leader of Erenköy. Osman Nuri Topbaş was born in 1942 in Erenköy and attended İmam-Hatip High School. Some of his teachers at high school were influential names such as Nureddin Topçu and Mahir İz, who are recognized as leading ideologues of Islamic thought in Turkey. Nureddin Topçu was particularly influential over the young Osman Nuri. Topçu received his doctorate in philosophy from the Sorbonne. He aimed to develop a moral philosophy based on Anatolian traditions.[55] Topçu's model linked Islam and Turkish identity as interdependent phenomena.[56] Under the deep influence of Henry Bergson, Topçu became a leading scholar who influenced all sorts of religious, nationalist, and conservative groups in Turkey. His ability to merge Islamic and European ideas was a major reason for his appeal among Islamic actors who appreciated the references to Western philosophy in his Islamic discourse.

As is apparent in his books, Osman Nuri Topbaş elaborates Islam as a structured philosophical discourse. Reflecting Topçu's legacy, Topbaş quotes Western philosophers to support his arguments. He wants to construct his own philosophical narrative while interpreting Islam. However, on the other hand, what we observe in the case of Osman Nuri Topbaş is a continuation of the Erenköy tradition, where the group elites have always been in close contact with the urban and well-educated Islamic elites. Erenköy has always been controlled by urban and upper-middle-class families.

As an influential group that links and mobilizes sophisticated network of merchants, Erenköy's approach to politics is contested. Erenköy has developed a balanced relationship with diverse political groups.[57] However, the impact of Erenköy on middle-class merchants has consistently attracted the interest of political actors. For example, Eymen Topbaş, a member of Topbaş family, occupied high-level administrative positions in the Motherland Party of Turgut Özal in the 1980s. However, the group has recently become more popular, particularly as a result of its close relations between Recep Tayyip Erdoğan and some prominent members of the Topbaş family. For example, Mustafa Latif Topbaş, a famous Turkish billionaire, is very close to Erdoğan.

Similarly, several other family members are known for their economic relations with politicians in the AKP. Companies owned by those members have won many government contracts. However, there is no perfect overlap between the Topbaş family and Erenköy. The clarification of the boundary between Erenköy and the Topbaş family in regard of the complex relations between religion and politics is beyond the limits of this study. However, the recent political activism of several family members has transformed the image of Erenköy, giving the impression that the group is deviating from its previous strategy of keeping a low profile politically.[58]

With full support from the ruling government, Erenköy has been able to mobilize many different elements within society. It is the Islamic group most favored by the government. Its status calls to mind the relationship between İskenderpaşa and the NSP, or the WP, in the 1970s and 1980s. As a result of the group's privileged status, Osman Nuri Topbaş has an unparalleled political legitimacy among political elites, which in turn creates many opportunities for the group's members. For example, many members of the group have recently been appointed to critical posts at Diyanet. Thus, what we see in Erenköy today is an Islamic group at its peak of influence.

5.5   THE REVIVALIST-RENEWALIST AXIS

We can classify as *revivalists* those Islamic movements that argue that the problems facing Muslims today emerge from their un-Islamic lifestyles, and that the solution is to bring Muslims back to Islam. We can classify as *renewalists* those who call for a new interpretation of Islam without completely rejecting the previous interpretations. Finally, we can classify as *reformists* those who believe that a radical agenda of religious reform is required, one that touches even the essential doctrines of Sunni Islam. Neither İskenderpaşa nor Işıkçılar nor Erenköy is reformist. These three groups stand somewhere between revivalism and renewalism. (The two other cases, Diyanet and compulsory religious courses, are excluded here, for they are embodiments of Sunni orthodoxy. In both cases, we observe the reproduction of Sunni Islamic theology supported by political authority.) (Table 5.1).

The Islamic tradition has mostly been skeptical to the idea of religious reform. That approach defines reformation as a distortion, based on an Islamic view of Western history, where the Reformation is defined as a distortion of original Christianity.[59] Besides, it emphasizes institutional differences between Islam and Christianity, arguing that since Islam has no "Catholic-style clerical class answering to a divinely appointed pope," it cannot undergo a similar reform.[60] According to Hüseyin Atay, an influential Turkish scholar of Islamic studies, such a reading of the Protestant Reformation was a result of ignorance of European history.[61] Based on a misreading of the Christian Reformation as a distortion of the very essence of religion (i.e. not just as a challenge to the authority of the Catholic Church), reform was understood to have the intention of changing the fundamentals of faith and was therefore rejected by many Islamic groups. Academics like Atay also remind that the Reformation was also about proposing new ideas that go beyond merely challenging the institutional powers of the Catholic Church.[62] Accordingly, reformists' ideas on various theological concepts such as free will—also relevant to this book—were also important issues through which they tried to realize their reformist agenda.[63]

Table 5.1 Classifying the Islamic movements

	Muslims' practice	Interpretation of Islam
Revivalist school	Problem is here	
Renewalist school		Problem is here

All three groups examined in this book take themselves to adhere to Sunni orthodoxy but occupy different positions along the spectrum revivalism and renewalism. They all recognize the theological framework of Sunni Islam as legitimate. They vehemently reject accounts that hold that Sunni Islam emerged through a historical process. Rather, they believe that true Islam has been constant in essence and does not bend to changing conditions. Consequently, they equate any reformist attempts that seek to disturb the Sunni orthodoxy with modernist efforts to shake the very foundations of Islam.

In this context, Işıkçılar stands as a radical revivalist: Hüseyin Hilmi Işık frequently stated that Islam is perfect, not subject to historical change, and has to be practiced without any new interpretation. He held that there was no need for new reasoning in Islam, since there is nothing left unexplained.[64] Işık stresses that his books do not contain any new interpretations and are simply collections of the work of previous scholars.[65] The root of Işık's radical revivalism is the belief in Islam's perfect transmission through history with no change, not even in interpretations based on cultural differences. For Işık, historical conditions have no ability to penetrate Islam, as it is ahistorical.

Having stated that "everything about religion comes from the Prophet," Işık swore that not even the Umayyad Caliphs did anything to change the religion.[66] Işık gives the Umayyads as a tactical example that proves that Islam has remained unchanged, because many Islamic scholars see them as a symbol of innovation in religion. Işık is confident that the Islam he promotes is the Prophet's Islam. Işık's perspective equation of Islam and Sunni orthodoxy excludes the possibility of any legitimate reformist thought.

İskenderpaşa is also a revivalist movement. However, compared with Işıkçılar, it is more open to renewalism. We do not observe in İskenderpaşa the Işıkçılar brand of radical rejection of new interpretations. Coşan's works do not emphasize the pure transmission of Islam through previous scholars. These works exhibit an openness to the role of historical and cultural factors in influencing the interpretation of Islam. However, this does not amount to an acceptance that historical dynamics are formative in Islam; Coşan still maintains that the Islamic tradition has retained its essence. However, Coşan accepts that people are interested in different interpretations of Islam based on particular circumstances and that, as a result, the genuine Islamic tradition has been polluted by various interpretations.[67] Thus, Coşan's method invites a critical engagement with Islamic literature in order to discern legitimate and illegitimate interpretations.

Erenköy's position on the revivalism-renewalism spectrum is less clear. The movement is in a process of moving toward a renewalist position and away from its original revivalism. There is no Işıkçılar brand of radical revivalism in Erenköy. In principle, Osman Nuri Topbaş is against new reasoning in religion.[68] On the other hand, in practice, we cannot but note that Topbaş seems to engage in new reasoning in his books.[69] Without explicitly presenting his discussions as new reasoning, Topbaş nevertheless expands the theological framework of Erenköy, which should be seen as a gradual departure from the revivalist lines of M. Sami Ramazanoğlu and Musa Topbaş. However, this slow progression toward renewalism should not be taken as a sign that the group has accepted reformism.

5.6   THE MATURIDI-ASH'ARI DEBATE

Theological schools are relevant when examining how Islam is interpreted by each group. It is therefore important to know how each group positions itself in the Maturidi-Ash'ari theological debate.

Işıkçılar defines itself as Hanafi and Maturidi.[70] Accordingly, it holds that the Hanafi *madhhab* is better than other Islamic schools.[71] The group believes that Abu Hanifa is not only the imam of Hanafis, but also of all Sunni Muslims.[72] Moreover, Abu Hanifa is the leader of all Sunni scholars.[73] To prove his superiority, Işık claims that Abu Hanifa "owns" three-quarters of the whole of Islamic knowledge.[74]

Işık does not approach Abu Hanifa as simply a great jurist who contributed to the formation of Islamic law. Rather, he perceives him to be a sacred figure with a divine mission. His mystic approach is visible, for example, when he claims that Jesus will follow Abu Hanifa's School once he returns from the heavens in the latter days.[75]

When it comes to Maturidism, Işık sees it as branch of the Hanafi *madhhab* rather than an independent school of theology.[76] Reflecting the traditional Ottoman ambiguity, Işık rejects the view that the differences between the Ash'ari and the Maturidi schools are important. Thus, while Işık opposes crossing the boundaries between the different Islamic schools of law—an act he considers heretical[77]—he is flexible when it comes to the border between Ash'ari and Maturidi theology. Reflecting his radical revivalism, Işık claims that neither al-Ash'ari nor al-Maturidi founded new schools; rather, what they did was to systematize the interpretations of early Muslims in different ways.[78] Linking Turks with the Hanafi-Maturidi tradition, Işık defines Turks as the protectors of Sunnism, affirming the Turkish cultural thesis.[79]

The confessional identity of İskenderpaşa is also Hanafi and Maturidi.[80] The differences between the Maturidi and the Ash'ari schools are again dismissed as minor disagreements. In a book on theology, Mehmed Zahid Kotku presented the general features of Sunni Islam according to Maturidi and Ash'ari and did not even mention the differences between the two thinkers' systems, wring as if there was consensus on all issues.[81] The traditional Ottoman-Turkish syncretism is thus visible in the ideology of İskenderpaşa. İskenderpaşa also affirms the Turkish cultural thesis and holds that the Turks preferred Islam for its compatibility with their values.[82]

Erenköy also takes Hanafism as its confessional identity. Osman Nuri Topbaş presents Abu Hanifa as "one of the greatest jurists the world has ever seen."[83] However, there is no direct mention of Maturidism in Topbaş's writings. Instead, Maturidism is understood as a part of Hanafism. Furthermore, in contrast to İskenderpaşa and Işıkçılar, Erenköy does not affirm the Turkish cultural thesis. Topbaş argues that that before Islam, Turks held a low position in the annals of history. Topbaş gives the example of Attila (the Hun) as a Turk who left only bloodshed and tears. It was Islam that changed the Turks into a civilized people.[84]

The Diyanet and Ministry of Education are not intended to have any confessional identity. The Diyanet presents itself as neutral with respect to the four schools of Sunni Islamic law.[85] However, if we imagine Diyanet as consisting of concentric ideological circles, there is no doubt that the outer circle is Sunni Islam, and the inner circle is Hanafism. Practically speaking, Diyanet teachings are based on Sunni Islam and the Hanafi *madhhab*. However, the Diyanet presents its Hanafi-dominated approach as a reflection of Turkey's demographic balance rather than as a doctrinal preference. Similarly, with regard to Islamic theology, in its catechism books the Diyanet defines itself as an adherent of the "an *ahl al-Sunna* school that follows the opinions of imam al-Maturidi."[86] Again, this is presented as a demographic reality rather than a doctrinal choice. Thus, Ash'arism is not emphasized as much as Maturidism in Diyanet materials. Also, with reference to Maturidism, the Diyanet's narrative stresses cultural dynamics and the special link between the Turks and Maturidi theology. For example, the rational nature of Maturidi's theology is attributed to the school's roots in Transoxiana.[87]

When it comes to religious textbooks, Abu Hanifa is presented undisputedly as the most influential scholar there.[88] He is presented as the key figure in shaping the Turks' relations with Islam and in spreading Islam among them. Abu Hanifa is credited for proving Islam's ability to solve humanity's problems in every age by systemizing the religion into a school of law.[89] Al-Maturidi comes second; he is presented as a follower of Abu Hanifa's theological teachings.[90] All textbooks also accept the narrative that presents Hanafi-Maturidi tradition as the most suitable theology for Turks. Accordingly, Abu Hanifa's moderate interpretation of Islam facilitated the Turk's adoption of and adherence to Islam.[91] Textbooks' emphasis on flexibility and practicability reflects the traditional Turkish approach to Hanafism as an accommodating school of law.

It is possible to detect the traditional Ottoman syncretic approach in the textbooks that are used in compulsory religious courses. Al-Maturidi is presented along with al-Ash'ari, for both are credited with playing important roles in systematizing the Islamic faith on the basis of reason and in defending Islam against heretic opinions.[92] They are presented as two figures who shared the same purpose, and there is no reference to their differences. In general, al-Ash'ari and al-Shafi'i are also presented as important figures in the formation of Turks' understanding of Islam.[93] But they occupy less space and receive less attention than Abu Hanafi and al-Maturidi. Like the Diyanet materials, the textbooks emphasize that Hanafism is the demographically and geographically dominant school in Turkey and explain that the Shafi'i School is dominant only in the "Eastern part of Anatolia."[94]

5.7   Conclusion

In this chapter, I have examined five cases, which I picked up to illustrate how the Islamic idea of nature is reproduced and transmitted in contemporary Turkey. In the following chapter, I will analyze the reproduction and transmission of the Islamic idea of nature in each case. As I have already underscored, the Islamic idea of nature is central to the interpretation of Islam propagated by each case. The agents of Islamic socialization and ingroup socialization in Turkey are very eager to transmit their particular version of the idea of nature to individuals who become the subjects of their Islamic activism. Thus, Islamic law does not monopolize the content of these five cases' religious narratives; each is also concerned with the idea of nature.

Notes

1. Coşan, *Hazineden Pırıltılar 3*, 243.
2. Waldman and Çalışkan, *The New Turkey and Its Discontents*, 83–118.
3. Barth, "Introduction," 15.

4. Long and Hadden, "A Reconception of Socialization," 43.
5. Kara, "Diyanet İşleri Başkanlığı," 47.
6. Gözaydın, *Diyanet Türkiye Cumhuriyeti'nde Dinin Tanzimi*, 1–24.
7. KONDA, *Diyanet İşleri Başkanlığı Araştırması*, 33.
8. Subaşı, *Türkiye'de Dini Hayat Araştırması*, 112.
9. On popular religion see: Teiser, "Popular Religion," 378.
10. Subaşı, *Türkiye'de Dini Hayat Araştırması*, 122.
11. Ibid., 113.
12. Ibid., 139.
13. Diyanet İşleri Başkanlığı, "İstatistikler", Accessed October 11, 2018. https://www.Diyanet.gov.tr/tr-TR/Kurumsal/Detay//6/Diyanet-isleri-baskanligi-istatistikleri.
14. Erdem, "Religious Services in Turkey," 199.
15. Kara, "Din ve Devlet Arasına Sıkışmış Bir Kurum," 29. Bardakoğlu, "'Moderate perception of Islam," 367–375.
16. Durkheim, *Education and Sociology*, 124.
17. Cesari, *The Awakening of Muslim Democracy*, 89.
18. Munson, "Islamic Mobilization," 500.
19. Tuğal, "Transforming Everyday Life," 423–458.
20. Sadiki, "Political Islam Theoretical Underpinnings," 2.
21. E. Cornell, "Headed East: Turkey's Education System," 52.
22. Buehler, "Ahmad Sirhindi," 141–162.
23. Weismann, *The Naqshbandiyya Orthodoxy*, 55.
24. Habib, "The Political Role of Sheikh Ahmad Sirhindi," 22–25.
25. Ansari, *Sufism and Shari'ah*, 29.
26. Gümüşhanevi, *Müceddid Risalesi*, 13.
27. Yaşar, "Mehmet Zahid Kotku," 328.
28. Mardin, "The Nakshibendi Order of Turkey," 222–223.
29. Yavuz, *Modernleşen Müslümanlar*, 279.
30. Tosun, "Nakşibendiyye," 652.
31. The rift was a typical one that reminds of confessional parties' experience with the church in the West. See: Kalyvas, *The Rise of Christian Democracy in Europe*, 24.
32. Yaşar, "Dergah'tan Parti'ye," 331.
33. Çakır, *Ne Şeriat Ne Demokrasi*, 60.
34. Çakır, *Ayet ve Slogan*, 37.
35. Mardin, *Türkiye, İslam ve Sekülerizm*, 189. Yaşar, "Esad Coşan," 332.
36. Coşan, "Gayemiz," 3.
37. Weisman, *The Naqshbandiyya Orthodoxy*, 153–154.
38. Coşan, *Hazineden Pırıltılar 3*, 485.
39. Erkaya, "Mahmud Es'ad Coşan'ın Hayatı," 32–34.
40. Bacik and Aras, "Exile: A Keyword in Understanding Turkish Politics," 487–406.

41. Özel, "Political Islam and Islamic Capital," 151.
42. Işık, *Tam İlmihal*, 4.
43. Tekin, "Işıkçılık," 344.
44. Mardin, *Türkiye'de Din ve Siyaset Makaleler 3*, 30. Karabiber compared *Işıkçılar* with the Lebanese Islamic movement *Ahbash*. See: Karabiber, "Lübnan Merkezli Çağdaş İslamî Bir Cemaat," 117–142. Another similarity is both groups' reaction to political Islam. However, *Işıkçılar* lowered their reaction to political Islam after the rise of the JDP. On Al-Ahbash brand of anti-Islamism see: Hamzeh and Dekmejian, "A Sufi Response to Political Islamism," 217–229.
45. Taslaman, *Küreselleşme Sürecinde Türkiye'de İslam*, 278.
46. Groc, "L'évolution de la presse écrite turque," 110.
47. Öztürk, "The Islamist Big Bourgeoisie in Turkey," 131.
48. Işık, *Faideli Bilgiler*, 200.
49. Kısakürek, *O ve Ben*, 112.
50. The relations between the Ottomans and the Naqshbandiyya had many ebbs and flows. See: Weismann, *Taste of Modernity*, 78.
51. Yılmaz, "Esad Erbili," 348.
52. Yavuz, *Modernleşen Müslümanlar*, 196. Çetinsaya, "The Caliph and the Shaykhs," 105.
53. Göktaş, "Es'ad Erbili ve Düşünceleri," 346.
54. Tosun, "Mahmut Sami Ramazanoğlu," 442.
55. Topçu's book *İsyan Ahlakı* is a key reference book, especially among conservative elites in Turkey. It is a Turkish translation of his PhD thesis, which was titled "*conformisme et révolte*". See: Topçu, *İsyan Ahlakı*.
56. Aydoğdu, "Ahlak Filozofu" ve "Hareket Adamı"," 439–463.
57. No mention of politics is found in the biography of Ramazanoğlu written by Musa Topbaş. Topbaş, *Sultan al-'Arifin*, 46–68. Also see: Çakır, *Ayet ve Slogan*, 58–59.
58. Efe, *Dini Gruplar Sosyolojisi*, 165–166.
59. Ozcan, "İslam'da Protestanlaşma Olmaz", 478.
60. Hasan, "Why Islam Doesn't Need a Reformation".
61. Atay, "Dinde Reform," 4.
62. Bernard, *A History of Christian Doctrine*, 27–28.
63. Trinkaus, "The Problem of Free Will," 303.
64. Işık, *Faideli Bilgiler*, 191.
65. Hüseyin Hilmi Işık, "Introduction," in al-Baghdadi, *Belief and Islam*, 3.
66. Süveydi, *Hak Sözün Vesikaları*, 153.
67. Coşan, *Tabakatü's-Sufiyye Sohbetleri 1*, 30–31.
68. Topbaş, *The Islamic Approach*, 5.
69. Topbaş, *Sufism A Path Towards The Internalization of Faith*, 64.
70. Izniki, *Miftah-ul Janna*, 23–24.

71. Işık, *Faideli Bilgiler*, 18.
72. Işık, *The Sunni Path*, 5.
73. *"ehli sünnet alimlerinin reisi"*. Işık, "Önsöz," in Müceddidi, *Dürr-ül Me'arif*, 3.
74. Işık, *Tam İlmihal*, 49.
75. Işık, *Kıymetsiz Yazılar*, 165.
76. Işık, *Tam İlmihal*, 1094. Hadimi, *İslam Ahlakı*, 192.
77. Hadimi, *İslam Ahlakı*, 201.
78. Işık, *Tam İlmihal*, 491. al-Baghdadi, *Belief and Islam*, 102.
79. Işık, *Faideli Bilgiler*, 47, 200.
80. Coşan, *Tabakatü's-Sufiyye Sohbetleri 1*, 347, 429. Kotku, *Ehl-i Sünnet Akaidi*, 16.
81. Kotku, *Ehl-i Sünnet Akaidi*, 141.
82. Coşan, *Hazineden Pırıltılar 4*, 223.
83. Topbaş, *Sufism*, 226. Topbaş, *Civilization of Virtues 2*, 416.
84. Topbaş, *Islam Spirit and Form*, 20.
85. Karaman, Bardakoğlu and Apaydın, *Ilmihal 1*, 44.
86. Ibid., 26.
87. Ibid.
88. Özdemir, *İlköğretim Din Kültürü ve Ahlak Bilgisi 6*, 121.
89. Pınarbaşı, *Ortaöğretim Din Kültürü ve Ahlak Bilgisi 9*, 111.
90. Yılmaz and et al., *Ortaöğretim Din Kültürü ve Ahlak Bilgisi 9*, 115.
91. Özdemir, *İlköğretim Din Kültürü ve Ahlak Bilgisi 6*, 122.
92. Ibid.
93. Pınarbaşı, *Ortaöğretim Din Kültürü ve Ahlak Bilgisi 9*, 111.
94. Yılmaz and et al., *Ortaöğretim Din Kültürü ve Ahlak Bilgisi 9*, 116.

REFERENCES

al-Baghdadi. 2015. Mawlana Diya ad-Din Khalid. *Belief and Islam: The Annotated Translation of Itiqadname [I'tiqad-nama]*. Translated by H.H. Işık. Istanbul: Hakikat.

Ali, Mubarak. 1996. *Ulema, Sufis and Intellectuals*. Lahore: Fiction House.

Ansari, Muhammad Abdul Hag. 1986. *Sufism and Shari'ah: A Study of Shaykh Ahmad Sirhindi's Effort to Reform Sufism*. Leicester: The Islamic Foundation.

Atay, Hüseyin. 2001. Dinde Reform. *Ankara Üniversitesi İlahiyat Fakültesi Dergisi* 43 (1): 1–26.

Aydoğdu, Hüseyin. 2009. 'Ahlak Filozofu' ve 'Hareket Adamı' Olarak Nurettin Topçu. *Türkiyat Araştırmaları Enstitüsü Dergisi* 40 (1): 439–463.

Bacik, Gokhan, and Bulent Aras. 2002. Exile: A Keyword in Understanding Turkish Politics. *The Muslim World* 92 (3/4): 387–406.

Bardakoğlu, Ali. 2004. 'Moderate Perception of Islam' and the Turkish Model of the Diyanet: The President's Statement. *Journal of Muslim Minority Affairs* 24 (2): 367–375.

Barth, Fredrick. 1969. Introduction. In *Ethnic Groups and Boundaries: The Social Organization of Culture Difference*, ed. Fredrick Barth, 9–38. Long Grove: Waveland.

Bernard, David K. 1996. *A History of Christian Doctrine: The Reformation to the Holiness Movement A. D. 1500–1900 Vol. 2*. Hazelwood: WAP Press.

Buehler, Arthur. 2012. Ahmad Sirhindi: Nationalist Hero, Good Sufi, or Bad Sufi? In *South Asian Sufis: Devotion, Deviation and Destiny*, ed. Clinton Bennet and Charles M. Ramsey, 141–162. London: Continuum.

Çakır, Ruşen. 1990. *Ayet ve Slogan: Türkiye'de İslami Oluşumlar*. Istanbul: Metis.

———. 1994. *Ne Şeriat Ne Demokrasi: Refah Partisi'ni Anlamak*. Istanbul: Metis.

Cesari, Jocelyne. 2014. *The Awakening of Muslim Democracy: Religion, Modernity and the State*. New York: Cambridge University Press.

Çetinsaya, Gökhan. 2005. The Caliph and the Shaykhs: Abdülhamid II's Policy towards the Qadiriyya of Mosul. In *Ottoman Reform and Muslim Regeneration*, ed. Itzchak Weismann and Fruma Zachs, 97–108. New York: I. B. Tauris.

Cornell, Svante E. 2018. Headed East: Turkey's Education System. *Turkish Policy Quarterly* 16 (4): 47–67.

Coşan, M. Esad. 1983. Gayemiz. *İslam* 1 (1): 3–5.

———. 2016a. *Hazineden Pırıltılar 3*. Ankara: M. Erkaya.

———. 2016b. *Hazineden Pırıltılar 4*. Ankara: M. Erkaya.

———. 2016c. *Tabakatü's-Sufiyye Sohbetleri 1*. Ankara: M. Erkaya.

Durkheim, Emile. 1956. *Education and Sociology*. New York: The Free Press.

Efe, Adem. 2013. *Dini Gruplar Sosyolojisi*. Istanbul: Dönem.

Emrullah, Ali bin, and Muhammad Hadimi. 2014. *İslam Ahlakı*. Istanbul: Hakikat.

Erdem, Gazi. 2008. Religious Services in Turkey: From the Office of Şeyhülislam to the *Diyanet*. *The Muslim World* 98 (2/3): 199–215.

Erkaya, M. Zahid. 2014. Mahmud Es'ad Coşan'ın Hayatı, Eserleri ve Tasavvuf Görüşleri. MA thesis, Ankara University.

Göktaş, Vahit. 2015. Es'ad Erbili ve Düşünceleri. In *Doğu'dan Batı'ya Düşüncenin Serüveni Medeniyet Projelerinin İnşa Sürecinde Çağdaş İslam Düşüncesi Vol. 9*, ed. Selim Eren and Ali Öztürk, 345–370. Istanbul: İnsan.

Gözaydın, İştar. 2009. *Diyanet: Türkiye Cumhuriyeti'nde Dinin Tanzimi*. Istanbul: İletişim.

Groc, Gerart. 1991. L'évolution de la presse écrite turque au cours de la décennie 1980. *CEMOTI* 11 (1): 89–118.

Gümüşhanevi, Ahmed Ziyaüddin. 2006. *Müceddid Risalesi, Vasiyetler ve Nasihatler*. Istanbul: Vuslat.

Habib, Irfan M. 1961. The Political Role of Sheikh Ahmad Sirhindi and Shah Waliullah. *Indian History Congress: Proceedings of the Twenty-third Session*, Calcutta, 209–223.

Hamzeh, A. Nizar, and R. Hrair Dekmejian. 1996. A Sufi Response to Political Islamism: Al-Aḥbash of Lebanon. *International Journal of Middle East Studies* 28 (2): 217–229.

Hasan, Mehdi. 2015. Why Islam Doesn't Need a Reformation. *The Guardian*, May 15. https://www.theguardian.com/commentisfree/2015/may/17/islam-reformation-extremism-muslim-martin-luther-europe

Işık, Hüseyin Hilmi. 2014a. *Faideli Bilgiler*. Istanbul: Hakikat.

———. 2014b. *Kıymetsiz Yazılar*. Istanbul: Hakikat.

———. 2014c. *Tam İlmihal Se'adet-i Ebediyye*. Istanbul: Hakikat.

———. 2015. *The Sunni Path*. Istanbul: Hakikat.

İzniki, Muhammad bin Qutbuddin. 2014. *Miftah al-Jannah*. Istanbul: Hakikat.

Kalyvas, Stathis N. 1996. *The Rise of Christian Democracy in Europe*. London: Cornell University Press.

Kara, İsmail. 2000. Din ve Devlet Arasına Sıkışmış Bir Kurum: Diyanet İşleri Başkanlığı. *Marmara İlahiyat Fakültesi Dergisi* 18 (1): 29–55.

———. 2005. Diyanet İşleri Başkanlığı. In *İslamcılık*, ed. Yasin Aktay, Tanıl Bora, and Murat Gültekingil, 45–66. Istanbul: İletişim.

Karabiber, N. Kemal. 2011. Lübnan Merkezli Çağdaş İslamî Bir Cemaat: AbdullâSerhendi el-Habeşî ve Ahbâş Cemaati. *Harran Üniversitesi İlahiyat Fakültesi Dergisi* 26 (2): 117–142.

Karaman, Hayreddin, Ali Bardakoğlu, and H. Yunus Apaydın. 1998. *Ilmihal 1*. Ankara: Diyanet İşleri Başkanlığı.

Kısakürek, Necip Fazıl. 2011. *O ve Ben*. Istanbul: Büyük Doğu.

KONDA. 2014. *Diyanet İşleri Başkanlığı Araştırması*. Istanbul: Konda.

Kotku, Mehmed Zahid. 1992. *Ehl-i Sünnet Akaidi*. Istanbul: Seha.

Long, Theodore E. Long, and Jeffrey K. Hadden. 1985. A Reconception of Socialization. *Sociological Theory* 3 (1): 39–49.

Mardin, Şerif. 1993. The Nakshibendi Order of Turkey. In *Fundamentalisms and Society*, ed. Martin E. Marty and R. Scott Appelby, 204–233. Chicago: University of Chicago Press.

———. 2012. *Türkiye, İslam ve Sekülerizm*. Istanbul: İletişim.

———. 2015. *Türkiye'de Din ve Siyaset Makalalar 3*. Istanbul: İletişim.

Müceddidi, Rauf Ahmed. 1998. *Dürr-ül Me'arif*. Istanbul: Hakikat.

Munson, Ziad. 2001. Islamic Mobilization: Social Movement Theory and the Egyptian Muslim Brotherhood. *The Sociological Quarterly* 42 (4): 487–510.

Özcan, Azmi. 2005. İslam'da Protestanlaşma Olmaz. *İslami Araştırmalar Dergisi*. 18 (4): 477–478.

Özdemir, Safiye. 2017. *İlköğretim Din Kültürü ve Ahlak Bilgisi 6*. Ankara: Dörtel.

Özel, Işık. 2010. Political Islam and Islamic Capital: The Case of Turkey. In *Religion and Politics in Europe, the Middle East and Africa*, ed. Jeffrey Haynes, 139–161. New York: Routledge.

Öztürk, Özgür. 2017. The Islamist Big Bourgeoisie in Turkey. In *The Neoliberal Landscape: The Rise of Islamist Capital in Turkey*, ed. Neşecan Balkan, Erol Balkan, and Ahmet Öncü, 117–141. New York: Berghahn.

Pınarbaşı, Bekir. 2016. *Ortaöğretim Din Kültürü ve Ahlak Bilgisi 9*. Ankara: Tutku.

Potter, G.R. 2008. *Zwingli*. London and New York: Cambridge University Press.

Sadiki, Larbi. 2011. Political Islam Theoretical Underpinnings. In *Interregional Challenges of Islamic Extremist Movements in North Africa*, ed. Muna Abdalla, 1–29. Pretoria: ISS.

Subaşı, Nejdet. 2014. *Türkiye'de Dini Hayat Araştırması*. Ankara: DİB.

Süveydi, E. Abdullah. 2014. *Hak Sözün Vesikaları*. Istanbul: Hakikat.

Taslaman, Caner. 2011. *Küreselleşme Sürecinde Türkiye'de İslam*. Istanbul: Istanbul Yayınevi.

Teiser, Stephen F. 1995. Popular Religion. *The Journal of Asian Studies* 54 (2): 378–395.

Tekin, Mustafa. 2005. Işıkçılık. In *İslamcılık*, ed. Yasin Aktay, Tanıl Bora, and Murat Gültekingil, 341–344. Istanbul: İletişim.

Topbaş, Musa. 2007. *Sultan al-'Arifin: Shaikh Mahmud Sami Ramazanoğlu the Sultan of Gnostics*. Istanbul: Erkam.

Topbaş, Osman Nuri. 2006. *Islam Spirit and Form*. Istanbul: Erkam.

———. 2009. *Civilization of Virtues 2*. Istanbul: Erkam.

———. 2012. *Sufism: A Path Towards the Internalization of Faith*. Istanbul: Erkam.

———. 2016. *The Islamic Approach to Reasoning and Philosophy*. Istanbul: Erkam.

Topçu, Nurettin. 2016. *İsyan Ahlakı*. Istanbul: Dergah.

Tosun, Necdet. 2011. Mahmut Sami Ramazanoğlu. In *İslam Ansiklopedisi Vol. 34*, ed. Türkiye Diyanet Vakfı, vol. 442. Ankara: TDV ISAM.

———. 2015. Nakşibendiyye. In *Türkiye'de Tarikatlar: Tarih ve Kültür*, ed. Semih Ceyhan, 611–692. Istanbul: İSAM.

Trinkaus, Charles. 1949. The Problem of Free Will in the Renaissance and the Reformation. *Journal of the History of Ideas* 10 (1): 51–62.

Tuğal, Cihan. 2009. Transforming Everyday Life: Islamism and Social Movement Theory. *Theory and Society* 38 (5): 423–458.

Waldman, Simon, and Emre Çalışkan. 2016. *The New Turkey and Its Discontents*. London: C. Hurst & Co.

Weismann, Itzchak. 2000. *Taste of Modernity: Sufism, Salafiyya, and Arabism in Late Ottoman Damascus*. Leiden: Brill.

———. 2007. *The Naqshbandiyya Orthodoxy and Activism in a Worldwide Sufi Tradition*. London and New York: Routledge.

Yaşar, M. Emin. 2005a. Dergah'tan Parti'ye, Vakıf'tan Şirkete Bir Kimliğin Oluşmuu ve Dönüşümü İskenderpaşa Cemaati. In *İslamcılık*, ed. Yasin Aktay, Tanıl Bora, and Murat Gültekingil, 323–340. Istanbul: İletişim.

———. 2005b. Esad Coşan. In *Islamcılık*, ed. Yasin Aktay, Tanıl Bora, and Murat Gültekingil, 332–333. Istanbul: İletişim.

———. 2005c. Mehmet Zahid Kotku. In *İslamcılık*, ed. Yasin Aktay, Tanıl Bora, and Murat Gültekingil, 326–329. Istanbul: İletişim.

Yavuz, Hakan. 2005. *Modernleşen Müslümanlar: Nurcular, Nakşiler, Milli Görüş ve AK Parti*. Istanbul: Kitap.

Yılmaz, Hasan Kamil. 2011. Esad Erbili. In *İslam Ansiklopedisi Vol. 11*, ed. Türkiye Diyanet Vakfı, 348–349. Ankara: TDV ISAM.

Yılmaz, Mustafa, Firdevs Arı, Veli Karataş, Tuğba K. Uysal, A. Yasin Okudan, Ayşe Macit, Dilek Menküç, et al. 2017. *Ortaöğretim Din Kültürü ve Ahlak Bilgisi 9*. Ankara: MEB Devlet Kitapları.

CHAPTER 6

The Islamic Idea of Nature in Contemporary Turkey

Like elsewhere, Islamic theology in Turkey has evolved in its particular sociohistorical context with its own scholars and texts. Contemporary Islamic actors in Turkey also interpret the Islamic idea of nature in terms of the dominant discourses of the times. Corroborating this insight are the several texts that have shaped theological knowledge for all five cases of this book.

In the case of three Islamic movements, we find reference books, or collections (*külliyat*), written by the present or the previous leaders, which define each movement's understanding of Islam. Fourteen books written by Hüseyin Hilmi Işık make up the Işıkçılar's *külliyat*. The Erenköy *külliyat* comprises the more than 60 books written by Osman Nuri Topbaş. The İskenderpaşa collection is composed of more than 40 books written by Mahmud Esad Coşan. Each *külliyat* also includes works written by earlier leaders, like M. Zahid Kotku in the case of İskenderpaşa and M. Sami Ramazanoğlu in the case of Erenköy. Reference books define the movements' Islamic interpretation, which is transmitted to the members as well as the public. Discussions of the idea of nature feature prominently in these reference books. Members are expected to regularly read these books, which also guide the activities of the movements.

The case of the Diyanet requires a different approach, since it is an official body. Among the many books and other materials published by the Diyanet, we focus on books that are specifically prepared to teach the public about the basics of Islamic theology, including the idea of nature.

© The Author(s) 2020   159
G. Bacik, *Islam and Muslim Resistance to Modernity in Turkey*,
https://doi.org/10.1007/978-3-030-25901-3_6

We will not examine more advanced works published by the Diyanet, for example one in which a scholar examines a technical question of theology. Rather, we are interested in what the Diyanet wants the people in general to learn about the Islamic idea of nature.

The two-volume catechist book entitled *İlmihal* is the Diyanet's chief religious guide for the public. The Diyanet widely distributes it to households, mosques, and schools. It is the fundamental guide in formulating the popular understanding of Islam. The other key work here is the *Tefsir*, a five-volume exegesis of the Qur'an, again written for the general public. As stated in the Introduction, the exegesis was written for "people of middle-level education and culture."[1] *Tefsir* covers topics such as causality, free will, and the idea of God and is therefore a good source for the study of the Islamic idea of nature as interpreted for and promoted among the general Turkish public.

A series of books with the title of *İnanç Kitapları* (Hereafter *Faith Series*) is another source for examining the Diyanet's articulation of the Islamic idea of nature. The series is composed of nine volumes, each of which covers an independent topic of Islamic theology. In the Introduction to the series, the purpose is defined as "[illuminating] the general public on Islamic faith."[2] The series is another resource to understand how the Diyanet interprets the Islamic idea of nature. In addition, the Diyanet has multiple means of conveying its Islamic message to the public: journals, Friday sermons, and radio and TV stations. These important arms of the mass media will be selectively observed as another route to understanding how the Islamic idea of nature is brought to the public.

Turning to the compulsory religious courses, I shall examine all Turkish textbooks for religious education from Grade 4 to Grade 12. Written for the purpose of delivering fundamental religious knowledge to students, these school textbooks cover all the critical content of the idea of nature. Textbooks are the prime resources for understanding how the Islamic idea of nature is interpreted and transmitted during religious socialization at the level of formal education.

In Chap. 2, I identified four critical subject areas of Islamic theology that collectively provide the basis for the Islamic idea of nature: causality, knowledge, free will, and the idea of God. I have devoted separate sections of this chapter to discuss these subjects. In each section, I will examine how materials representing each of the five cases—the three movements, the Diyanet, and the compulsory religious courses—deal with the particular subject, and more generally how each case interprets and incorporates these subjects into its Islamic narrative.

6.1   Islamic Movements on Causality and the Idea of God

6.1.1   Işıkçılar

The case of Işıkçılar demonstrates how a contemporary Islamic movement can promote the Ash'ari view of nature despite its Maturidi confessional identity. The movement's interpretation of Islam provides a clear Occasionalist view of causality, repeating nearly all of al-Ghazali's arguments.

Hüseyin Hilmi Işık's massive *Seadet-i Ebediyye* (Endless Bliss), the central book of the Işıkçılar movement, contains many long sections devoted to Islamic theology. Its treatment of theology completely rejects the concept of natural law. Reflecting an Occasionalist perspective, the book teaches that God moves everything, thus precluding the attribution of event to natural causation.[3] Işık's nature is al-Ghazali's nature; the universe operates with dual causality, natural and divine, but the latter is superior. God's customary creation (i.e. divine creation), which we cannot rationalize by means of human thought, causes natural events. Işık borrows many examples from al-Ghazali, including fire and burning cotton: the fire does not cause the cotton to burn—only God does. That cotton seemingly always burns upon contact with fire is a result of God's custom, that is, his habit of making it so, not of any natural law linking fire and burning. Işık denied the possibility of any necessary natural causes unequivocally: he emphasizes that neither fire, nor oxygen, nor heat, nor the electrons cause the burning—only God does. Denying such secondary causes, Işık reduced them to mere human illusions.[4]

Al-Ghazali's theory of movement virtually monopolizes religious thought in contemporary Turkey. Işık also recognizes this theory as the groundwork for his explanations of causality. Only a conscious agent with the ability to will can cause a movement. Lacking those faculties, a law cannot initiate a movement. Thus, law is simply a misnomer, since it is nothing but the custom of the actor (God) whose *will* is behind the movement or act. Thus, real causality is about the agent and his customs, not about secondary reasons, which have neither life nor power to will. God's customs are the only mechanisms that explain natural events.[5]

Işık posits that natural order is possible only when fixed natural laws generate the same results under the same conditions. However, defining God's customary works as the source of natural events, it is logically necessary to accept that God can change his custom as he wishes. Thus, belief in the suspension of nature is an essential part of faith.[6] Any conception of nature that implies limitations on God's sovereignty contradicts God's omnipotence. A proper conception of nature recognizes that God is able to act in nature as He wishes: no natural law binds him. The case is also important for demonstrating how some opinions about nature are still coded as principles of faith. Similarly, Işık frames debates about nature as matters of faith, not as matters of facts.

Having repudiated natural laws and put God's custom as the central authority, we have now a different notion of nature where God suspends order for some higher virtues.[7] The case of several pious people, like appearing in different places at the very same time, is only one example to prove how God suspends the natural order.[8] In fact, what we call natural is a fiction rather than a reality. So, if God lets someone fly, the man-made concept of natural presents the case as supernatural. This had nothing to do with the supernatural or the natural. Rather, a flying man is only a change in God's custom.[9]

Further reflecting the Occasionalist perspective, Işıkçılar's concept of the deity is that of a personal God who governs the universe without interruption through his divine attributes. This is a God who reacts instantaneously to various developments in one's life. God's special relations with people may lead him to change his custom, resulting in the suspension of the natural order. God is very much involved in daily life, knowing and following every detail. Işık is critical of Mu'tazili doctrine, which holds that God knows only through universals. Işık underlines that God knows particularities, including all details.[10] Adopting a personal conception of God, Işık has no doubt that people will see God in heaven.[11] Divine attributes in Işık's thought are not abstract; like al-Ash'ari, he explains them in concrete terms, suggesting a human-like image of the deity.

The influence of Ash'arism on Işık's thought is also clear in the latter's views on God's actions and morality. His stance on this intricate question of theology is clear: God does not have to do what is good and useful for his creatures, nor does he have to reward some people or torment others.[12] We remember these sentences from al-Ash'ari's *Kitab al-Luma'*.[13] Accordingly, God's intervention in nature cannot be subjected to a moral inquiry. Repudiating secondary causes require a personal God with divine attributes like seeing and knowing whose customs cause natural events but who is not subjected to a higher moral or natural law. Humans cannot possess or propose moral norms to understand God. Thus, the search for a logical explanation to God's custom on the basis of morality or rationality is not only meaningless but also heretical. God acts within a divine context, which is not comprehensible to the human mind.[14] To prove the irrelevance of a moral inquiry to God's actions, Işık again draws several examples from *Kitab al-Luma'*. For example, Işık explains that God is the possessor of everything, including human beings, and therefore has the absolute right to do with his possessions as he wills. No one has the right to question his conduct with regard to his possessions.[15] Or, since God is above every ruler and rule, God is not in a position to have to comply with any set of rules, since there is no power to ask this of him.[16] These are almost verbatim quotations from al-Ash'ari.[17]

To conclude, Işık formulates causality within the Ash'ari perspective, repudiating secondary causes. Işık's nature has God as its governor who creates and manages every event directly. Thus, people are expected to appeal directly to God, not to natural law, since God is the agent of every movement. Obviously, such an idea of nature invests more in the higher causality that is God's customs. Therefore, Işık could be interpreted as a scholar who reproduces al-Ghazali's Occasionalist ideas. Reflecting his deep respect for al-Ghazali, Işık praises the former's magnum opus, *Ihya*, as the most useful book.[18] Al-Ghazali's other books, like *Munkidh, Iljam al-'awam* and *Tahafut*, are also frequently quoted, sometimes in at length. Centuries after he passed away, al-Ghazali continues to be the most influential scholar in Işıkçılar's teachings on Islamic theology. By contrast, al-Maturidi has virtually no place in Işık's writings on causality.

6.1.2   İskenderpaşa

The study of how causality is interpreted in İskenderpaşa is comparatively difficult, since the religious discourse of that movement is dominated by piety and morality and rarely reflects the characteristics of a standard theological narrative. Theological issues are usually presented in their reference books indirectly. However, despite such hurdles, the İskenderpaşa reference books contain sections on the idea of causality. Like Işıkçılar, İskenderpaşa also proposes particular ideas about how nature works in the course of its religious instruction.

Al-Ghazali's theory of movement also provides the basis for M. Esad Coşan's approach to causality. Nature has no direct casual power, since it is a blind and created thing without the power to will. Everything in nature, such as trees and the sun, is under the direct governance of God.[19] God uses nature.[20] Having no consciousness, nature is an entity that is used by God as we use other objects. As a passive thing, it is subjected to God's agency and unable to will and therefore to cause any action. Coşan's frequent use of the term "blind nature" reflects the impact of al-Ghazali's theory of movement.[21] Coşan repudiates the role of natural law, that is, secondary causes, since God's agency is behind all natural events.

Following al-Ghazali's theory of movement, Coşan concludes that there is a double causality to explain natural events, and that it is the higher, divine causation that determines movement in nature. From this perspective, it is not clear what role the secondary causes can play. Thus, the investigation of nature in the context of İskenderpaşa's religious instruction is not like what is done in physic courses in universities, where investigators are oblivious to or ignore the dimension where God creates and does everything with his knowledge. The poverty of the methods of physic at explaining nature proves that God's custom, since it is not bound by regularity, is the real agent of natural events.[22]

Coşan does not yield to physics to explain nature; Islam monopolizes that task. Any scientific (or philosophical) attempt to explain nature without taking God's continuous agency into consideration ends in a wrong or incomplete judgment.[23] His proposal is also a contemporary example of how Islamic agents still reject the separation of religion and science.

Mehmed Zahid Kotku also adopts an Occasionalist perspective, as evidenced in his book on Islamic theology, *Ehli Sünnet Akaidi*. The book outlines a general framework of Sunni Islamic theology. Speculating on causal factors in nature, Kotku, partially expounding al-Ghazali's theory of movement, defines nature first as being a fixed or unchanging fact. Nature is fixed and motionless and thus cannot include or produce any causal dynamics that initiate the movement of things. So "black is black, white is white," and if there is any change, for example if "white becomes black," it is not because of nature or natural law, but because of God's will.[24] Kotku leaves little if any space for secondary causes, for he presents God as the agent of every motion, even the location of every individual raindrop and snowflake. To demonstrate his arguments, Kotku employs the raindrop example. God orders the place of each raindrop. Snow is no different, as God takes full charge there too. None of these natural events is autonomous, nor is there a natural law to cause them.[25] What we see as natural events are in fact the results of God's customs.

Following al-Ghazali's theory of movement, nature in İskenderpaşa is mostly seen through the lens of Ash'ari theology. For Coşan, nature is not able to initiate any movement, as it is a collection of unconsciousness and breathless things:

What is nature? Is it stone, tree or water? What is nature? It is the sum total of all these things. But, each of these things is different than the other. Nature is like a scene... It is not a unitary being to cause something. It is the collection of things. Thus, referring nature as a cause is illogical as there is nothing that exists as a unitary thing called nature.[26]

Logically, once nature is defined as lifeless, that is, *inanimate*, an alternate theory is needed to explain movements as the work of a real, conscious agent with the power of will. Recognizing an agent's will as the ontological cause of motion in nature leaves no space for natural law (since nature cannot will), but only the agent's customs. Thus, İskenderpaşa's Islamic teachings go beyond the narrative that postulates natural law as the basis of natural events. Instead, it requires a personal power that governs the universe behind the scenes.

Muslims instructed in these teachings are thus invited to develop an understanding of natural events as God's continuous agency in this world. Such an idea of nature entails a mysterious quality of natural events as well. Coşan locates this mysterious quality of nature somewhere beyond the limits of the knowledge that one acquires in physics lessons.[27] Contemplation of the mysterious reflections of God's ultimate power makes Muslims believe that everything is possible, irrespective of natural law. The possible is defined in terms not of natural law, but of God's limitless power.

The suspension of the natural order is another aspect of Coşan's understanding of causality.[28] Like Işık, Coşan insists that supernatural and natural are irrelevant categories when it comes to classifying God's actions. The emphasis on this topic is not trivial: it is a major argument for why natural law is merely a human illusion without any kind of effect or existence. Since events in nature are merely the habits of God, his actions could happen in any form and are not bound by any law. In other words, the argument of the suspension of natural law is a logical deduction of God's direct agency. But it is also employed to repudiate natural law. Coşan argues that, being out of time and space, God is not bound by anything. Thus, he is not held in chronological time or in any causal nexus; he can even enable people to see future events.[29] Coşan gives examples from Islamic history, especially the stories of saints, to prove that God does suspend the natural order.[30]

The God we read in İskenderpaşa is a highly personal God. Muslims will see him with their own eyes in the afterlife.[31] As a personal deity, God has certain attributes that are neither other than him nor part of him, yet which also have divine quality.[32] Belief in the divine attributes is essential of faith. Kotku writes that anyone who rejects that God has hands (like the Mu'tazila) deviates from the true teachings of Islam. He further insists that words like "God's hands" cannot be interpreted metaphorically as God's power.[33] God's absolute status above any law or morality renders impossible any attempt to evaluate his actions through moral inquiry. Very much like causality in nature, a moral causality—doing or not doing an action for a specific moral purpose—is not a legitimate framework for explaining God's actions. Kotku makes this clear by reminding that God is not bound to always do what is good for people. Kotku makes no mention of al-Maturidi's views on this subject. Instead he adheres to Ash'ari absolutism.[34]

The reference books of İskenderpaşa take things one-step further and fully anthropomorphize God. For example, if God loves one person, Coşan writes, he creates extraordinary conditions for him.[35] God not only governs the universe but also follows people's lives closely, even expressing divine emotions. Thus, God himself is emotional, like a human being: God can even be embarrassed (*utanmak*). To clarify what he means, Coşan explains that God can be embarrassed like a lady (*hanım*) or a child. He explains it can even be like the embarrassment of a person who does something wrong.[36]

As I have underlined above, the Islamic message İskenderpaşa transmits to its members, and to the larger public, is an Occasionalist idea of causality that repudiates natural law. The movement's message identifies a highly personal God as the central agent of daily events, as well as of other natural events. However, on causality, Coşan goes one step further and incorporates a new element where Islamic laws are able to affect events in nature. Defining revelation as the absolute truth and law, Coşan postulates a causal relation between revelation and natural events.[37] Interestingly, recognizing the effect of revealed laws is not held to contradict God's sovereignty. This perspective reflects the thesis that the Qur'an is not uncreated, a belief which has its origin in the divine nature of God's attributes. Accordingly, since attributes are divine, God's knowledge and his words (including the Qur'an) are also divine. Thus, while natural laws are repudiated—since anything that we observe in nature is created—revealed laws are seen as connected to God's divinity.

The origin of such a divine causality is the repudiation of natural law, as Sayyid Hussain Nasr notes, since it leads people to define God's revelation as the real law.[38] This should not be confused with the traditional Islamic argument that Islamic rules bring Muslims to a better life. Rather, this view proposes a causal link between religiosity and the course of events in the material world, for example, the volume of rainfall. Muslims' failure to live a religious life according to the revealed law can have material effects in nature.[39] Abiding by Islamic laws initiates God's direct intervention in nature in favor of people. God helps pious people, sometimes even directly through supernatural means.[40]

This sort of religious causality could be interpreted as the extreme extension of repudiating natural law. God governs nature through Islamic laws rather than natural law. Coşan formulates the essence of this special causation with a motto: if a person obeys God, everything obeys him (the person).[41] This is simply to incorporate Islamic principles into the relationship of man and nature, as if that relationship were another causal nexus.[42] As a matter of fact, Coşan frequently reminds the reader that *fiqh* (religious law) is the highest science.[43]

6.1.3   Erenköy

Like the two previous cases, Erenköy also adheres to the Ash'ari concept of causality, despite its Maturidi confessional identity. The movement transmits a typical God-first approach, where the divine power is explained as the sole cause of everything.[44] Osman Nuri Topbaş clearly warns that attributing a real effect to natural law is misleading, for it is God who governs the universe.[45]

Topbaş explains his understanding of nature with an analogy. He writes that nature is like a painting on a canvas. A painter paints dots, lines, and various shapes on the canvas. Shapes on the canvas have no ability to influence anything in the content of the painting. They cannot change size, shape, or color, nor can they affect appearances or places on the canvas. There is no authority on the canvas other than the painter's choice and will. No one can propose a causal link to explain shapes on the canvas other than the painter's custom or wishes. God is thus the painter of nature: He decides and makes everything in nature such that no object or element of it has any ability to cause itself or anything else.[46] All existing things in the universe are like the dots, lines, and shapes on a canvas. We are meant to extrapolate from this analogy that to understand nature we must focus on the artist, not the work of art.[47] We observe in the design of nature is God's absolute arbitrariness. As al-Ghazali once noted, God could have set nature differently, had he so wished.[48]

Earlier, we briefly analyzed Kotku's raindrop example, which recognizes no natural causes. As we will observe later in different contexts, the scholars of Islamic movements prefer analogies in which nature has no causal efficacy. Their analogies reflect the general precepts of the Ghazalian theory of movement. They cautiously avoid analogies where nature or natural law is assigned any role in the initiation of events. As I have elaborated in Chap. 2, Ibn Rushd criticized al-Ghazali and the Ash'ari view for excessive reliance on God's direct agency. For Ibn Rushd, there is "no counterpart to His will in the empirical world."[49] Thus, presenting God as the sole agent of natural events is flawed. God is not part of space and time, and thus it is impossible to find a counterpart of God's will in the empirical (space- and time-bound) world. Ibn Rushd suggests a differentiation between the empirical and the divine will. He argues that the agency of secondary causes is so clear that denying it is sophistry, as they are easily observed in sensible things.[50] On this debate, al-Maturidi's explanation is close to that of Ibn Rushd, and several passages of *Kitab al-Tawhid* suggest that al-Maturidi differs from al-Ash'ari on this point.[51] His explanation of nature recognizes that God created things with various features and structural qualities, and that one can thus speak of "rules" governing the natural order.[52] However, as we spot in all cases in this book, including the Diyanet, on causality, Ash'ari occasionalism prevails in Turkey, while al-Maturidi's approach is ignored.

Topbaş explains natural events as the results of God's creation through his unceasing interventions.[53] What is radical about his repudiation of natural law is that it entails a complete incapacity of humans to understand nature. Topbaş believes that understanding nature is not possible. Any attempt at explanation would require a causal nexus, and that would amount to the claim that God's custom is subject to that causal law. God is above any law, and thus any scientific framework that seeks to explain God's actions through natural law is a travesty. We cannot learn the exact reasons for the natural events that take place around us.[54] Topbaş demonstrates to us the consequence of the Occasionalist perspective: if the divine rules of governance rather than natural law determine natural events, then we cannot explain natural events with reference to the laws of nature.[55] The options now are either to develop an alternative method for learning the divine rules of governance, or to be satisfied with our deficiency.

Topbaş points to various natural events, like disasters, as hints of the divine aspect of nature. He claims that such events cannot be explained on the basis of observed natural phenomena.[56] Their explanation requires a type of knowledge quite different from that which science can furnish. Topbaş's interpretation of the Islamic idea to nature entails a denial of

natural law, thereby making space for an alternative order where the rule
is divine arbitrariness. It is a nature where God does anything he wishes,
sometimes even appearing as a supernatural being.[57]

Arguing along the same lines as Işık and Coşan, Topbaş defies the concept supernatural because it is a man made, and therefore of no relevance
to God's action. Man-made binaries like normal/abnormal and natural/
supernatural have nothing to do with God's custom. Again, the core of
the argument is rejection of any attempt to explain God's actions with
reference to a consistent framework. God acts as he wishes on the divine
level, which is not comprehensible by humans. The logical conclusion of
this view is an epistemic fatalism where the human mind cannot understand the movements and events in nature.[58] Following from this, Topbaş
also discards any moral framework that purports to evaluate God's acts.
God is above all law, so he is also outside any moral framework. His actions
are never questioned.[59] This epistemic argument is in principle the same as
the moral argument that rejects any attempt to explain God's decisions in
terms of a man-made framework. This approach is a typical expression of
the God-first theology, where the ultimate principle is to avoid any idea
that might appear to diminish God's absolute perfectness. Like the other
cases, on the issue of morality and God actions, Topbaş does not incorporate any Maturidi doctrines and instead adheres to Ash'ari absolutism.

In Topbaş's cosmology, the personal God of nature manages not only
the macro-level events of the universe but also the daily affairs of every
person. This is a personal God who cares about the universe; it is his continuous intervention (in the form of habit) that preserves the illusion of
natural law and prevents the descent into anarchy. God follows people
closely; he reacts to their decisions and deeds. Having no intermediaries,
God is an integral part of every person's daily life. Muslims in fact observe
the reflections of God's decisions in their daily lives. Topbaş proposes a
simple explanation that God manages people's lives and that people appeal
to God to favor them by acting piously.[60]

Topbaş is also in search of a religious causality: he is not satisfied with
natural law, for that concept presumes a natural order that exists independently of the revealed Islamic principles. He attempts to expand causality
by arguing that Islamic laws are the causes of effects in nature. So, natural
events like fires, plagues, and droughts are related to people's piety.
Religious causality is as follows:

> If most of the servants are on the right path, rain comes down as a mercy
> and a blessing, and happiness follows. However, if most of the community
> is inclined to their earthly desires, then floods, droughts or earthquakes

become inevitable. These sad events occur because of sins or rebelliousness committed by people. In other words, natural disasters happen only after spiritual quakes already took place due to corrupt hearts.[61]

Unlike with natural law, proposing an explanation of God's actions through religious laws does not diminish God's sovereignty. This is again a reflection of the Sunni orthodox view of the Qur'an as uncreated and divine. Recognizing the revealed laws as binding on nature does not contradict God' sovereignty, since the laws are also divine. Topbaş elaborates his idiosyncratic religious causality as follows:

> It cannot be denied that people's spiritual states and their actions—good or evil—play a role in the triggering or the deflection of earthquakes.[62]

Destroyed by God's direct agency and religious causality, natural law is now irrelevant. Thus, Topbaş wrote that it is wrong to exaggerate the role of physical rules by saying "if the buildings were strong enough, this earthquake would not have killed so many people," since things are dependent on the divine will, which manifests itself at all costs.[63] Here is the hierarchy of powers in nature as Topbaş explains to his followers:

> Those who have no clue of the divine presence wander around ordinary causes, idly latching on purely physical explanations, such as blaming tectonic faults for earthquakes.[64]

This is a world of direct divine governance, so Topbaş asks Muslims to organize their lives in accordance with the reality of a divine causation rather than on natural law, for natural laws are uncertain, while the divine rules and God's management are constant.[65]

6.2   Official Islam on Causality and the Idea of God

6.2.1   The Diyanet

The Diyanet's narrative on causality also reflects the general features of Occasionalism. Relevant books published by the Diyanet clearly display the prevalence of occasionalism in that official institution's interpretation of Islam.

Dinim İslam (Islam Is My Religion) is a typical example in this vein. Addressed particularly to young students, the book declares that everything good or bad, living or non-living, useful or not useful, is created by God's will, knowledge, and creation.[66] The book also includes sections that suggest that nature is governed by a religious causality, according to which God creates natural disasters or health problems to test human being.[67] Thus, the regular function of natural law surrenders to divine causation, which has its own customary framework. God is always able to do as he wishes. He can take back everything that a man has gained in his life. The text warns Muslims to bear in mind divine intervention, since it can affect everything in daily life. For instance, how people are given their sustenance is exclusively a matter of divine decision. However, the predominance of divine causation is not limited to these issues. It is the norm that governs the nature, so any action in nature needs God's consent to come into being.[68] I believe that the practical benefits of Occasionalism, that is, enabling Islamic agents to formulate their opinions in manner that is compatible with God's omnipotence, seem to make it an indispensable method. Occasionalism is practical and persuasive in bringing a God-centered explanation to the general public.

As is apparent in the book just analyzed, the Diyanet's narrative rejects the notion that natural law can cause the events and changes we see in nature. Indeed, even postulating natural law contradicts God's sovereignty. It is accepted that God directly and instantaneously governs natural events. The view equates any proposal that endows secondary causes with an autonomous efficacy with a claim to share in God's sovereignty, that is, *shirk*. Thus, in the case of the Diyanet, we again observe a typical problem of Sunni Islamic theology that is its inability to formulate a space for autonomous action.

To overcome the quandary, the Diyanet develops a narrative of harmony among God, natural law, and human will. However, one finds little information concerning the problematic aspects of this narrative. The style is declarative and carefully avoids the controversial issues. We observe the same narrative in *İnancım*, another typical book by Diyanet written for the public, where it is stated that faith requires belief in God's governance of nature through his "knowledge, design and creation."[69] However, this divine model is explained as if it does not raise any questions about natural law or man's free will. This style just makes statements without discussion, and the tricky issues are ignored.

The Diyanet's narrative does not explicitly repudiate natural law, as was the case with the three Islamic movements analyzed above. Even so, the priority of securing of God's sovereignty, that is, its God-first approach, results in similar consequences. Explaining natural events as the direct and instantaneous actions of God and passing over natural law with vague and ambiguous declarations, practically produces yet another Occasionalist outlook.

In this vein, the Diyanet's *Tefsir* offers detailed and dialectical discussions of causality. *Tefsir* is the pivotal exegesis that the Diyanet promotes and distributes in present-day Turkey. Four highly prestigious and leading Turkish scholars—Hayreddin Karaman, Mustafa Çağrıcı, İ. Kafi Dönmez, and Sadrettin Gümüş—were commissioned to write the *Tefsir*. They are recognized as eminent and well-credentialed religious scholars who have served the public in various religious and academic posts and who have been influential in governmental circles.[70]

Tefsir makes a sophisticated attempt to reconcile God's sovereignty and natural law. Yet even it still resorts to declaring assumptions and in some places contradictory reasoning in its effort to overcome a substantial quandary of Islamic thought, which is to formulate a space for autonomous action without violating God's sovereignty. *Tefsir* recognizes natural law as God's design. However, it still maintains that nature cannot limit God's will, and that God can suspend the natural order.[71] While the authors' goal is to reconcile natural law and divine sovereignty, the implication is that natural laws are efficient only so long as God does not intervene in nature. They thus uphold the Occasionalist conclusion that God manages the world and that his relations with the universe are continuous and direct.[72] The ultra-sensitivity to and respect for God's sovereignty remains the undisputed norm, leaving no possibility of formulating a consistent framework of autonomous action in nature. As a result, natural laws are still held to have no causal efficacy. Furthermore, it is again underlined that it is the human mind that imagines regularities in nature in the form of natural laws. In fact, various irregular events prove God's agency as the sole power to explain natural events.[73]

In another attempt at reconciliation, *Tefsir* appeals to the concept of *Sünnetullah* (Ar. *Sunnat Allah*) to explain the workings of nature. The Diyanet's *Encyclopedia of Islam* defines the term as the rules that God has laid down to sustain the social and natural orders.[74] This definition generates a causality that incorporates natural and social factors. Accordingly, if societies fail to comply with these laws in their social life, they can trigger certain natural events, such as disasters. But *Sünnetullah* refers to more general divine rules that determine both natural and social events in a supreme form of causation that is above natural law. The Diyanet's *Sünnetullah* is also based on the thesis that because the Qur'an is uncreated and divine, the rules it reveals govern nature. Thus, the Diyanet's cosmology also puts God's direct agency and his revealed rules at the center of natural order.

Tefsir then explains how God governs nature according to *Sünnetullah*. For every action, God first creates the cause and then creates the consequence, in keeping with divine wisdom.[75] On this account, a thing happening immediately following another thing does not mean that there is a causal link between them. Thus, the causal link we observe in nature is not autonomous but rather a reflection of God's agency. God's continuous creation of causes and consequences is his customary way of acting, albeit perceived as natural law by people. However, the attempt to accommodate God's agency with natural order results in a convoluted conclusion:

> The general immutable law (*sünnet*) enacted by God can only be changed by God with again a special law of God for an interim period in special cases.[76]

Analyzing the explanation, we read that order exists in nature thanks to God's general customs. However, even though *Tefsir* names them as the immutable general law, God changes them for interim periods. *Tefsir* here makes a distinction between *sünnet-i amme* (God's general laws) and *sünnet-i hassa* (God's exceptional laws) in order to reconcile natural order with God's sovereignty. Accordingly, a special law can suspend the immutable general laws in nature for a short time, and only in special cases. However, the case is now more complicated, since we have exceptional laws that can suspend the general laws that were defined as immutable.

What we observe here is a sophisticated Occasionalist perspective sifting God's sovereignty through various mechanisms. The outcome is again that God's absolute governance determines natural events. But it is obvious that the *Tefsir* authors want to minimize the suspension of the natural order: God only rarely changes his customs in *Tefsir*'s discourse on nature, and his actions are always in accord with wisdom. The quest here is to escape Ibn Rushd's criticism of Islamic scholars whose rejection of natural law leads to a tyrannical idea of God.[77] However, God's suspending natural order remains a recognized principle of the Islamic idea of nature in the Diyanet's interpretation of theology.[78]

The problem of this theological view is its inconsistency. For example, *Tefsir* accepts supernatural practices but cautiously reminds the reader that such events happen only on a special law of God. Indeed, despite such a cautious approach, is it hardly possible to read a biography of a contemporary Islamic saint or even many religious leaders that does not mention supernatural events, which proves that the *Tefsir*'s own theological caution fails. In fact, other books by the Diyanet, for example its chief catechism *İlmihal*, plainly recognize supernatural events. While summarizing the fundamentals of Islam in short sentences, *İlmihal* proclaims that the supernatural actions of saints are fact.[79] Reading many other books written for the general public, one quickly notices that the suspension of the natural order as well as various forms of supernatural events are essentials of Islamic faith in the Diyanet's interpretation of Islamic theology.[80]

Tefsir also makes use of analogy to explain nature. The analogy that illustrates the relationship of God and nature is the changing shadow of an object. It is an analogy we will remember from al-Ghazali's *The Incoherence of Philosophers*.[81] The shadow changes shape simultaneously with the change of position of the object that casts it. God's will and works in nature happen simultaneously, without a lapse of time, as do the concurrent changes of the shadow and the object. As in the painting analogy of Topbaş, the *Tefsir* shadow presents a nature without autonomy. The shadow cannot cause a change in its shape or position.

Accordingly, all we see in nature as changes and occurrences are simultaneous reflections of God's decisions. We observe God's governance as it is reflected in nature. Put differently, the only hypothetical difference is the missing dimension of divine governance, like the difference between the 3D object and its 2D shadow. Leaving no initiative to nature, the analogy reminds the Ghazalian theory of movement. Even the *Tefsir* analogy repeats the scheme of the Ghazalian theory almost verbatim: Nature is not an agent with a consciousness or will that initiates movement. What is more, there is no such thing as nature; it is merely an imagined concept. Nature is only a convenient collective name for things like trees, planets, stars, and animals. Thus, one cannot attribute a power to nature, which does not exist on any level other than that of a name.[82]

The Diyanet's *Faith Series* also perpetuates Occasionalism. Reading relevant volumes of the series, we quickly grasp that they are written in line with traditional Ottoman syncretism of the Ash'ari and the Maturidi schools again giving precedence to the former. The syncretic attempt in *Faith Series* therefore leads to some contradictory statements.

In the series, we are informed that there is normally an order in nature, but that order is subject to change depending on God's customs. Those changes are not abnormal or extraordinary developments. Rather, they are uncustomary (*adet dışı*) events, meaning changes in God's custom. Humans misunderstand them as extraordinary.[83] However, in some parts of *Faith Series*, the authors themselves define such changes in nature as extraordinary events.[84] Accordingly, such extraordinary events demonstrate God's absolute agency in nature, since they demonstrate the lack of any perpetual natural laws.[85]

According to *Faith Series*, God's direct agency causes all natural events. This logically requires the rejection of regular natural laws. Thus, it is frequently stated in the books that natural laws are not ontologically necessary, given God's direct agency in nature.[86] As a result, the knowledge of causes that we acquire through science "of which we are proud of"—an expression of disdain—is inadequate. True causality operates at the higher and absolute level of God's agency.[87] This conception of nature again resembles that of al-Ghazali, which holds that human sensation and reasoning have only a limited capacity to provide knowledge of causes. As a logical result of the occasionalist model, *Faith Series* reminds us that there are two worlds: visible and invisible. Man's senses and capacity fall short in understanding the invisible, which is the most critical one when it comes to causality.[88] All events in nature are governed at that invisible level, where God's agency rules nature, including man's acts.[89] Such a view of visible and invisible worlds is an important example to trace the Ash'ari impact in Diyanet's narrative. The dual conception of visible and invisible worlds is a Sufi perspective that al-Ghazali brought into Sunni theology. Recall that there was no such conception of the visible and invisible worlds in al-Maturidi's thought. For al-Maturidi, the visible world could be proposed as a proof to another; however, the idea of imagining man between the two worlds in terms of acquisition of any kind of knowledge is false.[90]

In another expression of its occasionalism, the Diyanet maintains the conception of a personal God. God is presented as a person (*zat*) in Diyanet books.[91] *İlmihal* gives many details about God's attributes.[92] *Tefsir* frequently reminds the reader that attributes are a requirement for God's perfectness.[93] By frequent references to leading Ash'ari scholars like al-Ghazali and al-Razi, divine attributes are explained as necessary for God's continuous contact with the universe.[94] The Diyanet vehemently challenges philosophical (and Mu'tazila) conceptualizations of God in the form of an abstract power or intellect.[95] God knows the particulars of every person's life,[96] and his actions have nothing to do with being good or bad.[97] The Diyanet's God is a typical reflection of Sunni Orthodox theology: God is the sole agent, which requires having attributes to explain his governing of the universe.

This explanation is simple and comprehensible to the average reader. However, this intelligibility comes at a cost: it comes close to anthropomorphizing God. Thus, as I have summarized in Chap. 3, in the case of Diyanet we face another problem of Sunni theology. Philosophers' abstract conceptions of God are not satisfactory for orthodox theologians, as they are neither comprehensible to the average reader not compatible with the Occasionalist view of nature. On the other hand, the piety-minded scholars' views approach anthropomorphism, which Ibn Rushd once derided as "turning God into an eternal man."[98] It is this nearly-anthropomorphized God that we find in many theological works written and promoted by a range of Islamic actors in contemporary Turkey.

6.2.2   School Textbooks

The idea of nature also occupies a large space in the textbooks of compulsory religious courses. Textbooks regard the issue of causality as a major subject of Islamic theology. Reading the relevant sections of religious course books, one might even feel that one is reading a science course book.

Thematically, the general debate on nature, particularly in the earlier years of study, is based on the concept of order.[99] Students are asked to ponder the order that they observe in nature. The purpose is to make them understand natural order as a sign of God's creation. Presented as a proof, natural order is defined as a result of the "measures and arrangements by God."[100] The idea of God's continuous agency is underlined to explain natural events. Mostly, textbooks up to the eighth year follow the same method of emphasizing natural order while teaching about God's relationship to nature. The emphasis on natural order, however, is presented along with a concept of personal God.[101] The personal God relates directly to everything in the universe and cares about every person's needs and problems. The continuous dialogue between God and nature is underlined.[102] Textbooks discuss divine attributes in detailed way; God sees, speaks, and intervenes in daily life.[103]

The narrative of the textbooks becomes dialectical after the eighth grade, and there is a concomitant shift in focus from natural order to causality. Natural law is now God's design. Students are taught that man should understand natural law as designed by God.[104] At this level, such explanation can be evaluated as a strategy to emphasize the significance of natural law without referring to any thorny theological issues. Basically, the method is to recognize natural law along with God's sovereignty. Textbooks skip traditional problems of Islamic theology concerning the compatibility of the autonomous natural law and God's sovereignty. Leaving those discussions aside, it is underlined that "the functioning of the universe depends on natural law" since God created everything in nature according to some measures.[105]

Particularly in the eighth-grade textbook, the narrative on causality comes close to a natural-law-first perspective. Physical laws are considered the most important factors for gaining an understanding of natural events, and it is made clear that if people fail to consider them, they will encounter various material problems such as environmental disaster or economic underdevelopment. This is a quite unusual recognition of natural law without resorting to any Occasionalist argument. Natural laws are held to cause events within their standard and mechanical procedure. Continuing the natural-laws-first approach, the book informs that the speed of the Earth's rotation, rain, snow, and all other natural events happen according to the laws of physics.[106] Not interested in the traditional problems of Islamic theology, the book has as its prime objective teaching students that understanding natural law is vital for developing better relations between man and nature. Consider the following question that one encounters in the textbook:

Why do people construct stronger houses in quake regions? Which physical laws should be considered in these areas?[107]

The semantics of the two questions suggest natural law causes events in nature. It does not mention the divine agency or the religious causality, which explains natural events like earthquakes as a function of religious impiety. The narrative is so precise that one sometimes has the impression that one is reading the transcript of a physics lecture. The book even defines what a physical event is in the fashion of a science textbook: a physical event happens because prevailing conditions determine the causal relations that govern the participating physical things. The textbook's intention is evidently to incorporate causality as an autonomous mechanism into Islamic theology without any qualification. To support its thesis, it reminds the reader that the Qur'an also directs men's attention to natural law. Life will be easier if one understands natural law.[108]

The eighth-grade textbook, presenting its causality-first-oriented opinions without mentioning any theological problem pertinent to God's relations with nature, offers the clearest stance on natural law of all books I have read while writing this book. No other book from the library of Turkish Islam that I have analyzed in this study can compete with its natural-law-first approach. It is the only book that raises no reservations on the role of natural laws in explaining nature.

However, the general feature of the narrative on causality is still an equivocal one if all textbooks are analyzed together. Thus, the causality-centered narrative that we observed in the eighth-grade book is exceptional in only one component of the official narrative, not a typical example of it. For example, we observe a clearly God-first approach on causality from the tenth-grade book onward. In the latter, it is underlined that all events in nature are reflections of God's continuous creation. God has a direct and continuous relationship with the universe.[109] Not surprisingly, God does everything in nature, such as bringing about rain or the blossoming of flowers.[110] The emphasis on natural law is largely absent in the latter textbooks.

The textbooks of different grades thus present an asymmetric approach to nature. The analysis of course books suggests that there is a planning only in terms of the topics to be included the curriculum. When it comes to the detailed content of topics such as causality or free will, what we find is variations of the Sunni theological narrative. For example, in the eleventh-grade book, there is a logical fallacy in the defense of the proposition that events in nature happen according to causal relations designed by God. Natural laws are subsequently defined as destiny, thus leaving the debate unresolved. Finally, after warning that if people fail to comply with religious laws, they will face natural disasters, the books end on the right side of the pendulum of Islamic theology, promoting pure religious causality.[111]

Given such equivocation, I categorize the narrative of textbooks as a moderately equivocal stance on natural law and causality. A synoptic analysis of textbooks does not provide a consistent idea of causality. This might be either the result of careless editing or a pedagogical intention to offer alternative perspectives. In any case, the textbooks can be credited with having sections that focus on natural law as well as a low-profile critical discourse of natural law that serves to secure God's sovereignty. It should be remembered here that secular education was a top Kemalist priority until the Islamist actors consolidated their power, and thus the moderate stance of religious textbooks can also be interpreted as remnants of the Kemalist influence on the Turkish education system.

In a wider perspective, however, the lengthy sections of religion course books exemplify Islam's difficult relationship with modernity, particularly when it comes to explaining nature. In the pertinent sections, we observe how the traditional authority of explaining Islam endures with regard to nature, refusing to yield to modern science. Consider, for example, how the tenth-grade textbook's section on nature begins with the following question: "What do you understand by law of nature?"[112] This rather confrontational approach implies that explaining nature is still the exclusive mandate of religious authorities, at the cost sometimes of clashing with relevant scientific explanations.

Why is a textbook in a course of religious studies even interested in raising this topic, given that schools offer courses like physics and chemistry in the natural sciences? The answer is that the ongoing interest of religious authorities in natural law is definitely in that Islam continues to hang on to its idea of nature. In other words, religious authorities still claim nature as its area of concern, not leaving it completely to modern science.

6.3 ISLAMIC MOVEMENTS ON FREE WILL

6.3.1 Işıkçılar

In Chap. 2, I quoted Mahmud Isfahani for his critical remark that Islamic scholars ceased to argue over free will and instead committed the knowledge of it to God.[113] Contemporary agents of Islamic theology in Turkey also practice this prudence. In general, their treatments of free will are short and vague, unlike their writings on other components of the Islamic idea of nature.

Our first case is the Işıkçılar, who adopt a strictly God-first approach on the free will issue. Hüseyin Hilmi Işık situates the movement's position on free will between that of the Jabriyya and the Mu'tazila. Accordingly, neither does God completely leave human actions to man's will, nor is man completely devoid of will.[114] However, when it comes to harmonizing man's will and God's sovereignty, his approach is almost a perfect replica of the Ash'ari perspective: Man's will has no ability to affect his deeds.

Işık defines God's absolute sovereignty over human actions as axiomatic in his approach to free will. If God does not will it, nobody can do, or even will to do, something good or bad. There are some instances, as Işık explains, where God does not allow people's acts to come into being even if they want to perpetrate those acts. Thus, ontologically, human action depends on God's will.[115] God's ultimate authority over man's deeds extends to man's own ideas and wishes. For Işık, even the doubts that come to one's mind are works of God.[116] If we imagine man's acts as consisting of two parts, willing (ideational) and doing (practical), Işık argues that God also creates the ideational segment. Logically, such overwhelming divine governance leaves no room for man's autonomy. Işık's priority is to secure God's sovereignty as the absolute agent of all human actions, including their ideational aspects.

While deliberating over his theological stance, Işık criticizes the Mu'tazila for engaging in polytheism by accepting man's freedom to create his own acts.[117] This famous criticism accuses the Mu'tazila of assigning many partners to God when they assert that each man is the creator of his acts. Man's full authority over his actions is not compatible with God's omnipotence.[118] For Işık, the belief that man creates his own will and actions is heresy.[119]

As noted above, a central feature of Işık's approach to free will is his extension of God's sovereignty over even the ideational aspect of people's actions.[120] Işık uses the concept of *kasb* by repeating the famous motto of al-Maturidi that pledges not to sacrifice man's freedom: "*Kasb* is from man, the creation is from God."[121] Accordingly, *kasb* results in man's actions, and it cannot be seen as created by God, since it is non-existent.[122] However, Işık's approach to *kasb*, which may be called a radical Ash'ari perspective, leaves us with the classic paradox of Islamic theology. Man is the doer of his actions thanks to *kasb*, which is not created by God. However, *kasb* itself does not exist. Işık's stance is even more confusing, since for him *kasb* is also not an act of man's willing, since God is the creator of man's will to do an act. In this framework, it is not clear how *kasb* makes man free and competent for his actions. Işık is also vague on the function of *kasb*, as it is sometimes man's will to choose, and sometimes a power that activates man's will to choose.[123] What we observe in Işık's writings is theological obscurantism that preserves God's role in creating even the ideational aspects of man's action[124] while attempting to avoid charges of fatalism.[125]

Işık's translation of the Ottoman scholar Kınalızade Ali Efendi (d. 1572)'s *Ahlak-ı Ala'i* (The Sublime Ethics) is a rare instance of the author adopting something close to the Maturidi perspective on free will.[126] Recognized as the first work on ethics in Turkish, the book is inspired by the writings of Nasir al-Din al-Tusi (1201–1275).[127] Credited with laying the foundations of Islamic ethics, al-Tusi was an Islamic scholar with a Shi'a background who attempted to synthesize Aristotelian and Islamic moral philosophy.

Like al-Tusi, Kınalızade relied on earlier Islamic philosophers (Ibn Sina and al-Farabi) and Greek philosophers such as Aristotle in developing his theory of ethics.[128] Reflecting the impact of rationalist philosophers, the dialectical discussion of free will in Kınalızade's book departs from the typical Ash'ari perspective. It is very likely that Işık incorporated Kınalızade's book into his movement's collection because of its discourse on morality, not for its theological content. Indeed, Işık did not hold back from expressing his reservations about the author, claiming for example that al-Tusi—who inspired Kınalızade—was responsible for many people's deaths during Hulagu's torching of Baghdad. Işık also intervenes in the text by repeating typical Ash'ari opinions on various topics like free will to counterbalance Kınalızade's rationalist views.[129]

Although Işık proposes an Ash'ari explanation on free will, which theologically is risk-free perspective since it makes no qualification to God's sovereignty and creation, he does admit that the free will issue is "the trickiest puzzle on earth."[130] Not satisfied with assigning almost no role to man in the creation of his own actions, Işık wants to reframe free will beyond the scope of human reason. Thus, Işık's stance on free will is different than those of several scholars like Khalidi al-Baghdadi, whom the Işıkçılar movement recognizes as an inspiration.[131] Al-Baghdadi's books, like *Itiqadname* and *Mektubat*, are selectively quoted in Işıkçılar's reference books. For example, in the ninth letter of *Mektubat* (The Letters), al-Baghdadi presents a detailed discussion on human will, in which he provides balanced and critical assessments of various approaches, including that of al-Ash'ari.[132] However, Işık's interpretation of the free will issue is more conservative than even that of al-Baghdadi.

6.3.2   İskenderpaşa

Reflecting the same reservation, the reference books of İskenderpaşa have no direct, lengthy discussions of free will. Free will is almost left untreated in movement's reference books. For example, the term *irade-i cüziyye* (the classical Islamic concept defining man's will) is used only once in Coşan four-volume *Tefsir Sohbetleri*, a thematic exegesis of the Qur'an. In the first volume of this exegesis, Coşan had only a one-sentence statement to the effect that God gave human beings an *irade-i cüziyye* and the freedom to act as they wish.[133] Coşan gives no elaboration or defense of this statement. The free will issue in the case of İskenderpaşa can thus be read as part of the movement's moralist narrative where Islamic messages are communicated through parables.

The general survey of Coşan's major books, such as the nine-volume *Hazineden Pırıltılar*, the four-volume *Tabakata's-Sufiiyye Sohbetleri*, and the four-volume *Tefsir Sohbetleri*, reveals that he unequivocally articulates a God-oriented (divinely determinist) theology in which God's will is axiomatic, and therefore free will is excluded.[134] On the other hand, the reference books do not explicitly reject free will. Coşan is satisfied by reminding the reader of man's responsibility for his actions and God's sovereignty over man's actions. Leaving his stance at this, Coşan is not interested in the details of the potential problems of reconciling man's will and God's sovereignty. However, he does not endorse a full-blown defense of man's freedom of action. While predestination is a keyword in Coşan's interpretation of Islam, free will is not treated as a fundamental concept, and in many parts is even ignored.[135]

Mehmed Zahid Kotku's approach is similar to Coşan's. Kotku first argues that the theological differences on free will between the various theological schools are minor and merely semantic. For example, while presenting the general features of Sunni faith according to both the Maturidi and the Ash'ari schools, he does not even mention their differences and proceeds as if they are in consensus on all issues.[136] Kotku's approach could be interpreted as a continuation of the Ottoman syncretic approach to the Islamic schools of theology. However, it is also an important indicator of the movements' shift to a more conservative theological position. To compare, Ahmed Ziyaüddin, the influential leader of the Ottoman Naqshbandiyya order who I discussed briefly in Chap. 5, was a staunch Hanafi-Maturidi whose intellectual position could be defined as Ash'ari-skeptical, if not anti-Ash'ari. While recognizing the Ash'ari contribution to Islamic orthodoxy, Ziyaüddin did not count adherents of that school as part of *Ahl al-Sunna*.[137] By contrast, the present articulation of free will in İskenderpaşa's reference works no longer reflects that anti-Ash'ari attitude.

Kotku does not devote much space to it in his works. It occupies only half a page in *Ehli Sünnet Akaidi*, a 300-page book on Islamic theology. Like Coşan, Kotku employs a declarative style that does not inform us about the details of his reasoning. He holds that all actions are contained in God's will and order, but that man also has a personal will. However, does this not elaborate on the details of this seemingly contradictory account, such as the status of man's volition *vis-à-vis* God's will.[138]

One striking point in Kotku's writings is his quotation of al-Maturidi's arguments. For example, he repeats the Maturidi motto that man is the doer of his actions, but not the creator. He also writes that God creates whatever a man wants, another Maturidi explanation of the relationship between man and God in the creation of man's deeds.[139] Though he does not provide a clear and consistent defense or explanation of these quotations, they can be interpreted as evidence of Kotku's attempt to somehow connect himself and his movement with the Maturidi approach to free will. However, immediately following these short discussions, Kotku turns to criticize the Mu'tazila theses on free will and argues that man cannot be the commander (*kumandan*) of his deeds. In another section, he argues that human acquisition (*kasb*) has no role in creating human actions.[140] Such controversial arguments could also be the ongoing reflection of the traditional Ottoman syncretic method of concurrently and contradictorily repeating the Ash'ari and the Maturidi arguments.

İskenderpaşa's account of free will does not include a full recognition of human agency. Though it differs in terms of its reference to several Maturidi resources, it ultimately only admits a qualified form of human agency and is for the most part committed to the God-first approach. Furthermore, the İskenderpaşa reference books avoid detailed engagement with the free will issue providing only a vague narrative. Thus, the movement's works are mostly silent on free will, and when they do address the issue, they emphasize the limit's human agency.

6.3.3   Erenköy

Erenköy exhibits a similar reluctance to address the free will issue. Sections directly or indirectly dealing with this issue are comparatively few in the reference of books of the movement. Osman Nuri Topbaş covers free will without detail or argument.[141] Topbaş maintains the God-first approach, insisting that free will is non-existent and that God is the sole agent.[142]

Having secured his position by showing interest in the God-first approach, Topbaş then continues with a reluctant and prudent narrative that holds that free will lies beyond human comprehension. Accordingly, it is better to believe in free will without asking for details or proof. Theological topics like the free will issue are compared to a "bottomless and shoreless sea."[143]

Unlike their bold attacks on natural law in defense of the God-first approach, the Islamic actors I analyze in this book are more reserved when it comes to the issue of free will. Though they do not strongly defend free will, they do not criticize it in the name of God's ultimate sovereignty. They tend to opt for what can be thought of as a safe narrative. The repudiation of free will would introduce serious problems concerning human responsibility. Proposing God's agency in explaining human's actions is not as logically persuasive as doing the same in repudiating natural law. However, reflecting different degrees of the God-first approach, they do not recognize man's absolute ability to determine his actions. The strategy probably originated in the fear of Islamic scholars that their standard theological arguments might fail to persuade Muslims, which might result either in a crisis of faith or in the adoption of more rationalistic opinions.

In this vein, Topbaş rejects rational arguments as valid instruments for investigating the free will issue. He believes that they lead to dead-ends and offer no solution, just like the arguments of philosophers.[144] Having defined the topic as beyond reason, Topbaş clarifies his safe narrative on free will: neither those who say that man has no will nor those who claim that man's will is absolutely free are correct. Topbaş states that the truth is somewhere in between, but again, he provides no detail. He is satisfied to remind that man has will and choice in a way that we are not able to grasp fully.[145] Topbaş refrains from promoting a dialectical narrative, since it is not possible to advance in an understanding of an issue that reason cannot comprehend. He frequently repeats that the topic is beyond the capacity of the human intellect.[146] He suggests that the limits of this issue should not be strained due to man's obligatory respect for God.[147] Topbaş also advises the reader also that free will is not an issue in which one can find useful knowledge.[148]

To conclude, Erenköy repeats the usual prudent narrative on free will. The prime method of securing God's sovereignty leaves the movement's narrative in a quite traditional position on the free will issue. Thus, Erenköy's stance on free will is the parallel of its position on natural law: overvaluing free will is a sign of ignorance, therefore one must always keep in mind that it is totally non-existent in the face of God's absolute will.[149] It is again interesting to observe an Islamist movement with a Maturidi confessional identity not proposing strong arguments on free will and instead siding with traditional arguments on free will, which are not compatible with the Maturidi perspective.

6.4   Official Islam on Free Will

6.4.1   Diyanet

We also encounter the traditional prudence on the free will issue in the publications of the Diyanet. *İlmihal* warns that only God can know the inner reality of free will. Thus, asking for a clear solution here is to ask the impossible of human beings.[150] After stating the impossibility of grasping free will, *İlmihal* states that all events and things in the universe come into existence by God's creation. Thus, man decides or chooses his action within the boundaries that are given to him by God.[151] There is no complete freedom. This is in fact the exact strategy that we observe in Erenköy and İskenderpaşa: since the general characteristic of Turkish Islam is the God-first approach, the prime interest is usually to make it explicitly clear that a proposed argument does not violate God's sovereignty.

Having secured God's sovereignty, *İlmihal* examines the subject of free will under two subtitles of a section, in line with the Maturidi view, where the ideational and practical segments of man's actions are analyzed separately. Under the first subtitle, "Man's Will and Its Role in Action," the ideational aspect is explained. Accordingly, God created man with free will so man can act as he (man) wishes. This bold statement is, however, qualified in the following way: man's will does not dominate the act; instead, it has only a limited effect on man's action. This text implies that man is able to dominate his acts enough to be responsible for them. Instead of presenting dialectical debates to clarify what is meant by these arguments, the text is satisfied with the traditional motto: the acquisition (*kasb*) is from man, and creation is from God.[152] Critically, *İlmihal* does not give any information about what *kasb* is beyond the assertion that it originates in man.

The first subsection thus offers what can be called a reserved stance on free will. However, the difficulty of reconciling man's autonomous ability to will and God's ultimate sovereignty appears to be a perennial topic in the Diyanet's books. Though the narrative acknowledges man's ability to will, that ability is compromised as soon as it is juxtaposed with God's sovereignty. The dilemma is the impossibility of imagining any act, even the act of wishing something, independent of God's sovereignty. Everything is not only part of God's knowledge but also part of his will. The Diyanet's interpretation of Islamic theology is thus reluctant to recognize man's autonomy even in the ideational segment of his actions. For example, a Diyanet book on destiny for the general reader first invokes the Qur'anic verse "you cannot will it unless God wills" and then concludes that it is not possible for any development to take place independent of God's will.[153]

After explaining the ideational aspect of action, *İlmihal* examines how actions come into existence. The section "The Creation of Man's Actions" counterbalances the previous section. One is again reminded that according to Sunni Islam, only God can create, and thus one cannot think of man as creating his actions.[154] Man is able to choose by using his free will. However, God's eternal knowledge already knows man's choice and creates according to man's choice and will.[155] The idea of God creating what man wills reflects the classical Maturidi opinion, though it is not clear whether this division of labor between man and God gives ultimate freedom to man. Yet, the reference to God's knowledge empowers God's role without negating man's volition. It puts God into the context *via* his knowing rather than his sovereignty. God knows everything eternally because he is outside of time.[156] Yet, his knowing is not like acting and does not compromise man's will. Although *İlmihal* does not develop this argument, its reference to God's involvement by stressing God's knowledge rather than his power could be evaluated as a proof displaying *İlmihal*'s reserved endorsement of a man-first approach to free will.

The exegetic work *Tefsir* explicitly affirms the Maturidi perspective, which is presented as being theologically different from all the other schools—Ash'ari, Mu'tazila, and Jabriyya.[157] *Tefsir* states clearly that human will is real and exists along with God's will.[158] The relevant sections on free will in *Tefsir* exhibit two important characteristics: first, the exegesis includes many declarative remarks. For example, it is frequently stated straightforwardly that man has the will to act and that God is the creator of everything, as if these two facts do not raise any theological dilemmas.[159] We are not informed about how this compatibility is possible. Thus, the exegesis presents a minimalist approach to free will, despite the framing of the debate according to the Maturidi perspective. Thus, *Tefsir* gives the impression that it wants to arrest the impact of man's will precisely at the point where it is adequately positioned to counter fatalism.

A striking example of this minimalism is the exegesis explanation of man's action in relation to God's involvement: man's power and will are somehow (*bir şekilde*) influential in man's actions.[160] The sentence is an indirect one, presenting its meaning through interrelated arguments' clauses. By attributing the effect of man's will somehow (*bir şekilde*) to his own act with, it recognizes the limited explanatory power of reason. In Turkish, *bir şekilde* refers to a situation in which we know the facts but lack information about how they work or relate to one another. Thus, man exerts some influence on his actions, but our intellect fails to grasp how that actually occurs. This is a typical example of Maturidi obscurantism that secures man's freedom without attempting to solve its apparently contradiction with God's sovereignty.

As elaborated in previous chapters, al-Maturidi conceded that man is an agent who acquires his power to act but did not make it clear how man is differentiated from God, who retains the power to create everything including man's acts.[161] No matter the reality, al-Maturidi asks us to believe in a model where man is a free doer, even though God is the creator of all actions. Al-Maturidi is satisfied by having made his position on free will clear and sets other problems aside. Reflecting this classical Maturidi method, *Tefsir* declares that man's will influences his actions and wants us to believe that it is occurs in some way (*bir şekilde*) that we cannot comprehend.

Faith Series has also several sections on free will that generally adhere to Ash'ari theology. *Faith Series* also explicitly admits that it is not possible to completely explain the free will issue.[162]

If we recall that the series is a recent project by the Diyanet to educate the public about Islamic faith, it is striking to observe that Fakhr al-Razi, the most prominent Ash'ari scholar after al-Ghazali, dominates many volumes of the series.[163] For example, a volume of the series that contains long sections on free will starts with a parable from al-Razi where Caliph Ali's opinions on free will are explicated. Ironically, the message of the parable refutes the main arguments of Maturidi and the Mu'tazila on free will. A man came to Ali and said that he is able to perform both good and bad deeds. Ali asked the man whether he does so along with God or independent of God. Ali then warned that if one thinks he performs any act along with God, it is simply polytheism, since to do so is to assign a partner to God. On the other hand, if one thinks one is able to act independently, it is tantamount to deifying oneself.[164] The Ash'ari message of the parable is clear; the first part attacks the Maturidi position, while the second part attacks on Mu'tazila position. After the parable, we are warned that the gist of the free will issue is the question of whether man is able to do anything independent of God or not. Having successfully located the free will issue within God's creation, the explanation is given: man has no ability of completely independent action.[165] Then it is stated that all deeds of man from birth to death are under God's absolute control. God is the absolute authority in planning and governing everything in the universe, including man's volition and deeds.[166] Though *Faith Series* includes some typical examples of discussions on free will, the general approach is very critical of man's freedom in his volition and deeds. Yet, we are warned against being misled by alternative arguments, since human action is created by God. It is underlined that man's relationship to his own actions is only a façade.[167]

6.4.2   School Textbooks

Following the same principle of prudence, school textbooks devote almost no space to the free will issue. Reading the relevant pages, one feels that textbook authors consciously refrain any detailed engagement with the free will issue. Analysis of the very short, relevant sections indicates that the general feature of the textbooks' treatment of free will is similar to that of the Diyanet's materials. Textbooks recognize that man has an ability to choose according to his will. However, it is also noted that man's will is partial (*cüz'i*), and that the absolute will (*kulli*) belongs only to God.[168] However, there is no information about how the two wills relate to man's actions. The relevant sections in the textbooks aim to teach students that man has free will, which is compatible with God's sovereignty, but they do so without explaining how that compatibility is possible.

6.5   ISLAMIC MOVEMENTS ON KNOWLEDGE

6.5.1   Işıkçılar

Inner knowledge is an important component of the Işıkçılar interpretation of Islam. In the movement, the concept refers to the sublime form of learning, different from rational knowledge, that lay people can acquire.[169] Accordingly, the reason why we need inner knowledge is the limited capacity of human reason; there are many things that reason cannot grasp. Similarly, human sensation is not capable of perceiving the divine governance of nature.[170] Thus, there is a need for an alternate knowledge to connect man with invisible rules that govern the universe.

Işıkçılar employs Ghazalian arguments to demonstrate the limits of human reason and sensation. The Işıkçılar reference books are full of quotations from al-Ghazali. We encounter Al-Ghazali's famous example of the limits of the human eye.[171] Elsewhere, Işık quotes at length al-Ghazali's *Al-Munkidh* to argue that there are critical things beyond the scope of reason.[172] Moreover, inner knowledge in Işıkçılar is no longer limited to the spiritual experiences of Sufis; instead, everyone requires it, as human reason cannot fully comprehend the real, divine rules that determine the natural order.

Işıkçılar writings give reason a subservient place, a view, we have already seen in the writings of al-Ghazali. Human reason is an instrument that operates according to mechanical principles and has no ability to generate reliable knowledge. On this model, reason's limits disqualify it as a means of acquiring reliable knowledge.[173] Reason is just "an instrument of measurement," a passive apparatus lacking the ability to generate truth.[174] It therefore cannot play a serious role in matters regarding knowledge about God. Reason is not able to discover truth on its own; it needs the help of a higher authority. At best, it can only choose between alternatives, and then only if it is given true guidance. Thus, if not properly guided, subservient reason can even become an instrument of delusion.

Işıkçılar does not only subordinate reason to God's guidance. The movement's teachings dismiss reason altogether as an authority, particularly on but not limited to religious issues. Işık condemns as infidel those who interpret the Qur'an according to reason, for the only legitimate and correct meanings are those interpreted by the Sunni scholars.[175]

To challenge Işık by asking whether those scholars employ reason when interpreted meaning is pointless, since Işık holds that *ahl al-Sunna* scholars interpreted Islam according to what they learned from the Prophet, not according to reason.[176] In Işık's approach to knowledge, the only reliable method is inner knowledge. In fact, revelation itself is proof of the limits of human reason: "Had reason been enough to find truth, there would have been no need for prophets," writes Işık.[177] This point is another major deviation from Maturidi theology; for al-Maturidi, reason can know good on its own, even without revelation. By contrast, Işık follows al-Ash'ari and concludes that attempting to understand Islam through the guidance of reason is a rejection of prophethood.[178] Pursuing inner knowledge is identified as a method of overcoming the deficiencies of human reasoning and sensation. The only limitation is Islamic law, with which inner knowledge is expected to comply.[179] Islamic law, unlike scientific knowledge, has its origin in revelation, making it the highest norm, to which all other types of knowledge and opinions are subjected.

Işık emphasis's emphasis on inner knowledge suggests a preference for traditions over reasoning. Knowledge acquired by the traditions is superior to human reason.[180] This is yet another difference between the Ash'ari and the Maturidi schools, proving how the Işıkçılar, notwithstanding their Maturidi confessional identity, has evolved along an Ash'ari line. Unlike al-Ash'ari, who required the acceptance of all traditions the traditionists reported,[181] al-Maturidi held that narrators are fallible people and that their traditions can not necessarily be accepted.[182] Once it is established that human reason is deficient in various ways, Işık warns that its employment as a central element might lead to innovations in Islam.[183] Thus, he asks Muslims to be satisfied with the established body of Islamic knowledge.

As I have explicated in Chap. 3, the limits of human senses and reason are key evidence for al-Ghazali that inner knowledge must exist. By contrast, al-Maturidi, though he admitted such limits, argued that they could not disprove the validity of rational knowledge. For al-Maturidi, rational knowledge through sensation and reasoning is the best available method.[184] Thus, the popularity of al-Ghazali's theses on the limits of senses and reason in Turkey, as we observe in the case of Işıkçılar, demonstrates the deep influence of Ash'ari theology even in a country known with a predominantly Maturidi confessional identity. One would not expect confessional Maturidis to compromise on al-Maturidi's stance on rational knowledge, which itself is essential to Maturidi theology. However, as we observe in all the cases examined in this chapter, al-Ghazali's theses on knowledge have eclipsed those of Maturidi in contemporary Turkey.

The incorporation of inner knowledge into mainstream Islam paved the way for an idiosyncratic approach to the heart—a replica of al-Ghazali's approach, as discussed in Chap. 3—which requires further attention, since it also prevails in all the cases we study in this book. According to this view, the heart is the pivotal organ with the ability to experience sensation and to think alongside its function of pumping blood. As al-Ghazali wrote, "the five senses" are "conveying water to [*the heart*]," which is the main organ to process them.[185] This description is based on an interpretation of the Qur'an. In the Qur'an, the heart is the central organ of comprehension as well as the generation of emotions and senses.[186] For example, a verse in Surat al-A'raf depicts the heart as an organ with a purpose of acquiring understanding, but also counts it with other organs, like eyes and ears, and mentions their prime functions of seeing and hearing: "They have hearts with which they do not understand, they have eyes with which they do not see, and they have ears with which they do not hear."[187] The semantics of this verse suggest that, as eyes see and ears hear, so the heart understands. Based on such an interpretation, the Islamic tradition of Occasionalism identifies the heart as the organ able to acquire inner knowledge: Since secondary causes are repudiated, a new type of knowledge is required to connect man with the divine rules of the universe. Thus the heart emerges as man's means of connecting to and acquiring inner knowledge.

To clarify the issue of heart in this vein, I propose the following theoretical framework for analyzing the various interpretations of the function of the heart. The first approach to the question of the heart in the Qur'an argues that such verses are allegorical and ought not to be read literally. The second approach is historicist and explains the cardiocentric model—which argued that the heart is in fact the organ of intelligence, in the Qur'an as the result of the view of the Arabs who (in the seventh century) believed that the heart is the center of thinking and believing.[188] Thus, not the brain-centered conception of the body (the encephalocentric theory) but the Aristotelian idea of the human body with the heart as the center of sensation and thinking was the dominant one.[189] While the heart is the most important organ in the Aristotelian conception of the body, in the Hippocratic conception, the brain is central. For the historicist approach, revelation followed the cardiocentric track only to make its message understandable, as that was the norm among Arabs at the time. Thus, the term heart in the Qur'an should be read today as "brain" or "reasoning." The third approach is literalist and accepts the heart as an organ with some kind of sense-experience capacity, and even of reasoning, without rejecting the role of brain.[190]

Supporters of inner knowledge have generally adhered to the literal interpretation of the Qur'anic verses that address the function of the heart. Işıkçılar likewise claims that the heart is not only a blood-pumping organ but also the generator of knowledge that affects one's belief.[191] Işıkçılar identifies the heart as the organ of love, hate, and fear, and as the locus of belief or disbelief.[192] Similarly, the heart plays the central role in inner knowledge: divine light comes to the heart to deliver the knowledge that helps us understand what God and the Prophet mean by their words.[193]

Işık wrote that the heart is the president of the human body. Having a lower status, the brain can only inform the heart about man's emotions. Accordingly, when man receives some information about outer things through senses, the brain quickly reports them to the heart, that is, the final processor.[194] (I should note here that Işık had a modern education in medicine and chemistry.)

In a wider context, in the case of Işıkçılar, we also see how a contemporary Islamic movement maintains antagonism to philosophy and rational knowledge. Işıkçılar reference books define philosophers as heretics for having ideas that threaten Islamic faith. In its attack on philosophy, Işıkçılar repeats the arguments and examples of al-Ghazali. Upholding his antagonism to philosophy, the movement relies on al-Ghazali's arguments and examples rather than reconstructing their challenge by referring to the ideas of contemporary philosophers. They still understand and conceptualize Islam's relations with philosophy in the terms al-Ghazali formulated almost ten centuries ago. Thus, Işıkçılar exemplifies how some contemporary Islamic movements continue the fight with philosophers, even the Greek ones.

Greek philosophers are heretic scholars, Işık frequently tells the reader.[195] However, Işık also wants to demonstrate their intellectual poverty: "The Greek philosophers are the most ignorant people on earth."[196] Such comments represent the present-day animosity toward philosophy. Işık makes no allowance even for the greats of classical philosophy. He calls Plato an *ahmak* (idiot, stupid) and derides Aristotle for depending on reason rather than experience. Işık blames these two giants of Greek philosophy for delay of Europe's technological development, which, he argues, would have happened much earlier than eighteenth century had it not been for their poor intellectual guidance.[197]

While criticizing the philosophers, Işık uses populist jargon rather than engaging directly with ideas. His arguments that denigrate the philosophers are simple and appealing to his followers. He advises them not to read the Greek philosophers. Instead, they should be satisfied with Islam, for even a simple tradition that grew from the Prophet's utterances is worth more than the talk of all the old Greek philosophers.[198]

Işık's stance on Muslim philosophers is equally harsh. The list of Muslim philosophers who are labeled heretics includes many famous names. Ibn Hazm is a heretic.[199] Ibn al-Haytham and Abu Bakr al-Razi were influenced by Greek philosophy.[200] Unsurprisingly, Işık also targets the Mu'tazila: they, too, are defined as a heretic sect, owing in part to their rationalist philosophy. Işık reserves a special place for Ibn Sina in the list of heretics as the "leader" of those who follow reason.[201]

Işık accuses Ibn Sina and al-Farabi in particular of sharing Aristotle's opinion that matter is eternal and then declares that were disbelievers.[202] Işık often cannot control his anger toward the Muslim philosophers. For example, Ibn Sina was of limited vision. This caused his lesser share of Islam, and he stayed in the "dirt of philosophy" (*felsefe pisliği*).[203]

Işık draws heavily on al-Ghazali while condemning the philosophers.[204] Declaring Ibn Sina as faithless, Işık quotes Al-Ghazali directly.[205] Similarly, he quotes Al-Ghazali while when al-Farabi as infidel.[206] Such cases indicate the continuing impact of al-Ghazali on Muslims in contemporary Turkey. While pushing philosophy out of Islam, Işık also quotes several Islamic scholars like al-Shafi'i, who is reported to have denounced *kalam* as a great sin, and Abu Yusuf, who is reported to have declared that those who are interested in *kalam* cannot lead prayer.[207]

Işık praises al-Ghazali for purging Islamic thought of philosophers' errors.[208] He presents al-Ghazali as a savior of orthodox Islam in an age of chaos, when heretical ideas, like those of the Fatimids and the Mu'tazila, infected Muslim lands.[209] He also credits al-Ghazali for incorporating inner knowledge into Islam as part of his fight against the philosophers.[210]

To strengthen his attack on philosophy, Işık proposes a narrative about Islamic history in which he marks the period that I call the Age of Autonomy as the source of many problem, including the contamination of the Islamic faith with scientific knowledge and philosophical thinking.[211] The origin of the problem for Işık is in the interaction of Islamic and Greek thought: this is what paved the way for erroneous interpretations of religion.[212]

By contrast, Işık salutes the latter period, the age in which the roots of Sunni orthodoxy took hold, as the restoration period when Islam's contamination was cured. According to him, Islam was rescued from contamination in the eleventh century.[213] He interprets the reorganization of Muslim societies in the post-Abbasid period as the restoration process that returned Muslims to the authentic Islam, that is, to its original form before Greek thought contaminated it.

Let us visualize two brackets of time in Islamic history: the first begins under the reign of Ma'mun in 813, when the Abbasid Bayt al-Hikma was at its peak in translating Greek books and soliciting scholars' original contributions; the second beginnings in 1111, when Al-Ghazali died and Sunni orthodoxy was consolidating. In the first bracket, which I name the Age of Autonomy, we see a burgeoning rationalist scholarship. In the second bracket, hailed as the restoration period of Islamic history, we see the rise of the piety-minded religious authorities and the rejection of Greek thought. The years 813 and 1111 epitomized the cultural trajectories of each bracket, respectively. Today, there are those who look back on the first bracket and sigh sadly; others, like Işık, look back at the second bracket and sigh with relief.

Işık's narrative is a typical example of this piety-minded perspective, which is shared by many contemporary Islamic revivalists in Turkey. For instance, Said Nursi supports this narrative, claiming that Greek thought contaminated Islam and created chaos in Islamic thought.[214] The Age of Autonomy is regarded by present-day piety-minded scholars as the *ancien régime* when Islam was contaminated.

Işık completely rejects philosophy, considering it to be the agent of the contamination of the Islamic faith. To him, there is no such thing as truly Islamic philosophy. No true Islamic scholar was a philosopher, and no true philosopher can be an Islamic scholar.[215] For example, al-Ghazali was not a philosopher, nor was he under the influence of Greek philosophy.[216] Philosophy is the opposite of prophecy, because pure reason rejects revelation.[217] Philosophical statements are nothing but diversion from the right path.[218]

Işık defines the religiously correct path as dependent first on revelation and then on the transmitted teachings of the Islamic scholars. For him, dependence on reason leads to rejection of prophethood.[219] Leaving no room for philosophy in Islamic thought, Işık maintains the Ghazalian mindset.

6.5.2   İskenderpaşa

İskenderpaşa also adopts the Ghazalian approach to inner knowledge: man is able to acquire inner knowledge after going through several religious procedures. The movement's works hold inner knowledge above rational knowledge and frequently emphasize the differences between the two types of knowledge. Coşan warned that inner knowledge should not be confused with the knowledge that is acquired by listening to or reading the works of university professors.[220]

Inner knowledge and rational knowledge are stratified. If the key agents of Sunni Islam are the piety-minded religious scholars, then inner knowledge has played a key role in consolidating their status. Reflecting this stratification, Coşan incorporates al-Ghazali's label "men of words," used pejoratively for rationalist philosophers who depend on reason and senses, into his writings.[221]

Coşan underlines the substantial differences between rational and inner knowledge: the latter can only be obtained through a personal process. This is what Al-Ghazali wrote of inner knowledge in *al-Munkidh*, that it did not come from "systematic demonstration or marshalled argument."[222] Similarly, Coşan argues that inner knowledge does not originate in systematic methods, for it is not separated from one's state of mind or religiosity. Emphasizing this difference, Coşan often uses the example of the university professors, since they are the agents of rational knowledge, which can be acquired by everyone who practices the relevant systematic method. In explaining this point, Coşan gives another meaning to Al-Ghazali's remark that science is not about words.[223] He holds that it is not always possible to translate the truth of nature and other things in terms of causal links into the ordered system of language. Science is more a state of mind. Just as the Occasionalist viewpoint requires fuzzy logic to explain the events of nature by defining God's habit as the only cause, so inner knowledge destroys the more stable nature of rational knowledge and introduces a similarly fuzzy knowledge by proposing the subjective process of knowledge acquisition. Inner knowledge rises above rational knowledge inasmuch as it deals with the supreme form of knowledge: the knowledge on God, the sole agent of all actions.[224]

Coşan views human reason as a subservient reason, which needs the guidance of superior religious knowledge. Accordingly, reason does not have power to discover absolute truths; it is able to recognize only the principles defined by God. However, because reason is without the capacity to understand God's knowledge directly, it should pursue this quest by learning from inner knowledge, which Coşan calls the real science (*asıl ilim*).[225] Reason is expected to recognize truths presented through the agents of inner knowledge. The repudiation of reason's autonomous ability to discover truths in turn requires a theory of the brain and the heart.

Coşan recognizes the heart as the organ of thought, contemplation, and perception.[226] For example, interpreting the above-cited verse from the Qur'an in which it is said, "they have hearts with which they do not comprehend," Coşan explains that "we understand from the verse that the heart is an organ of comprehension." Though Coşan does not reject the brain's role, and his approach to the heart bears spiritual elements, he still recognizes that the heart can comprehend while also being the chief organ that keeps man carrying on (*çekip çevirmek*).[227] Kotku similarly wrote that the center of reason is the heart and not the brain.[228]

In their treatments of inner knowledge, Islamic actors in contemporary Turkey usually cite al-Ghazali's arguments. Al-Ghazali's ideas have also influenced İskenderpaşa's interpretation of Islam. However, we observe a special case where the writings of another Islamic scholar, who lived even before al-Ghazali, also inform the movement's understanding of inner knowledge. Abu 'Abd al-Rahman al-Sulami (942–1021), who was raised in a Shafi'i-Ash'ari intellectual circle, is a critical thinker for İskenderpaşa.[229] Al-Sulami believed in the possibility of experiential knowledge of divine reality through Sufi methods of inner education. He focused on mystical theology.[230] As Alexander Kynsh explains, al-Sulami played a key role in the systemization of the Sufi science of his age.[231] He also wrote an exegesis of the Qur'an, based on Sufi methods.[232]

The central status of inner knowledge and the skepticism toward rational knowledge associated with it have led İskenderpaşa to repeat traditional Ghazalian arguments against philosophy as well. Coşan criticizes philosophers for proposing alternatives to revelation and for being satisfied solely with reason.[233] Coşan harshly criticizes philosophy and writes that philosophers' knowledge should be abandoned.[234] Kotku also frequently warns his followers not to obey philosophers, particularly on what they say about nature.[235] For Kotku, philosophers are those who fill in their books with "empty words."[236]

İskenderpaşa's writings are also critical of the Mu'tazila, framed as a heretical sect that is wrong on all issues. Like Işık, Kotku mentions the *fatwa* that prohibits praying behind a Mu'tazila.[237] Kotku also warned that Muslims should not marry them or even go to their funerals.[238] Given that there are no Mu'tazila around, we may read "Mu'tazila" as a label for any and all rationalists of the present age.

İskenderpaşa writings also repeatedly deny the intellectual caliber of philosophers. Coşan for instance considers philosophers like Strabo, Aristotle, and Plato to be insincere and unoriginal thinkers.[239] "The philosopher is a man like you," says Coşan, to challenge their prestige, implying their inability to acquire absolute knowledge through revelation as well as inner knowledge. Philosophers, this logic holds, are just like anyone who formulates his thoughts on the basis of sensation and reasoning.

Moreover, for Coşan, philosophy books are full of contradictions and mistakes, since they are simply collections of various philosophers' opinions, which change over time. Each philosopher taught his own ideas, which might be corrected or revised by peers or successors. The history of philosophy is a collection of corrections, proving that philosophers have always changed their minds.[240] Changes and differences in their knowledge are proof of the imperfect nature of rational knowledge. Coşan asks rhetorically, "so is not the path of reason always one?" To him, differences among philosophers are proof of reason's limits, which in turn demonstrates why inner reason is required.[241]

Coşan implies that, in contrast to the always-shifting teachings of the philosophers, inner knowledge does not change and is therefore reliable. We should note, however, that Coşan never brings up the intellectual differences among Islamic scholars, nor of the Islamic principle that disagreement among scholars reflects the mercy of God.

The only context where Coşan speaks positively about philosophers is when he contemplates the Muslim contribution to Western civilization. While arguing that Islamic scholars' ideas contributed to European successes, Coşan speaks appreciatively of, for example, Ibn Rushd.[242]

The İskenderpaşa reference books maintain the traditional stance on philosophy. Coşan's approach annihilates any chance of incorporating rationalist methods into the movement's interpretation of Islam. The only legitimate place for rational thought is subservient reason, which is the guided by superior religious knowledge.

6.5.3   Erenköy

Like the other cases, Erenköy interprets inner knowledge within the framework of its Occasionalist idea of nature. There is need for real insight to acquire divine knowledge of the universe and its divine governance. Inner knowledge is the alternate method of examining and comprehending the real causes that operate in nature.[243] In general, the theological ideas on rational knowledge and inner knowledge that Erenköy teaches reflect the influence of al-Ghazali. Some particular accents or discursive elements notwithstanding, Erenköy upholds the Ghazalian idea of inner knowledge.

According to the reference books of Erenköy, inner knowledge is acquired through a subjective process without standard rules and becomes accessible only upon spiritual maturation.[244] It is received directly through the heart. Unlike rational knowledge, inner knowledge depends on a personal and subjective procedure, and thus only those who possess a purified soul can attain such knowledge.[245]

The ontological necessity of inner knowledge comes again from the limits of human senses and reason. According to Topbaş, positivism constructs truth on the five senses. However, Islam is also about the unseen, where human senses have no capacity at all.[246] However, the issue of deficiency is also a valid point about human reason: like every bodily organ, the intellect also has its limits.[247] As a result, a human being cannot gain perfect knowledge, due to the limited nature of sensation and reasoning. Thus, employing means such as reasoning, or other methods like analogy, is never enough to grasp knowledge of matters that are beyond human intellect.[248]

Topbaş frequently quotes al-Ghazali while arguing that reasoning and sensation cannot be sufficient for finding the knowledge that is behind the "curtain that covers the invisible side of things."[249] Accordingly, while reason and the senses can be used to investigate the visible realm, another instrument is required to learn about the things that reason and the senses cannot grasp. Only with inner knowledge is man able to see and understand what his senses cannot see and his mind cannot understand.[250] In this thinking, as stated above, the unseen realm is in fact the ontological reason for proposing inner knowledge.[251] We again observe how al-Ghazali's arguments on the limits of senses and reason play a central role in the interpretation of Islamic theology in Erenköy. Analyzing various cases on this subject, one concludes that Islamic actors in contemporary Turkey have given up a substantial element of the Maturidi interpretation in favor of an Ash'ari standpoint on this topic.

Topbaş also defends the concept of subservient reason. Reason is only able to find, know, and comprehend things in a limited realm of the visible world.[252] Thus, revelation's help is always required.[253] In fact, God's sending thousands of prophets is proof of the deficiency of the human intellect. Reason is necessary but insufficient. Human reason or intellect is *naqis al-'aql* (inadequate intellect), or *'aql al-juz'i* (partial intellect).[254] Since it fails to grasp reality in its totality, the subservient reason may generate conclusions mixed with "doubt, hesitation, error, deficiency and delusion." Thus, it is better for reason to stay "within its natural limits." The logical solution is acceptance by reason of the assistance of revelation. That is the only mechanism to save the former from being dragged into contradiction.[255] Topbaş thus suggests putting reason into the service of religion. If this is not done, and reason is taken as the only instrument, the result will be disaster for humanity.[256]

Erenköy also shares the cardiocentric perspective on human cognition: The heart is not only the spiritual but also the cognitive center of the body. It is the organ that is able to obtain real knowledge. Therefore, the heart is usually defined in the Erenköy reference books as the instrument of knowledge.[257] There is also a hierarchical relationship between the heart and reason: since reason has limits in processing knowledge, the heart takes the lead exactly at the point where reason can go no further in find-ing a solution.[258] The heart occupies the higher place in the hierarchy: the brain presents proofs to the heart, which unifies them for perfect compres-sion of the truth. It is up to the heart to amend the inadequacies of the brain in this process.[259] Without the heart, what the brain produces is only raw knowledge.[260] Reason is dependent on the heart; without the heart, reason has no value.[261] Given the central and the higher role of the heart, Topbaş concludes that "Islam is a religion of the heart rather than merely a religion of reason."[262]

Erenköy also maintains the traditional skepticism toward philosophy and rational knowledge. Topbaş's works argue that philosophy causes people to confuse the prohibited and the permissible because it offers (among other procedures of reasoning) analogical deduction, which allows people to avoid submission to divine revelation. Philosophy is portrayed as weakening the human ability to engage with absolute knowledge. For Topbaş, to prac-tice philosophy is to be enslaved to the limited senses and human intel-lect.[263] The extreme skepticism toward human senses and reasoning, a legacy of al-Ghazali, prevails in Erenköy. In no passage does Topbaş enter-tain any argument about knowledge that might resonate with al-Maturidi.

To give one example of his criticism of reasoning: Topbaş writes that it is Satan who introduced analogical reasoning.[264] Topbaş bases this view on a Qur'anic verse where, after creating Adam, God ordered the angels to prostrate themselves before him. Satan did not comply, though all the oth-ers did. When asked, Satan reasoned to legitimate his disobedience as fol-lows: "I am better than Adam: you created me from fire, and you created him from clay."[265] Muslim scholars usually interpret this verse as proof that reasoning might generate wrong results and lead one away from obeying God's orders. A logical derivative of Satan's argument is the lesson that the absolute knowledge that comes from God must be obeyed, and rea-soning must be distrusted, because it has no ability to acquire knowledge.

Topbaş's second move, very much like a point made by Coşan, is to point out that the disagreements among philosophers are proof of the inadequacy of reason and philosophy.[266] Philosophers prove their own limitations in their constant debates and falsification of each other's views.[267] Again, it is their lack of ability to acquire absolute knowledge that makes them engaged in endless and pointless debate. The argument that philosophers busy themselves with empty arguments has its roots in al-Ghazali's *The Incoherence of Philosophers*, where he complained that to plunge into narrating the differences among the philosophers would involve too long a tale.[268] Since then, on the assumption that there can be only one truth, philosophers' disagreements have been interpreted as proof of their falseness.

Like Coşan and Işık, Topbaş too questions the intellectual quality of philosophers. However, Topbaş focuses more on the applicability of their ideas: he claims that not even one person can be found who has attained happiness through belief in and practice of Aristotle's philosophy.[269] Challenging philosophers for their failure to produce useful knowledge also reflects the influence of al-Ghazali and brings to mind his "men of words" characterization of philosophers, which implies their uselessness. For Topbaş, philosophers are simply "men of words," not purveyors of ideas that can be put to work to cure social problems or guide people to salvation.

Topbaş applies the same criticism to Muslim philosophers. For example, he states that al-Farabi's ideas have no practical application.[270] Thus, having worked through several examples of Greek as well as Islamic philosophy, Topbaş then claims that in the history of humanity, no society has achieved peace and happiness by implementing the views of a particular philosopher.[271] On the contrary, he argues, philosophers have often provoked distress among people.[272]

Islamic ingroup socialization in the case of Erenköy is therefore based on the traditional antagonism to philosophy. The reference books repeatedly state that philosophy is not compatible with Islam. Topbaş recounts the story of Muhammad Iqbal, who read Ibn Sina and al-Farabi. Not satisfied with their dry sentences, Iqbal found himself "a traveler in their nightmare dead-end streets."[273] Like Iqbal, Topbaş is alarmed by the weakness of philosophy and reason.[274] Thus, he issues his judgment: "May reason be sacrificed for Muhammad."[275]

6.6   Official Islam on Knowledge

6.6.1   *Diyanet*

The official narrative of Islam as presented by the Diyanet strives to propose a balanced approach to the question of inner knowledge. The Diyanet's writings do indeed offer a relatively balanced and less one-sided account of the role and importance of inner knowledge. As a result, the Diyanet's articulations of official Islam recognize inner knowledge incorporate it into its religious narrative while also striving to keep it in check.

As a principle, Diyanet writings present inner knowledge to the Turkish public as an important element of Islamic faith. In a section on knowledge, *İlmihal* clearly defines official Islam's standpoint on inner knowledge by declaring that it is possible to access various special types of information through certain procedures called *kashf* and *ilham*.[276] *Kashf* and *ilham* are forms of a self-realization of reality that do not rely on senses or reasoning. Unlike the standard knowledge that we acquire through sensation and reasoning, knowledge reveals itself in its original absoluteness beyond all spatio-temporal determinants in an alternate form like *kashf*.[277] (This is again what al-Ghazali summarized in *Al Munkidh* as the knowledge that "did not come about by systematic demonstration or marshalled argument."[278])

Tefsir takes the same approach to inner knowledge. As long as it is does not clash with revelation, people can get knowledge through inner knowledge.[279] Though Diyanet's attempt to keep inner knowledge within limits is important, the explicit recognition of those limits is even more significant. This is because, given the enormous social impact and prestige that inner knowledge generates. This point is critical in understanding contemporary Islamic socialization as well as Islamic movements in Turkey. Almost all movements believe that their interpretation of Islam, articulated in their reference books, is somehow directly inspired from God. For example, Said Nursi, deeply influential among Islamic movements in contemporary Turkey, wrote that his 6000-page *Risale-i Nur*, which includes long sections on non-religious issues like biology, was a direct inspiration from God.[280]

The reason why Islamic actors emphasize inner knowledge, as we clearly see in the Diyanet materials, is that Sunni orthodox theology does not accept that direct contact between God and men has ceased. *Tefsir* defines God's divine will and revelation as active whereas human reason is passive and subject to revelation and divine will.[281]

Tefsir then contextualizes inner knowledge in the Islamic tradition. The text explains that the Islamic tradition includes the concept of *ledünni 'ilm* (intuitive knowledge or inner knowledge), a type of "knowledge that comes from God without an intermediary or instrument."[282] This knowledge comes to one's cognition not through the standard instruments of the senses. Inner knowledge is classified into two groups, objective-general and subjective-personal. Revelations received from God give objective-general knowledge, whereas all other modes of knowledge reception are subjective-personal. However, both categories of knowledge originate at "God's side" (*Allah katı*).[283]

The classification in *Tefsir* reveals how inner knowledge is defined in Sunni orthodoxy. Revelation, that is, the transmission of objective-general knowledge, ceased with the death of the Prophet Muhammad, but inner knowledge has continued to be transmitted. We can thus finalize the definition of inner knowledge according to Sunni orthodoxy in contemporary Turkey: It is knowledge directly from God transmitted in ways other than revelation.

The Diyanet materials also teach people that the heart is the central organ of inner knowledge. In *Tefsir*, we read that inner knowledge comes through the heart when the "eye of one's heart" opens.[284] To clarify the role of the heart in the acquisition of inner knowledge, *Tefsir* quotes al-Ghazali's *Ihya*. Man's heart and *lehv-i mahfuz* (the divine book that includes all knowledge, including knowledge of the future) are like two mirrors facing each other, but with many curtains in between. Once the curtains are removed, the heart is able to reflect the content of the divine book.[285] Man's heart has the potential to engage directly (without an intermediary) with the divine source of knowledge. However, such narrative through the analogy of a mirror where man communicates between the two worlds contradicts Maturidi epistemology. Al-Maturidi does not recognize such a communication between the two worlds through human beings. For him, as I have stated before, this world could be a proof of another world; however, it cannot inform us about the nature or knowledge of that world.[286]

The interpretation of Islam that the Diyanet promotes among the Turkish public also emphasizes that the heart is the main receiver-organ of inner knowledge. For example, it is very easy to encounter a Friday sermon—written by a central commission under the control of the Diyanet and read in the same way in all mosques in Turkey—that describes the heart as an organ that not only circulates blood but also orients spiritual life, the source of faith and faithlessness, love and hate, good and bad.[287]

Faith Series adopts the same stance on inner knowledge. The series reproduces the traditional skepticism toward rational knowledge. Referring to various Ash'ari resources, *Faith Series* explains that inner knowledge is reliable. The texts also include several warnings on the subjective nature of inner knowledge, but inner knowledge is never categorically rejected.[288] Sufi practices are appreciated as means of acquiring inner knowledge. Reading relevant parts of the series, one does not detect a strong Maturidi reservation, which would be more skeptical toward, or at least less enthusiastic about, inner knowledge. Instead, the general approach of faith series maintains the Ghazalian skepticism toward rational knowledge.

Inner knowledge is emphasized as a pillar of the Islamic faith.[289] *Faith Series* also concludes that a theory of knowledge that depends solely on empirical observation is invalid. One must include metaphysical inquiry, without which any theory of knowledge is reductionist and narrow.[290] The series repeatedly mentions that observation and experience are not the sole source of knowledge. Knowledge, in this account, should not only include the events of this world but also metaphysical experience.[291] Having repeated the narrative on the limits of human knowledge, *Faith Series* then explains that religion complements science.[292] We here see the typical hierarchy of Sunni Orthodox theology, where religion retains ultimate authority over science.

The Diyanet's narrative functions to incorporate inner knowledge into the mainstream interpretation of Islam. This is clear even in those works by authors known for their appreciation for Maturidi theology. Consider for example the volume coauthored by Bekir Topaloğlu, a scholar who translated Maturidi's *Kitab al-Tawhid* into Turkish. The volume states that Maturidi theology is superior to that of al-Ash'ari. An early section that lists sense, reasoning as the major sources of knowledge accords perfectly with Maturidi theology.[293] The reader is also warned that knowledge acquired through inner knowledge is not reliable. However, the text never explicitly rejects inner knowledge.[294] On the other hand, later on inner knowledge is recognized as the second method of proving the existence of God. Inner knowledge here is described as a direct method where one removes curtains to obtain absolute knowledge. Inner knowledge is the knowledge that God directly puts into the human heart without resorting the normal means of knowledge acquisition, meaning observation and reasoning.[295] In addition, inner knowledge is described as a more sublime form of knowledge acquisition. Reason is able to know indirectly through some means, whereas the heart knows directly by inner knowledge without resorting any secondary means.[296]

Thus, some minor qualifications notwithstanding, the Diyanet's materials clearly recognize and value inner knowledge. In 2013, *Diyanet Aylık Dergi*, the Diyanet's monthly journal for a general readership, published a special issue on *irfan* (gnostic knowledge), an indication of the important place of inner knowledge in the Diyanet's messaging to the Turkish public. In the editorial column, Mehmed Görmez—who was the head of the Diyanet in 2013—emphasized that man grasps some truths through spiritual senses.[297] Görmez's argument takes the Ghazalian approach to explaining the need for an alternative form of knowledge. Also noteworthy in this vein is the Diyanet's persistent recognition of alternative knowledge and its policy of disregarding the views of various Turkish scholars who are critical of inner knowledge.[298] While disseminating its interpretation of Islam to the public, the Diyanet does not incorporate such rejections or criticism of inner knowledge.

In this vein, the Diyanet employs two different narratives to explain the relationship between philosophy and science. In the first narrative, philosophers are treated as part of the greater Islamic civilization and discussed in a careful, moderate tone. For example, *İlmihal* favorably cites Ibn Sina, al-Farabi, and Ibn Rushd.[299] At no point does the Diyanet's first narrative point out the criticisms levied against philosophers like al-Farabi. *Tefsir* shares this positive evaluation and even recognizes philosophical argumentation as a valid method in religious study.[300] This positive approach even includes the Mu'tazila and does not call the group heretical. Their arguments are selectively quoted throughout *Tefsir*.[301] *Tefsir* even legitimates the Mu'tazila by mentioning that *ahl al-Sunna* scholars relied on some of their arguments.[302] *İlmihal* also refer to Mu'tazila arguments in various sections.[303] Given the public status of *İlmihal* as the major Islamic catechism, its neutral (and arguably favorable) stance on the Mu'tazila is significant. The positive narrative on philosophy and rationalism continues, even with regard to the historical period when Islam and Greek philosophy interacted. *İlmihal* points to this period as the origin of the Islamic rational schools.[304]

This first narrative accommodates the philosophers into Islamic cultural heritage without addressing their debates with piety-minded scholars. Diyanet materials never quote philosophers in ways that might appear to undermine Sunni orthodoxy. These texts give the general impression that Islamic intellectual history has been a smooth, uncontroversial progression toward the formation of Sunni theology. They downplay intra-Islamic debate and avoid suggesting that different scholars reached radically different conclusions about theology and epistemology.

However, the Diyanet's second narrative on the philosophers, which focuses on matters of theology, reflects the influence of al-Ghazali. It harshly criticizes philosophy and even modern science. *Faith Series* articulates this second narrative. The series, as the general rule, rejects modern science's authority in explaining nature. It is underlined that there is no science independent of metaphysics.[305] Accordingly, religion has authority to interrogate even scientific conclusions. Citing al-Ghazali, the series warns readers that certain scientific assumptions may even constitute or result in heresy. For example, philosophers such as Phyrrhon, Protagoras, and Descartes are criticized on the grounds that their epistemological skepticism leads to atheistic conclusions.[306] Sigmund Freud is presented as a *"sapkın"*[307]—a term that can mean both deviant and pervert in Turkish. The text repeatedly condemns Darwinism, positivism, and skepticism.[308] The series posits a hierarchy of knowledge with religion at the top. The rationale behind such thinking is clear: "Philosopher's opinions and scientists' observations and technical innovations" are unsatisfactory. Thus, at most they can be simple "stepping stones" (*atlama taşı*) toward the true reality of religion.[309] Various forms of inner knowledge are frequently explained and defended: experimental knowledge excluding metaphysical experience is held to be not only misleading but also unscientific. Science is redefined to include metaphysical experience and knowledge; thus, as the series argues, if metaphysics is removed, what we get is not science but mere positivism.[310] However, the scope of metaphysics is so wide that it even includes dreams as a source of knowledge.[311]

6.6.2   School Textbooks

School textbooks differ considerably from the other cases in terms of their treatment of the issue of inner knowledge. There is no section of any mandatory religious course textbook that explicitly recognizes inner knowledge. Instead, textbooks merely advise that Muslims should seek true knowledge (*doğru bilgi*).[312] This phrasing suggests that religion does have some role in verifying true knowledge. However, though the adjective "true" (*doğru*) has a religious connotation, it cannot be interpreted as recognition of inner knowledge. On the other hand, the textbooks do repeat the traditional argument that human reason is not sufficient for the acquisition of true knowledge, and that revelation is therefore necessary. However, such warnings in textbooks do not amount to a call for inner knowledge to compensate for the deficiency of human reason. Instead, a cooperative model between revelation and reason is suggested. Man is said to reach truth and beauty more easily when reason and revelation are both used.[313]

The textbooks do include long sections on Sufi orders, whose major concern is to acquire inner knowledge. In this vein, Sufism is defined as "a branch of science that belongs to Islamic culture."[314] The focus on Sufism as a branch of science within Islamic culture is indeed important. However, there is no further information about what is meant by the phrase "a branch of science that belongs to Islamic culture." The general discourse implies an intention to incorporate Sufism into the Islamic tradition. We encounter special chapters on Sufi orders like the Naqshbandiyya and Qadiriyya. Thus, it is normal to read sections with the title of "Interpretations in Islamic Thought" that explain how and why Islam has been interpreted throughout history. Such sections usually focus on various Sufi traditions, but mainly on the Qadiri and Naqshbandiyya orders as the two representative traditions.[315] They are presented as examples of "Sufi Interpretations of Islamic Thought."[316]

The textbooks also cite al-Ghazali as an Islamic scholar who systemized and developed Sufi thought.[317] However, in presenting a detailed discussion of Sufi orders and al-Ghazali, textbooks do not include any discussion of inner knowledge. Instead, such topics presented as examples of the richness of Islamic tradition and culture. In any case, the growing enthusiasm in textbooks to incorporate Sufism into the official Islamic narrative should be noted. Textbooks present Sufism as a pillar of Islam.[318]

Textbooks display a negative view of the historical period during which the encounter between Islam and Greek philosophy took place. The textbooks locate the origin of Islamic philosophy in the encounter among Islamic, Greek, Persian, and Indian culture. The interaction is presented in negative terms and is said to have had several problematic consequences. For example, the textbook asserts that new Muslims introduced their old beliefs and cultures to Islam. This created deep philosophical problems. This is the "contamination" problem that we examined in the contexts of the Erenköy and Işıkçılar accounts of Islamic history.

The religion course textbooks point to translations of the works of Greek philosophers as the major reason for the contamination of Islam. Contamination led to intellectual chaos, during which "some people with bad intentions" began questioning Islamic principles, sowing *fitna* in the Muslim community.[319] This period is deemed a time of cultural chaos (*kültürel kargaşa*) when doubts clouded Muslim minds. This chaos brought forth the rationalist defense of Islam in the light of the Qur'an and the hadith.[320] Thus, the narrative about the genealogy of Islamic philosophy centers on the defense of Islam. It implies that Islam's cultural interaction with other cultures, particularly Greek culture, created serious social problems. The textbooks in turn praise the post-Abbasid developments that gave birth to Sunni orthodoxy.

However, textbooks do not take a dim view of philosophers themselves. They present the philosophers as part of the Islamic cultural heritage, but they do not go into detail about their theological arguments. Thus, text-books show appreciation for philosophers like al-Farabi and Ibn Sina as great contributors to Islamic civilization.[321] The comparatively balanced narrative of the textbooks is also evident when it comes to the Mu'tazila. Textbooks quote the major characteristics of Mu'tazila thought, such as the emphasis on man's freedom, and the belief in man's ability to create his own actions, and do not accuse them of heresy.[322] In this narrative, Mu'tazila disputes with the piety-minded scholars, or their transmission of Greek thought, are not mentioned. Philosophers are appreciated for their contributions to Islamic civilization, but they are not the focus of atten-tion. None of them is lauded like Abu Hanifa or al-Shafi'i. In textbooks, the representatives of official Islam are Abu Hanifa, al-Shafi'i, al-Maturidi, al-Ash'ari, Bahauddin Nakshibendi, and Ahmad Yesevi, not al-Farabi or Ibn Sina.

As a striking example, not a single textbook includes any information about Ibn Rushd. Ironically, his name appears only once, under a portrait of him by the fourteenth-century Florentine painter Andrea Bounaiuti.[323] The brief inscription under it is the only information that students read about Ibn Rushd. Satisfied with only mentioning the philosophers' names and noting that they are a part of the Islamic heritage, textbooks center the narrative of Islamic history on figures like Abu Hanifa and al-Shafi'i.

6.7   Conclusion

The Islamic cases I analyzed demonstrate that the traditional Ottoman syncretic approach to the Ash'ari and the Maturidi theological schools remains strong. Despite the popular identification of Turks as Maturidi, Ash'ari thought remains influential in each of our five cases' interpretation of the Islamic idea of nature. If we imagine a spectrum with Ash'ari's *Kitab Al-Luma'* and Maturidi's *Kitab al-Tawhid* on opposite sides, the literature of the Turkish Islam as we have observed in five cases is closer to the Ash'ari side on all aspects of the Islamic idea of nature. We find virtu-ally no strong Maturidi views on knowledge and free will where we would most expect them. Even in the cases like the school textbooks, where we detect a comparatively Maturidi perspective, the message is compromised by many qualifications. In no case is there a systematic, consistent, and firm Maturidi interpretation of the Islamic idea of nature.

Al-Ghazali is the key scholar in all five cases. Occasionalism as inter-preted by al-Ghazali is the dominant paradigm across the board. Though

Turks are known for their Maturidi confessional identity, it is al-Ghazali, a leading Ash'ari thinker, who is the chief influence on many texts that shape contemporary Islamic theology in Turkey. Al-Ghazali ties Turkish Islam to Ash'arism while marginalizing the influence of Maturidi theology.[324]

Looking synoptically into its content, the nature we encounter in five cases is an order in which natural law has limited power, since nature is governed by divine causation. At times one even detects an embarrassment about natural law. Natural law is often presented as if it is illusory, enticing human beings away from an understanding of the real causal relations in the universe. Turkish theologians teach students to reject natural causality or at least maintain a rigorous skepticism toward it. The overarching message is God's direct rule. As a personal deity, God governs nature with constant intervention that results in the suspension of the natural order. God is very much involved in daily life. Piety-minded scholars advise Muslims to appeal directly God, for he is the ultimate cause of all things.

All five cases recognize that there are people who can acquire inner knowledge with their hearts through various spiritual methods. The Islamic narrative as observed in the five cases takes the limits of rational knowledge as proof of man's need for a religious understanding of nature. Thus, challenging, and even sometimes despising, modern science is a common aspect of these Islamic actors' interpretations of nature.

Finally, due to its emphasis on God's sovereignty, the Islamic idea of nature in Turkish Islam does not recognize an autonomous space for man's will. Its priority is to secure God's sovereignty, so man's freedom is either a secondary issue or merely a matter of moral responsibility.

NOTES

1. Karaman et al., *Kur'an Yolu Türkçe Meal ve Tefsir I*, 29.
2. Kılavuz, *Allah'a İman*, 6–7.
3. Işık, *Tam İlmihal*, 82.
4. Işık, *Belief and Islam*, 77–78.
5. Işık, *Kıymetsiz Yazılar*, 14, 224.
6. Işık, *Faideli Bilgiler*, 39, 68.
7. Işık, *Tam İlmihal*, 47.
8. Emrullah and Hadimi, *İslam Ahlakı*, 24.
9. Süveydi, *Hak Sözün Vesikaları*, 306–309.
10. Işık, *Tam İlmihal*, 55–56.
11. Emrullah and Hadimi, *İslam Ahlakı*, 143

12. Işık, *Belief and Islam*, 29.
13. al-Ash'ari, *Kitab al-Luma'*, 99.
14. Süveydi, *Hak Sözün Vesikaları*, 27–28.
15. Emrullah and Hadimi, *İslam Ahlakı*, 24.
16. Işık, *Tam İlmihal*, 403.
17. al-Ash'ari, *Kitab al-Luma'*, 99.
18. Işık, *Kıyamet ve Ahiret*, 62. Işık's political views also reflect the influence of al-Ghazali. He holds that although the rightly guided caliphs transmitted Islam's spiritual messages to hearts perfectly and implemented the rules of Islam, gradually, it became impossible to carry out the two tasks simultaneously. Subsequently, a division of labor between state and religion developed, where religious scholars were given the mission of explaining and preaching the rules of Islam, and kings were charged with the implementation of Islamic rules. Işık's narrative is a contemporary reflection of the new alliance between state and society within the Sunni orthodoxy. Işık quoted in Müceddidi, *Dürr-ül Me'arif*, 3. Emrullah and Hadimi, *İslam Ahlakı*, 153. Işık, *The Sunni Path*, 7.
19. Coşan, *Tabakatü's-Sufiyye Sohbetleri II*, 582. Coşan, *Tabakatü's-Sufiyye Sohbetleri I*, 61.
20. Coşan, *Hazineden Pırıltılar III*, 240.
21. Ibid., 241.
22. Ibid., 242.
23. Ibid., 240–245.
24. Kotku, *Ehl-i Sünnet Akaidi*, 152.
25. Ibid., 2.
26. Coşan, *Hazineden Pırıltılar III*, 243.
27. Coşan, *Tabakatü's-Sufiyye Sohbetleri III*, 54.
28. Kotku, *Ehl-i Sünnet Akaidi*, 201.
29. Coşan, *Tabakatü's-Sufiyye Sohbetleri I*, 361.
30. Ibid., 293.
31. Ibid., 48.
32. Kotku, *Ehl-i Sünnet Akaidi*, 126, 160.
33. Ibid., 56, 91.
34. Ibid., 142, 199.
35. Coşan, *Tabakatü's-Sufiyye Sohbetleri IV*, 46.
36. Coşan, *Hazineden Pırıltılar III*, 247.
37. Coşan, *Tabakatü's-Sufiyye Sohbetleri I*, 186.
38. Nasr, *An Introduction to Islamic Cosmological Doctrines*, 9.
39. Coşan, *Tabakatü's-Sufiyye Sohbetleri I*, 328.
40. Coşan, *Hazineden Pırıltılar IV*, 228. Coşan, *Hazineden Pırıltılar III*, 166, 124.
41. Coşan, *Tabakatü's-Sufiyye Sohbetleri I*, 491.

42. Coşan, *Tabakatü's-Sufiyye Sohbetleri III*, 386–390.
43. Ibid., 143. Coşan, *Hazineden Pırıltılar IV*, 284.
44. Topbaş, *Islam Spirit and Form*, 61.
45. Topbaş, *The Secret in the Love for God*, 62.
46. Topbaş, *Gönül Bahçesinden Son Nefes*, 176.
47. Topbaş, *The Islamic Approach to Reasoning and Philosophy*, 67.
48. Kukkonen, "Plenitude, Possibility, and the Limits of Reason," 546.
49. Ibn Rushd, *The Incoherence of the Incoherence*, 88.
50. Ibid., 318.
51. al-Maturidi, *Kitabü't-Tevhid*, 207, 244, 251.
52. Ibid., 305, 311.
53. Topbaş, *Sufism A Path Towards The Internalization of Faith*, 238.
54. Topbaş, *Islam Spirit and Form*, 58.
55. Topbaş, *Sufism A Path Towards The Internalization of Faith*, 238.
56. Topbaş, *The Secret in the Love for God*, 62.
57. Topbaş, *Sufism A Path Towards The Internalization of Faith*, 238–248.
58. Topbaş, *Islam Spirit and Form*, 15
59. Ibid., 58.
60. Topbaş, *The Golden Chain of Transmission Masters*, 176.
61. Topbaş, *The Secret in the Love for God*, 65–66.
62. Ibid., 66.
63. Ibid., 67.
64. Ibid., 63.
65. Ibid.
66. Aydın, *Dinim İslam*, 330.
67. Ibid., 334.
68. Ibid., 330–334.
69. Özafşar and Doğan, *İnancım*, 152.
70. Hayrettin Karaman is particularly important. He is influential among Islamist political elites. Karaman's authority over other Islamic scholars, including Diyanet members, is undisputed. Karaman is among the authors of *İlmihal* and *Tefsir*, a testament to his authority in the formulation of the official Islamic narrative presented to the public. Ideologically, Karaman can be classified as an Islamist. See: Aktay, "Hayreddin Karaman," 349.
71. Karaman et al, *Kur'an Yolu Türkçe Meal ve Tefsir I*, 187.
72. Ibid., 401, 62.
73. Ibid., 487, 545.
74. Çelebi, "Sünnetullah," 158–159.
75. Karaman et al., *Kur'an Yolu Türkçe Meal ve Tefsir I*, 676.
76. "Allah tarafından konan bu değişmez genel kanun (sünnet-i âmme), ancak özel durumlarda yine Allah'n özel bir sünnetiyle (sünnet-i hâssa) ve geçici olarak değişebilir". Ibid.

77. Ibn Rushd, *The Incoherence of the Incoherence*, 325.
78. Yiğit, *Kuran'dan Öğütler I*, 321.
79. "Velîlerin kerameti vardır ve haktır". Karaman, Bardakoğlu and Apaydın, *Ilmihal I*, 66.
80. Özafşar and Doğan, *İnancım*, 122.
81. al-Ghazali, *The Incoherence of the Philosophers*, 31, 56.
82. Karaman et al., *Kur'an Yolu Türkçe Meal ve Tefsir III*, 405. Also see: Özdemir, *İlahi Adalet ve Rahmet Penceresinden*, 30. Kılavuz, *Allah'a İman*, 89.
83. Topaloğlu, Yavuz and Çelebi, *İslam'da İman Esasları*, 31–32.
84. Ibid.
85. Özdemir, *İlahi Adalet ve Rahmet Penceresinden*, 148.
86. Ibid., 193, 31.
87. Yeşilyurt, *Çağdaş İnanç Problemleri*, 24.
88. Topaloğlu, Yavuz and Çelebi, *İslam'da İman Esasları*, 37.
89. Karadaş, *Kadere İman*, 6–17.
90. al-Maturidi, *Kitabü't-Tevhid*, 100–101.
91. Karaman et al., *Kur'an Yolu Türkçe Meal ve Tefsir III*, 61.
92. Karaman, Bardakoğlu and Apaydın, *Ilmihal I*, 87.
93. Karaman et al, *Kur'an Yolu Türkçe Meal ve Tefsir I*, 30.
94. Kılavuz, *Allah'a İman*, 32, 38. Karaman et al, *Kur'an Yolu Türkçe Meal ve Tefsir I*, 62.
95. Topaloğlu, Yavuz and Çelebi, *İslam'da İman Esasları*, 166.
96. Ibid., 500. Kılavuz, *Allah'a İman*, 82.
97. Karadaş, *Kadere İman*, 13.
98. Ibn Rushd, *The Incoherence of the Incoherence*, 285.
99. Baştürk and Özdemir, *İlköğretim Din Kültürü ve Ahlak Bilgisi 5*, 14.
100. Ibid., 15.
101. Güleş, Güleç and Taşkın, *Ortaöğretim Din Kültürü ve Ahlak Bilgisi 10*, 15.
102. Yılmaz, Arı ve Karataş, *Ortaöğretim Din Kültürü ve Ahlak Bilgisi 10*, 13.
103. Ibid., 23–24.
104. Eroğlu, *İlköğretim Din Kültürü ve Ahlak Bilgisi 8*, 13–16
105. Ibid., 11–15.
106. Ibid., 15–16.
107. Ibid.
108. Ibid.
109. Yılmaz, Arı ve Karataş, *Ortaöğretim Din Kültürü ve Ahlak Bilgisi 10*, 12–19.
110. Güleş, Güleç and Taşkın, *Ortaöğretim Din Kültürü ve Ahlak Bilgisi 10*, 15.
111. Genç, *Ortaöğretim Din Kültürü ve Ahlak Bilgisi 11*, 10–17.
112. Yılmaz et al., *Ortaöğretim Din Kültürü ve Ahlak Bilgisi 10*, 11.
113. Calverley and Pollock, *Nature, Man and God in Medieval Islam*, 931.

114. Işık, *Faideli Bilgiler*, 233.
115. Işık, *Tam İlmihal*, 4.
116. Işık, *Faideli Bilgiler*, 38.
117. Işık, *Tam İlmihal*, 701.
118. Ibid., 57.
119. Işık, *Faideli Bilgiler*, 188.
120. Ibid., 235.
121. Işık, *Kıymetsiz Yazılar*, 244.
122. Işık, *Faideli Bilgiler*, 236. Işık, *Tam İlmihal*, 702.
123. Işık, *Kıymetsiz Yazılar*, 347, 407.
124. Işık, *Belief and Islam*, 29, 79. Işık, *Tam İlmihal*, 701.
125. Işık, *Tam İlmihal*, 15.
126. Emrullah and Hadimi, *İslam Ahlakı*, 46.
127. Kınalızade, *Ahlak-ı Ala'i*, 48.
128. Öztürk, *Kınalizade Ali Çelebi'de Aile Ahlakı*, 36–50.
129. Emrullah and Hadimi, *İslam Ahlakı*, 9, 45.
130. Işık, *Faideli Bilgiler*, 238.
131. Işık, *Belief and Islam*, 31.
132. Bağdadi [al-Baghdadi], *Mektubat*, 11–17.
133. Coşan, *Tefsir Sohbetleri I*, 171.
134. Ibid, 339.
135. Coşan, *Tefsir Sohbetleri IV*, 267, 458, 585.
136. Kotku, *Ehli Sünnet Akaidi*, 141.
137. Koçoğlu, "Ahmed Ziyaüddin Gümüşhanevi'nin İslam Mezheplerine Bakışı", 123. Gencer, "Bir Müceddid Olarak Ahmed Ziyaeddin-i Gümüşhanevi", 63
138. Kotku, *Ehli Sünnet Akaidi*, 142.
139. Ibid., 25, 157.
140. Ibid., 163, 66.
141. Topbaş, *Islam Spirit and Form*, 96–100.
142. Topbaş, *Gönül Bahçesinden*, 177.
143. Ibid., 179.
144. Topbaş, *Sufism A Path Towards the Internationalization of Faith*, 74.
145. Topbaş, *Gönül Bahçesinden*, 179.
146. Topbaş, *Islam Spirit and Form*, 91.
147. Topbaş, *Gönül Bahçesinden*, 179–180.
148. Topbaş, *Islam Spirit and Form*, 90.
149. Ibid., 99
150. Karaman, Bardakoğlu and Apaydın, *Ilmihal I*, 133.
151. Ibid., 135.
152. Ibid., 136.
153. Karadaş, *Kadere İman*, 25.

154. Karaman, Bardakoğlu and Apaydın, *Ilmihal I*, 136, 137.
155. Ibid.
156. Ibid., 133.
157. Karaman et al., *Kur'an Yolu Türkçe Meal ve Tefsir I*, 455.
158. Karaman et al., *Kur'an Yolu Türkçe Meal ve Tefsir II*, 678.
159. Karaman et al., *Kur'an Yolu Türkçe Meal ve Tefsir I*, 455.
160. Karaman et al., *Kur'an Yolu Türkçe Meal ve Tefsir II*, 675.
161. Pessagno, "Irada, Ikhtihayar, Qudra, Kasb," 190.
162. Karadaş, *Kadere İman*, 10.
163. Ibid., 20.
164. Ibid., 18.
165. Karadaş, *Kadere İman*, 20–21.
166. Ibid., 18, 14.
167. Ibid., 35.
168. Eroğlu, *İlköğretim Din Kültürü ve Ahlak Bilgisi 8*, 21.
169. Süveydi, *Hak Sözün Vesikaları*, 329.
170. Işık, *Tam İlmihal*, 41.
171. Ibid., 26.
172. Işık, *Faideli Bilgiler*, 458–458.
173. Süveydi, *Hak Sözün Vesikaları*, 288.
174. Işık, *Tam İlmihal*, 104.
175. Ibid., 406, 23.
176. İzniki, *Miftah-ul Janna*, 10, 175.
177. Işık, *Tam İlmihal*, 41.
178. Işık, *Kıymetsiz Yazılar*, 11.
179. Işık, *Tam İlmihal*, 50.
180. Ibid., 25, 48.
181. al-Ash'ari, *Al-Ibanah 'An Usul Ad-Diyanah*, 53.
182. al-Maturidi, *Kitabü't-Tevhid*, 61.
183. Izniki, *Miftah-ul Janna*, 29.
184. al-Maturidi, *Kitabü't-Tevhid*, 309–310. al-Subki, *Al-Sayf Al-Mashur*, 4.
185. al-Ghazali, *The Alchemy of Happiness*, 28.
186. Tahmasebi, "The Concept of Heart in Quran," 391.
187. *Qur'an*, Al-A'raf: 179.
188. Lazić et al., "Brain and art," 248.
189. Crivellato and Ribatti, "Soul, mind, brain," 245–246.
190. Hussain, "'Heart-talk': Considering the Role of Heart in Therapy," 1203–1210. For a recent example of this literature, see: Mushtaq, *The Intelligent Heart*.
191. Işık, *Belief and Islam*, 13.
192. Süveydi, *Hak Sözün Vesikaları*, 323.
193. Işık, *Belief and Islam*, 59.

194. Izniki, *Miftah-ul Janna*, 13, 47.
195. Işık, *Namaz*, 155.
196. Işık, *Kıymetsiz Yazılar*, 137. Izniki, *Miftah-ul Janna*, 19.
197. Işık, *Tam İlmihal*, 955, 1078, 758.
198. Ibid., 409, 69.
199. Izniki, *Miftah-ul Janna*, 81.
200. Işık, *Tam İlmihal*, 539.
201. Izniki, *Miftah-ul Janna*, 145.
202. Işık, *Belief and Islam*, 96. The Ghazalian impact unto contemporary Turkish Islamic scholars' understanding of al-Farabi and Ibn Sina is strong. For example, Said Nursi labeled them as having only the rank of an ordinary Muslims (*adi bir mümin derecesi*) for being espoused to naturalist ideas. While criticizing them, Nursi also quotes Al-Ghazali's critical stance on al-Farabi and Ibn Sina. Nursi, *Sözler*, 335.
203. Işık, *Kıymetsiz Yazılar*, 9.
204. Işık, *Tam İlmihal*, 962.
205. Ibid., 116.
206. Işık, *Kıymetsiz Yazılar*, 236.
207. Işık, *Tam İlmihal*, 414.
208. Işık, *Belief and Islam*, 102–103.
209. Accessed March 12, 2017. http://www.hakikatkitabevi.net/book. php?bookCode=132.
210. Işık, *Kıyamet ve Ahiret*, 107.
211. Işık, *Namaz*, 15. Süveydi, Hak Sözün Vesikaları, 323.
212. Işık, *Faideli Bilgiler*, 5.
213. Işık, *Belief and Islam*, 61.
214. Nursi, *Muhakemat*, 18–19.
215. Işık, *Tam İlmihal*, 1102.
216. Emrullah and Hadimi, *İslam Ahlakı*, 546–547. Işık, *Tam İlmihal*, 1102.
217. Işık, *Kıymetsiz Yazılar*, 137.
218. Işık, *Belief and Islam*, 113.
219. Işık, *Tam İlmihal*, 41.
220. Coşan, *Tabakatü's-Sufiyye Sohbetleri I*, 643, 95.
221. al-Ghazali, *Al Munkidh*, 55.
222. Ibid., 25.
223. Coşan, *Tabakatü's-Sufiyye Sohbetleri III*, 209.
224. Coşan, *Tabakatü's-Sufiyye Sohbetleri II*, 197.
225. Coşan, *Tabakatü's-Sufiyye Sohbetleri I*, 476–477, 642.
226. Coşan, *Hazineden Pırıltılar I*, 336.
227. Karaman et al., *Kur'an Yolu Türkçe Meal ve Tefsir I*, 331.
228. Kotku, *Ehli Sünnet Akaidi.*, 240.

229. Radtke, "as-Sulami, Abu 'Abd al-rahman," 744. Coşan, *Tabakatü's-Sufiyye Sohbetleri I*, 30–31.
230. Honerkamp, "A Sufi Itinerary of Tenth Century Nishapur," 48.
231. Kynsh, *Islamic Mysticism: A Short History*, 125.
232. Rustom, "Forms of Gnosis in Sulami's Sufi Exegesis," 327–344.
233. Camii, *Şevahid-ün Nübüvve Peygamberlik Müjdeleri*, 14.
234. Coşan, *Tabakatü's-Sufiyye Sohbetleri II*, 232.
235. Kotku, *Ehli Sünnet Akaidi*, 255.
236. Ibid., 272.
237. Ibid., 258, 111.
238. Ibid., 112.
239. Coşan, *Tabakatü's-Sufiyye Sohbetleri II*, 146.
240. Coşan, *Hazineden Pırıltılar V*, 62.
241. Coşan, *Hazineden Pırıltılar IX*, 117.
242. Coşan, *Hazineden Pırıltılar VIII*, 54.
243. Topbaş, *Sufism A Path Towards the Internationalization of Faith*, 47, 32.
244. Ibid., 70.
245. Ibid., 81, 12–24.
246. Topbaş, *The Islamic Approach*, 63.
247. Topbaş, *Islam The Religion of Truth*, 68.
248. Topbaş, *The Secret in the Love for God*, 15. Topbaş, *The Islamic Approach*, 21, 86–87.
249. Topbaş, *Sufism A Path Towards the Internationalization of Faith*, 65–66.
250. Topbaş, *The Secret in the Love for God*, 189.
251. Topbaş, *The Islamic Approach*, 41.
252. Topbaş, *The Golden Chain*, 420.
253. Topbaş, *Contemplation in Islam*, 17.
254. Topbaş, *The Islamic Approach*, 54, 19.
255. Ibid., 59, 17, 47.
256. Topbaş, *Sufism A Path Towards the Internationalization of Faith*, 46. Topbaş, *Gönül Bahçesinden*, 56.
257. Topbaş, *Sufism A Path Towards the Internationalization of Faith*, 99, 64, 47.
258. Ibid., 46.
259. Topbaş, *Contemplation in Islam*, 19–20.
260. Ibid., 19–20.
261. Ibid., 21
262. Topbaş, *Islam Spirit and Form*, 10.
263. Ibid., 9.
264. Topbaş, *The Islamic Approach*, 5.
265. *Qur'an*: Al-A'raf 12.
266. Topbaş, *Islam Spirit and Form*, 18.

267. Topbaş, *Sufism A Path Towards The Internalization of Faith*, 64.
268. al-Ghazali, *The Incoherence of the Philosophers*, 4.
269. Topbaş, *The Islamic Approach*, 48.
270. Ibid., 49.
271. Ibid., 48.
272. Topbaş, *Contemplation in Islam*, 16.
273. Topbaş, *Civilization of Virtues II*, 437.
274. Topbaş, *Sufism A Path Towards the Internationalization of Faith*, 54–55.
275. Topbaş, *The Islamic Approach*, 99.
276. Karaman, Bardakoğlu and Apaydın, *Ilmihal I*, 66.
277. Izutsu, *Creation and the Timeless Order of Things*, 1–37.
278. al-Ghazali, *Al Munkidh*, 25.
279. Karaman et al., *Kur'an Yolu Türkçe Meal ve Tefsir I*, 15.
280. Nursi, *Mektubat*, 416–418.
281. Karaman, Bardakoğlu and Apaydın, *Ilmihal II*, 16.
282. Karaman et al., *Kur'an Yolu Türkçe Meal ve Tefsir III*, 573–574.
283. Ibid.
284. Karaman et al., *Kur'an Yolu Türkçe Meal ve Tefsir I*, 71–72.
285. Karaman et al., *Kur'an Yolu Türkçe Meal ve Tefsir III*, 215. al-Ghazali also uses the mirror metaphor. In fact, it is a typical example of neo-Platinian impact. See: al-Ghazali, *The Alchemy of Happiness*, 48.
286. al-Maturidi, *Kitabü't-Tevhid*, 103.
287. Accessed May 2, 2018, http://www2.Diyanet.gov.tr/DinHizmetler-iGenelMudurlugu/HutbelerListesi/Beden%20Ülkesinin%20Sultanı%20Kalp.pdf.
288. Kılavuz, *Allah'a İman*, 26.
289. Karadaş, *Kadere İman*, 56. Yeşilyurt, *Çağdaş İnanç Problemleri*, 131–132.
290. Yeşilyurt, *Çağdaş İnanç Problemleri*, 44.
291. Ibid., 46.
292. Ibid., 48.
293. Topaloğlu, Yavuz and Çelebi, *İslam'da İman Esasları*, 18–30.
294. Ibid., 24.
295. Ibid., 91.
296. Ibid., 91.
297. Görmez, "İrfan Geleneğimiz," 1.
298. Yeşilyurt, "Kutsiye, Velayet ve Keramet Kavramları," 294.
299. For example: Karaman, Bardakoğlu and Apaydın, *Ilmihal II*, 496, 430, 461, 495.
300. Karaman et al., *Kur'an Yolu Türkçe Meal ve Tefsir I*, 188.
301. Karaman et al., *Kur'an Yolu Türkçe Meal ve Tefsir II*, 624, 390, 449.
302. Karaman et al., *Kur'an Yolu Türkçe Meal ve Tefsir III*, 107.

303. Karaman, Bardakoğlu and Apaydın, *Ilmihal I*, 28.
304. Ibid., 20–21.
305. Yeşilyurt, *Çağdaş İnanç Problemleri*, 23, 28.
306. Ibid, 38, 36.
307. Ibid., 54.
308. Topaloğlu, Yavuz and Çelebi, *İslam'da İman Esasları*, 73–82.
309. Ibid., 43.
310. Yeşilyurt, *Çağdaş İnanç Problemleri*, 47.
311. Ibid., 127.
312. Eroğlu, İlköğretim Din Kültürü ve Ahlak Bilgisi 8, 74. Yılmaz and et al., *Ortaöğretim Din Kültürü ve Ahlak Bilgisi 10*, 76.
313. Ibid., 80, 122.
314. Yaldız, *Din Kültürü ve Ahlak Bilgisi 7*, 71.
315. Ibid., 63–97.
316. Demirtaş, *Ortaöğretim Din Kültürü ve Ahlak Bilgisi 12*, 54.
317. Ibid., 56.
318. Ibid., 54–78.
319. Yaldız, *Din Kültürü ve Ahlak Bilgisi*, 768.
320. Ibid., 769.
321. Pınarbaşı, *Ortaöğretim Din Kültürü ve Ahlak Bilgisi 9*, 112 and Yılmaz and et al., *Ortaöğretim Din Kültürü ve Ahlak Bilgisi 9*, 122.
322. Genç, *Ortaöğretim Din Kültürü ve Ahlak Bilgisi 11*, 64.
323. Yılmaz and et al., *Ortaöğretim Din Kültürü ve Ahlak Bilgisi 10*, 130.
324. In Chap. 3, I have summarized the revisionist literature on al-Ghazali (see, Footnote 53). My findings in this book are quite relevant for this debate: There is not a single case that confirms the revisionist literature on al-Ghazali. The cases of this book suggest that the revisionist literature on al-Ghazali is merely an invention of academic scholarship.

References

Aktay, Yasin. 2005. Hayreddin Karaman. In *İslamcılık*, ed. Yasin Aktay, Tanıl Bora, and Murat Gültekingil, 348–373. Istanbul: İletişim.

al-Ash'ari. 1940. *Al-Ibanah 'An Usul Ad-Diyanah [The Elucidation of Islam's Foundation]*. Translated by Walter C. Klein. New Haven: American Oriental Society.

———. 1953. *Kitab al-Luma' [The Luminous Book]*. Translated by Richard J. McCarthy. Beirut: Imprimerie Catholique.

al-Ghazali. 1963. *Deliverance From Error [Al Munkidh min Ad Dallal]*. Translated by W.M. Watt. Lahore: Sh. Muhammad Ashraf.

———. 1991. *The Alchemy of Happiness [Kimiya-yi Sa'adat]*. Translated by Claud Field. Lahore: Sh. M. Ashraf.

218   G. BACIK

―――. 2000. *The Incoherence of the Philosophers [Tahafut al-falasifa]*. Translated by Michael E. Marmura. Utah: Brigham Young University Press.

al-Maturidi. 2018. *Kitabü't-Tevhid Açıklamalı Tercüme [Kitab al-Tawhid]*. Translated by Bekir Topaloğlu. Ankara: İSAM.

al-Subki, Tac al-Din. 2015. *Al-Sayf Al-Mashur fi Sarh 'aqida Abu Mansur*. Ankara: TDV.

Aydın, Muhammet Şevki. 2014. *Dinim İslam*. Ankara: Diyanet İşleri Başkanlığı.

Bağdadi [Baghdadi], Mevlana Halid. 2000. *Mektubat [Maktubat]*. Translated by D.K. Yıldız. Istanbul: Sey Tac.

Baştürk, Ayhan, and Murat Özdemir. 2017. *İlköğretim Din Kültürü ve Ahlak Bilgisi 5*. Ankara: İlke.

Calverley, Edwin E., and James W. Pollock. 2002. *Nature, Man and God in Medieval Islam: 'Abd Allah Baydawi's Text Tawali' al-Anwar min Matali' al-Anzar Along With Mahmud Isfahani's Commentary Matali' al-Anzar, Sharh Tawali' al-Anwar*. Leiden: Brill.

Camii, Mevlana Abdurrahman. 2014. *Şevahid-ün Nübüvve Peygamberlik Müjdeleri*. Istanbul: Hakikat.

Çelebi, İlyas. 2006. Sünnetullah. In *İslam Ansiklopedisi 38*, ed. Türkiye Diyanet Vakfı, 158–159. Istanbul: TDV ISAM.

Coşan, M. Esad. 2016a. *Hazineden Pırıltılar I*. Ankara: M. Erkaya.

―――. 2016b. *Hazineden Pırıltılar II*. Ankara: M. Erkaya.

―――. 2016c. *Hazineden Pırıltılar III*. Ankara: M. Erkaya.

―――. 2016d. *Hazineden Pırıltılar IV*. Ankara: M. Erkaya.

―――. 2016e. *Hazineden Pırıltılar V*. Ankara: M. Erkaya.

―――. 2016f. *Hazineden Pırıltılar VI*. Ankara: M. Erkaya.

―――. 2016g. *Hazineden Pırıltılar VII*. Ankara: M. Erkaya.

―――. 2016h. *Hazineden Pırıltılar VIII*. Ankara: M. Erkaya.

―――. 2016i. *Hazineden Pırıltılar IX*. Ankara: M. Erkaya.

―――. 2016j. *Tabakatü's-Sufiyye Sohbetleri I*. Ankara: M. Erkaya.

―――. 2016k. *Tabakatü's-Sufiyye Sohbetleri II*. Ankara: M. Erkaya.

―――. 2016l. *Tabakatü's-Sufiyye Sohbetleri III*. Ankara: M. Erkaya.

―――. 2016m. *Tabakatü's-Sufiyye Sohbetleri IV*. Ankara: M. Erkaya.

―――. 2016n. *Tefsir Sohbetleri I*. Ankara: M. Erkaya.

―――. 2016o. *Tefsir Sohbetleri II*. Ankara: M. Erkaya.

―――. 2016p. *Tefsir Sohbetleri III*. Ankara: M. Erkaya.

―――. 2016q. *Tefsir Sohbetleri IV*. Ankara: M. Erkaya.

Crivellato, Enrico, and Domenico Ribatti. 2007. Soul, Mind, Brain: Greek Philosophy and the Birth of Neuroscience. *Brain Research Bulletin 71* (4): 327–336.

Demirtaş, Kenan. 2017. *Ortaöğretim Din Kültürü ve Ahlak Bilgisi 12*. Ankara: Özgün.

Emrullah, Ali bin, and Muhammad Hadimi. 2014. *İslam Ahlakı*. Istanbul: Hakikat.

Eroğlu, Arif Hikmet. 2017. *İlköğretim Din Kültürü ve Ahlak Bilgisi 8*. Ankara: Tuna.

Genç, Nazım. 2017. *Ortaöğretim Din Kültürü ve Ahlak Bilgisi 11.* Istanbul: Netbil.

Gencer, Bedri. 2013. Bir Müceddid Olarak Ahmed Ziyaeddin-i Gümüşhanevi. In *Uluslararası Gümüşhanevi Sempozyumu,* ed. H. Mahmut Yücer, 46–77. Istanbul: Bağcılar Belediyesi.

Görmez, Mehmet. 2013. İrfan Geleneğimiz. *Diyanet Aylık Dergi* 272 (1): 1–3.

Gross, Charles G. 1995. Aristotle on the Brain. *The Neuroscientist* 1 (4): 245–250.

Güleş, Bayram, Güler Güleç, and Zekai Taşkın. 2017. *Ortaöğretim Din Kültürü ve Ahlak Bilgisi 10.* Ankara: Bilim ve Kültür.

Honerkamp, Kenneth. 2006. A Sufi Itinerary of Tenth Century Nishapur Based on a Treatise by Abu 'Abd al-Rahman al-Sulami. *Journal of Islamic Studies* 17 (1): 43–67.

Hussain, Feryad. 2013. 'Heart-talk': Considering the Role of Heart in Therapy as Evidenced in the Quran and Medical Research. *Journal of Religious Health* 52 (4): 1203–1210.

Ibn Rushd. 1987. *The Incoherence of the Incoherence [Tahafut al-Tahafut].* Translated by Simon Van Den Bergh. Cambridge: EJW Gibb Memorial Trust.

Işık, Hüseyin Hilmi. 2014a. *Faideli Bilgiler.* Istanbul: Hakikat.

———. 2014b. *Kıymetsiz Yazılar.* Istanbul: Hakikat.

———. 2014c. *Tam İlmihal Se'adet-i Ebediyye.* Istanbul: Hakikat.

———. 2015a. *Belief and Islam.* Istanbul: Hakikat.

———. 2015b. *The Sunni Path.* Istanbul: Hakikat.

———. 2017. *Kıyamet ve Ahiret.* Istanbul: Hakikat.

Izutsu, Toshiko. 1994. *Creation and the Timeless Order of Things: Essays in Islamic Mystical Philosophy.* Ashland: White Cloud Press.

Karadaş, Cağfer. 2015. *Kadere İman.* Ankara: Diyanet İşleri Başkanlığı.

Karaman, Hayreddin, Ali Bardakoğlu, and H. Yunus Apaydın. 1998. *Ilmihal I.* Ankara: Diyanet İşleri Başkanlığı.

Karaman, Hayrettin, Mustafa Çağrıcı, İ. Kafi Dönmez, and Sadrettin Gümüş. 2012a. *Kur'an Yolu Türkçe Meal ve Tefsir I.* Ankara: Diyanet İşleri Başkanlığı.

———. 2012b. *Kur'an Yolu Türkçe Meal ve Tefsir III.* Ankara: Diyanet İşleri Başkanlığı.

Kılavuz, Ulvi Murat. 2015. *Allah'a İman.* Ankara: Diyanet İşleri Başkanlığı.

Kınalızade, Ali Efendi. 1982. *Ahlak-ı Ala'i.* Istanbul: Tercüman.

Koçoğlu, Kiyasettin. 2010. Ahmed Ziyaüddin Gümüşhanevi'nin İslam Mezheplerine Bakışı. *Milel ve Nihal* 7 (3): 109–144.

Kotku, Mehmed Zahid. 1992. *Ehl-i Sünnet Akaidi.* Istanbul: Seha.

Kukkonen, Taneli. 2000. Possible Worlds in the Tahafut al-tahafut: Averroes on Plenitude and Possibility. *Journal of the History of Philosophy* 38 (3): 329–347.

Kynsh, Alexander. 1999. *Islamic Mysticism: A Short History.* Leiden: Brill.

Lazić, D., S. Marinković, I. Tomić, D. Mitrović, A. Starčević, I. Milić, M. Grujičić, and B. Marković. 2014. Brain and Art: Illustrations of the Cerebral Convolutions. A Review. *Folia Morphol* 73 (3): 247–258.

Müceddidi, Rauf Ahmed. 1998. *Dürr-ül Me'arif.* Istanbul: Hakikat.

Muhammad bin Qutbuddin İzniki. 2014. *Miftah-ul Janna*. Istanbul: Hakikat.

Mushtaq, Gohar. 2012. *The Intelligent Heart, the Pure Heart: An Insight into the Heart Based on the Qur'an, Sunnah and Modern Science*. London: Ta-Ha.

Nasr, S.H. 1978. *An Introduction to Islamic Cosmological Doctrines*. London: Thames and Hudson.

Nursi, Said. 1995a. *Muhakemat*. Istanbul: Envar.

———. 1995b. *Sözler*. Istanbul: Envar.

———. 2014. *Mektubat*. Şahdamar: İzmir.

Özafşar, M. Emin, and Doğan Recai. 2010. *İnancım*. Ankara: Diyanet İşleri Başkanlığı.

Özdemir, Metin. 2015. *İlahi Adalet ve Rahmet Penceresinden Kötülük ve Musibetler*. Ankara: Diyanet İşleri Başkanlığı.

Öztürk, Hüseyin. 1990. *Kınalizade Ali Çelebi'de Aile Ahlakı*. Ankara: Aile Araştırma Kurumu.

Pessagno, J. Meric. 1984. Irada, Ikhtihayar, Qudra, Kasb The View of Abu Mansur Al-Maturidi. *Journal of the American Oriental Society* 104 (1): 177–191.

Pınarbaşı, Bekir. 2016. *Ortaöğretim Din Kültürü ve Ahlak Bilgisi 9*. Ankara: Tutku.

Radtke, B. 1998. al-Sulami, Abu 'Abd al-rahman. In *Encyclopedia of Arabic Literature II*, ed. Julic Scott Mcisami and Paul Starkey, vol. 744. London: Routledge.

Rustom, Mohammed. 2005. Forms of Gnosis in Sulami's Sufi Exegesis of the Fatiha. *Islam and Christian-Muslim Relations* 16 (4): 327–344.

Süveydi, E. Abdullah Süveydi. 2014. *Hak Sözün Vesikaları*. Istanbul: Hakikat.

Tahmasebi, Zahra. 2015. The Concept of Heart in Quran. *Journal of Applied Environmental Biological Sciences* 5 (10): 386–391.

Topaloğlu, Bekir, Y. Şevki Yavuz, and İlyas Çelebi. 2015. *İslam'da İman Esasları*. Diyanet İşleri Başkanlığı: Ankara.

Topbaş, Osman Nuri. 2006. *Islam: Spirit and Form*. Istanbul: Erkam.

———. 2009a. *Civilization of Virtues II*. Istanbul: Erkam.

———. 2009b. *The Secret in the Love for God*. Istanbul: Erkam.

———. 2011. *Contemplation in Islam*. Istanbul: Erkam.

———. 2012. *Sufism: A Path Towards The Internalization of Faith*. Istanbul: Erkam.

———. 2015. *Islam: The Religion of Truth*. Istanbul: Erkam.

———. 2016a. *Gönül Bahçesinden Son Nefes*. Istanbul: Erkam.

———. 2016b. *The Golden Chain of Transmission Masters of the Naqshibandi Way*. Istanbul: Erkam.

———. 2016c. *The Islamic Approach to Reasoning and Philosophy*. Istanbul: Erkan.

Yaldız, Hacer. 2017. *Din Kültürü ve Ahlak Bilgisi 7*. Ankara: Gün.

Yeşilyurt, Temel. 2013. *Çağdaş İnanç Problemleri*. Ankara: Diyanet İşleri Başkanlığı.

————. 2017. Kutsiye, Velayet ve Keramet Kavramları. In *İslam Düşünce ve Geleneğinde Kutsiyet Velayet Keramet*, ed. Şevki Yavuz Yusuf, 289–296. Istanbul: 29 Mayıs Üniversitesi Yayınları.

Yiğit, Yaşar. 2011. *Kuran'dan Öğütler I*. Ankara: Diyanet İşleri Başkanlığı.

Yılmaz, Mustafa, Firdevs Arı, and Veli Karataş. 2017a. *Ortaöğretim Din Kültürü ve Ahlak Bilgisi 10*. Ankara: MEB Devlet Kitapları.

Yılmaz, Mustafa, Firdevs Arı, Veli Karataş, Tuğba Kevser Uysal, Ahmet Yasin Okudan, Ayşe Macit, Dilek Menküç, et al. 2017b. *Ortaöğretim Din Kültürü ve Ahlak Bilgisi Ders Kitabı 10. Sınıf*. Ankara: MEB.

CHAPTER 7

Conclusion

One purpose of this book is to show that problems and issues in the inter-pretation of Islam go beyond law and politics; the Islamic idea of nature also plays key role in Muslims' understanding of Islam. Accordingly, our analysis of five cases demonstrated that the Islamic idea of nature as imparted to Turkish Muslims contributes to:

- a highly skeptical stance on causality, and a belief in a divine causa-tion that determines natural events;
- A deep suspicion about the capacity of human reasoning and sensa-tion and a consequent belief in the existence and necessity of inner knowledge;
- a limited recognition of human autonomy over human deeds;
- and a highly personal conception of God.

In a broader perspective, the Turkish case displays the historical conti-nuity of the Islamic idea of nature from the Middle Ages to the present day. Despite their historical affiliation with the Maturidi school, writings of the five cases examined here bear the deep influence of Ash'ari theology when it comes to the idea of nature, which constitutes an important part of Islamic socialization. Thus, the classical quandary of Islamic theology, what William J. Courtenay once defined as sacrificing natural causality and human volition on the altar of divine omnipotence, persists in contempo-rary Turkey.[1] Having recognized the imposition of a higher causation

© The Author(s) 2020   223
G. Bacik, *Islam and Muslim Resistance to Modernity in Turkey*,
https://Doi.org/10.1007/978-3-030-25901-3_7

upon natural processes, it is presumed that there are mechanisms operating between the metaphysical and physical realm of the created universe, as well as within each of them.[2]

In 1503, Gregor Reisch presented a woodcut depicting the levels of scholastic learning. As the work indicates, students study the grammar at the lower levels and then move up to logic, rhetoric, and other sciences. The summit of knowledge that students reach at the highest level includes theology and metaphysics.[3] If we were to draw a similar model but for what Islamic learning in present-day Turkey teaches about nature, it would simply be this (Fig. 7.1).

Recall one of the grand debates of Islamic philosophy, expressed in al-Ghazali's attack on Aristotelian Muslim scholars in *The Incoherence* and Ibn Rushd's response to him with *The Incoherence of the Incoherence*. The Islamic idea of nature that we observe in the Turkish case aligns with al-Ghazali's position, particularly his refutation of the Aristotelian concept of causality. In *Physics*, Aristotle, having recognized that there are natural laws governing nature, wrote that to know something is to know its causes.[4] Unlike the Aristotelian method, the Islamic idea of nature in contemporary Turkey repudiates natural law and argues that to know something requires going beyond natural causality. Having defined God's agency as the sole cause of natural events, in harmony what al-Ghazali wrote centuries ago, the ultimate form of knowing is knowledge of God, that is, *ma'rifatullah*.[5]

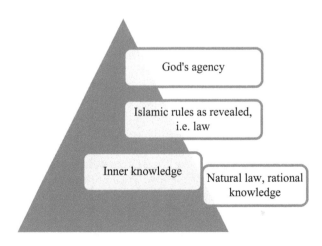

Fig. 7.1   The Islamic idea of nature as taught in contemporary Turkey

The analysis of the Turkish case also sheds light on some general problems of Muslim societies in regard to the Islamic idea of nature. To begin with, the survival of certain interpretations of Islam has never been only the result of its intellectual appeal. The alliance between state and Islam, a key element of Sunni orthodoxy, still prevails across the Muslim world, contributing to the persistence of particular interpretations of Islam over others. Enjoying the opportunities of the alliance, the Sunni clergy are able to promote their particular interpretation and shape the daily practice and beliefs of the general population.

Secondly, by not yielding to modern science in regard to the explanation of nature, as we observed in the Turkish case, the Islamic idea of nature inhibits the disassociation of realms that is characteristic of modern societies. Thus, the Islamic idea of nature is an important case to observe how Muslims still insist on its continuing traditional authority in all fields of life. The standard religious outlook still opposes the notion of confining Islam to a single, spiritual domain and leaving some fields to alternate paradigms such as secular law and modern science. The Sunni orthodox view is ready to recognize science or law only on the condition that they accept Islam as the ultimate authority.

This situation generates a deeper clash with modernity at the paradigmatic level. Historically, Muslims have followed a pragmatic path toward modernity at the institutional level. As a result, they have not been rigidly against adapting to modernity's various institutional forms, even the modern state.[6] Also, as we observed in the Turkish case by studying various Islamic movements, Muslims have no qualms about adapting to the institutional aspect of modernity. By contrast, Muslims have reservations about modernity at the paradigmatic level, as is clear in the various Islamic actors' interpretations of the Islamic idea of nature. Islamic movements, with modern instruments such as the mass media and modern schools, propagate ideas that are clearly incompatible with modernity. For example, it is very typical to observe Islamic actors rejecting causality in explanations of natural events while readily employing modern instruments or having modern institutions.

The Islamic idea of nature, which had its origins in the encounter of Islamic and Greek thought, is today part of Islamic faith. Muslims acquire it in their Islamic socialization (as we observed in several cases in this book) as a standard Islamic belief that trusts faith more than the articulations of man. Reformist attempts to modify the Islamic idea of nature collide with the hard shell of Islamic faith. We should remember also that the legitimacy of the philosopher, and even the scientist, has declined alongside the consolidation of Sunni orthodoxy. Thus, there is no effective mechanism within the Islamic tradition to update the Islamic idea of nature in line with recent scientific or philosophic approaches. This has led to the dissemination of vague scientific content and outdated arguments, which in turn are exploited by religious agents as they insist on the supremacy of Islam in all fields of life.

Thus, the dilemma of Islamic thought with respect to the idea of nature is clear: Islam has not completely ceded its traditional authority to explain nature to modern science. At the same time, the mechanism for updating according to the most recent scientific data is simply not in place today. The result is the interpretation of Islam according to a conglomeration of contending ideas and arguments, including some outdated ones, leading to serious problems in terms of how Muslims think of nature and causation.

One such problem is the persistence of previous Muslim scholars' ideas on nature. For example, *Marifetname*, a book written in 1757 and full of information about geography and medicine, the content of which cannot be accepted as reliable by any contemporary standard, is still a best-selling book in Turkey and influences contemporary Muslims' understanding of nature. Such an old book should be of interest only to historians and antiquarians; its popularity, however, is proof that old ideas are still authoritative. In fact, book's scientific merit is problematic even by the standards of 1757.[7]

Commenting on the Aristotelian idea of nature, Bertrand Russell noted that, today, in light of modern science, that grand and influential paradigm can no longer be accepted.[8] The problem is that an idea of nature is a reflection of what people's knowledge is about "the natural world they live in" or "the cosmos they imagined."[9] On this account, the key arguments of the Islamic idea of nature were developed before the rise of modern scientific revolution. Updating is a crucial issue for a religion that still claims traditional authority in various fields like nature. The case is not different when it comes to several Muslim scholars' ideas that are still influential in shaping contemporary Turkish Muslims' understanding of nature. However, since Muslim scholars' ideas on nature are also treated as part of the canonical tradition, Muslims are reluctant to give them up, despite their outdated content. As a result, the Islamic idea of nature has become a stagnant set of assumptions and arguments about nature transmitted without major update from one generation to the next. This transmission resembles what Marshall G.S. Hodgson called the degeneration of a tradition.[10] Indeed, my examination of five cases demonstrated that what happens in the Turkish context is mere transmission, since Islamic agents reproduce the Islamic idea of nature without substantial update. Reading the reference texts of Islamic actors in Turkey, one may even get the feeling that no time has elapsed since al-Ghazali walked the Earth.

So what solution might one propose, in the light of these impediments?

Seemingly, the most popular proposal is to revitalize the link between Islam and science (or rationalist thought in the broader context) in order to rehabilitate Muslims adversely affected by stale religious thinking. The belief that underlies this proposal is that a new and effective mechanism can be devised to energize the weak connection between Islam and science.

Though it might sound interesting, such a proposal has little chance, given some sizable obstacles. To begin with, the proposal assumes too boldly that the piety-minded Muslim scholars can be persuaded to recognize the need to expand the definition of who is a scholar with a legitimate role in shaping Islamic thought.[11] One would be naïve to expect to realize such a change, given the current sociological and intellectual profile of mainstream religious scholars. The highest status for a scholar in Islam is *'alim*, and it is said without any special reservation that the term normally refers to a religious scholar. Neither the mainstream Islamic movements nor the general Muslim population see, for example, a sociologist or a chemist as *'alim*. Moreover, the piety-minded scholars are so convinced of the superiority of their resources that their efficient cooperation with even piety-minded scientists is unlikely. Even people with an extensive modern academic education in religion fail to get the title of *'alim*.[12]

So, who are the actors? Who will connect Islamic thought with the most up-to-date science and knowledge? Who are the capable actors to sustain dialogue between Islam and science? Since the rationalist scholars have already been delegitimated, there is no group to fulfill this mission in the Islamic world. The inevitable option is to continue the mission through the traditionalist Muslim scholars, a group whose professional skills are certainly not adequate to sustain a dialogue with modern science and philosophy. As a matter of fact, this option has been the main mechanism in bringing the findings of recent scientific developments into the Islamic field, resulting in the dissemination by Islamic actors of populist and often times distorted or misunderstood interpretations of recent scientific developments.

There are other obstacles to the first proposal: Today, the idea of communication between religion and science through actors is anachronistic. Science has developed into a profession that sets its own terms for training scientists. The shift from the natural philosopher to the professional scientist has led to conflicts with leaders of organized religion.[13] The gap between the religious scholars and modern scientists has widened to an unprecedented level, which makes systematic cooperation between scientist and religious scholars almost impossible. It is true that there is a nostalgia among Muslims for the past's charismatic *'alim* who held expertise in many disciplines:

> Throughout Islamic history, the central figure in the transmission of the sciences has been the wise man, or *hakim*. He has usually been a physician, a writer and a poet, an astronomer and mathematician, and above all, a sage. In the figure of the hakim, one can see the unity of the sciences as so many branches of a tree of which the trunk is the wisdom embodied in the sage in this figure of the *hakim*, or sage.[14]

However, expecting such a profile in modern times, when the sciences have undergone a deep differentiation, is naïve. Modern science may be open to interdisciplinary or trans-disciplinary studies. But the idea of the unity of the sciences is now a rarely discussed concept.

A second proposal is to follow the Western model, which requires that Islam cede its traditional authority of explaining nature to modern science. This option requires accepting that religion and science are exclusive realms. In 1972, the US National Academy of Sciences passed a resolution stating that religion and science are separate and mutually exclusive realms of human thought.[15] The resolution echoed the well-known approach proposed by various scholars like Etienne Gilson, the French philosopher who argued that science and faith should be held as two distinct kinds of thought. They are two distinct species of knowledge, and thus neither of them has to question the function of the other.[16]

However, as this book has shown, a similar agenda in the Muslim world requires a clash with the pillars of religious orthodoxy. Islam claims authority to shape Muslims' idea of nature. To give a very recent example from Turkey of how Islam still claims absolute authority over all fields, including science, consider a book by Ali Bulaç's, a prominent author very influential in Islamist circles across the country. In his recently published exegesis of the Qur'an, *Dirasatu'l-Kur'an*, Bulaç insists that scientific knowledge that is acquired by observation or reasoning should be processed through the filter of the Qur'an. In case of a clash between scientific knowledge and the Qur'an, Bulaç proposes that it must be because of some deficiency in human observation or reasoning, for a clash between the Qur'an and absolute truth is impossible. For Bulaç, the Qur'an remains the ultimate authority to evaluate even scientific knowledge.[17] Bulaç's stance is no different than that of al-Ghazali, who also saw the Qur'an as a book from which "the sciences of the ancients and contemporaries branch off."[18] Representing the mainstream view in Turkey, Bulaç's stance on the issue proves that the traditional reservation about scientific knowledge has remained virtually unchanged since age of Ibn al-Haytham (d. 1045), whose demand for the autonomous authority of scientific knowledge was rejected.

The prospects of this proposal are also poor given the sociological realities of the Muslim world. No mainstream interpretation of religion has emerged in the Muslim world that calls for religious authorities to cede their traditional powers. What is more, Islamization of Muslim societies today is gaining even more momentum. For this reason, calling upon religious authorities to cede their traditional powers would nowadays be as weak an echo in Muslim societies as was the traditional secularization thesis of the 1930s.

Finally, the analysis of this book reveals a general insight on Islamic reform. Change in the interpretation of Islam requires more than intellectual intervention. Many ideas we define today as reformist were already said before the nineteenth century. As early as the eighteenth century, Islamic thinkers like Hasan al-Attar (1766–1835) demanded radical changes within the Islamic tradition.[19] Other reformists have also written books back then full of sharp criticism of the current paradigms of Islam. However, they failed to persuade the Muslim public of the rightness of their ideas. Thus, the legitimation or embrace of a new Islamic interpretation on a societal level requires more than intellectual intervention; it is also a matter of power relations between Sunni orthodoxy and the state. These power relations have enabled only certain interpretations of Islam to become the normative content of religious education and socialization. As a result, people who are subject to Islamic socialization acquire a view of nature as an essential part of their religious faith. The Islamic idea of nature is thus woven into the thick fabric of religious culture. Not surprisingly, al-Ghazali was aware of this strategic point:

Indeed, true faith (*al iman al rasikh*) is the faith of the masses that develops in their hearts from childhood due to their constant exposure (to religious material), or that accrues to them after they have reached the age of majority as a result of experiences that they cannot fully articulate.[20]

He knew that most people attain their belief by following their parents and teachers.[21] Al-Ghazali's opinions remind us that religious orthodoxy is an issue not merely of intellectual persuasion but also of socialization within a supportive social and political system. In the absence of this support, as cases of the Mu'tazila as well as contemporary reformers show, the broad propagation of alternative, critical views, and subsequent society-wide reform is extremely difficult to achieve. It is not realistic to expect that reformist Islamic scholars will overturn the religious *status quo* in the politically, socially, and economically hierarchical Muslim world. Thus, what we need is a more balanced approach of actors and structures to formulate explanations of how certain social and political complexities cause the formation of certain religious paradigms in the Muslim world. We might be critical of how Muslims interpret Islam to solve problems in terms of their understanding of nature. However, a realistic perspective requires the admission that change is not easy and is only possible with parallel transformations in Muslim societies' social and political organizations.

NOTES

1. Courtenay, "The Critique on Natural Causality," 83.
2. I borrow these frames from Amina Wadud, who is known as a Muslim reformist. Her explanation demonstrates how even reformists adopt the mainstream Islamic idea of nature and construct their reformist narrative exclusively on the basis of Islamic law. Wadud, *Inside The Gender Jihad*, 24.
3. Ozment, *The Age of Reform*, 43.
4. Aristotle, *Physics*, 2.
5. al-Ghazali, *The Alchemy of Happiness*, 55.
6. Belkeziz, *The State in Contemporary Islamic Thought*, 122.
7. Hakkı, *Marifetname*, 1–25.
8. Russell, *The History of Western Philosophy*, 226.
9. Taylor, *A Secular Age*, 25.
10. Hodgson, *The Venture of Islam Vol. 1*, 79.
11. Schimmel, "Islam," 190.
12. Guessoum, "Issues and Agendas of Islam and Science," 375.

13. Drees, "Academic Freedom and the Symbolic Significance of Evolution," 67.
14. Nasr, *Science and Civilization in Islam*, 41.
15. Grose, *Science But Not Scientists*, 655. Also see: Solberg, "Science and Religion in Early America," 73–92.
16. Gilson, *Reason and Revelation in the Middle Ages*, 72–74. To remember, for Aquinas "faith and science are not about the same thing". Hastings, *Medieval European Society, 1000–1450*, 143.
17. Bulaç, *Kur'an Dersleri*, 10.
18. al-Ghazali, *The Jewels of the Qur'an*, 19.
19. Gesink, *Islamic Reform and Conservatism*, 24.
20. al-Ghazali, *On the Boundaries of Theological Tolerance*, 124.
21. Abrahamov, "Al-Ghazali's Supreme Way to Know God," 144.

References

Abrahamov, Binyamin. 1993. Al-Ghazali's Supreme Way to Know God. *Studia Islamica* 77 (1): 141–168.
al-Ghazali. 1977. *The Jewels of the Qur'an: Al-Ghazali's Theory [Kitab Jawahir al–Quran]*. Translated by Muhammad Abul Quasem. Kuala Lumpur: University of Malaya Press.
———. 1991. *The Alchemy of Happiness [Kimiya-yi Sa'adat]*. Translated by Claud Field. Lahore: Sh. M. Ashraf.
———. 2002. *On the Boundaries of Theological Tolerance in Islam: Abu Hamid al Ghazali's Faysal al Tafriqa [Faysal al Tafriqa]*. Translated by Sherman A. Jackson. New York: Oxford University Press.
Aristotle. 2018. *Physics*. Indianapolis: Hackett.
Belkeziz, Abdelilah. 2009. *The State in Contemporary Islamic Thought: A Historical Survey of the Major Muslim Political Thinkers of the Modern Era*. New York: I. B. Tauris.
Bulaç, Ali. 2016. *Kur'an Dersleri: Dirasatu'l-Kur'an Vol. 2*. Istanbul: Çıra.
Courtenay, William J. 1973. The Critique on Natural Causality in the Mutakallimun and Nominalism. *The Harvard Theological Review* 66 (1): 77–94.
Drees, Willem B. 2008. Academic Freedom and the Symbolic Significance of Evolution. In *The Study of Religion and the Training of Muslim Clergy in Europe*, ed. Willem B. Drees and Pieter Sjoerd van Koningsweld, 67–70. Leiden: Leiden University Press.
Gesink, Indira Falk. 2010. *Islamic Reform and Conservatism: Al-Azhar ad the Evolution of Modern Sunni Islam*. London: I. B. Tauris.
Gilson, Etienne. 1939. *Reason and Revelation in the Middle Ages*. London and New York: Charles Scribner's Sons.
Grose, Vernon L. 2006. *Science But Not Scientists*. Bloomington: Author House.

Guessoum, Nidhal. 2012. Issues and Agendas of Islam and Science. *Zygon* 47 (2): 367–387.

Hakkı, Erzurumlu İbrahim. 1984. *Marifetname*. Istanbul: Kitsan.

Hastings, Margareth. 1971. *Medieval European Society, 1000–1450*. New York: Random House.

Hodgson, Marshall G.S. 1977. *The Venture of Islam Vol. 1*. Chicago: The University of Chicago Press.

Nasr, Sayed H. 1987. *Science and Civilization in Islam*. Cambridge: The Islamic Texts Society.

Ozment, Steven. 1980. *The Age of Reform 1250–1550: An Intellectual and Religious History of Late Medieval and Reformation Europe*. London: Yale University Press.

Russell, Bertrand. 1946. *The History of Western Philosophy*. New York: George Allen & Unwin.

Schimmel, Annemarie. 1971. Islam. In *Historia Religionum Handbook for the History of Religions Vol. II*, ed. Jouco Bleeker and Geo Widengren, 125–210. Leiden: E. J. Brill.

Solberg, Winton U. 1987. Science and Religion in Early America: Cotton Mather's 'Christian Philosopher'. *Church History* 56 (1): 73–92.

Taylor, Charles. 2007. *A Secular Age*. New York: Belknap.

Wadud, Amina. 2013. *Inside The Gender Jihad: Women' Reform in Islam*. London: Oneworld.

INDEX

© The Author(s) 2020
G. Bacik, *Islam and Muslim Resistance to Modernity in Turkey*,
https://doi.org/10.1007/978-3-030-25901-3